BTEC FIRST

Public Services
(Uniformed)

Helen Cook, Debra Gray, Graham Saffery,
Ray Barker, Roger Paul

www.heinemann.co.uk

✓ Free online support
✓ Useful weblinks
✓ 24 hour online ordering

01865 888058

Heinemann
Inspiring generations

Heinemann Educational Publishers
Halley Court, Jordan Hill, Oxford OX2 8EJ
Part of Harcourt Education

Heinemann is the registered trademark of
Harcourt Education Limited

Text © Debra Gray, Ray Barker, Graham Saffery, Helen Cook, Roger Paul 2004

First published 2004

09 08 07 06 05 04
10 9 8 7 6 5 4 3 2 1

British Library Cataloguing in Publication Data is available
from the British Library on request.

ISBN 0 435 45459 5

Typeset by 🗚 Tek-Art, Croydon, Surrey
Printed by the Bath Press Ltd
Cover photo © Alamy

Contents

Unit 12
This unit is not in this student book, however you can access it on the
Heinemann website. See the Introduction for instructions.

Introduction

How to use this textbook

The public services offer a vast range of opportunities for careers, in services such as the police, fire, ambulance, army and navy. Whatever service you decide to join there will be numerous chances for career and personal development. You will learn new skills and develop your abilities, you will learn more about the community in which you live and work, and you will make a valuable contribution to the welfare of the people who live in that community through the job you do. Remember, the public services are the biggest employer in this country and are essential to the well-being of the nation.

Your BTEC First Diploma in Public Services course is certificated by Edexcel, one of the country's leading awarding bodies for vocational qualifications. This student book covers the three core units and six other units from which you will choose three required for the qualification. The units covered are:

Unit 1: The public services
Unit 2: Public service skills
Unit 3: Public service fitness
Unit 5: Workplace welfare
Unit 7: Outdoor activities and the public services
Unit 8: Sport and recreation
Unit 11: Crime and its effects
Unit 12: Community and cultural awareness
Unit 14: Expedition skills

Unit 12 is not included in the book but is available for you to download from our website at www.heinemann.co.uk/vocational. Click on: Public services in the subject list on the left-hand column on the page. From there click on: Free resources in Resource centre box in the right-hand corner of the page.

Assessment

You will be assessed by a series of assignments. Each assignment is designed so that you can show your understanding of a number of **learning outcomes** for each unit. Each unit is assessed by a series of assessment activities designed to cover certain grading points (Refer to the *Grading Criteria* for each unit in your course handbook for further guidance on these grading points.) You will see that for each unit there is a pass, merit, and distinction grade. Within each grade there a number of criteria for which evidence is required. To gain a pass, you will need to provide sufficient evidence for each criteria in the pass grade. To gain a merit, you will need to gain not only all the pass criteria but the merit criteria as well. For a distinction grade, you will need to provide evidence for all the pass, merit and distinction criteria.

How will this book help you?

Through the text there are a number of features designed to encourage you to reflect on the issues raised, relate the theory to your practice and assist you to understand the relevant concepts and theories. These features are:

Think about it	questions designed to encourage reflection or discussion with others
Let's do it	activities that encourage you to go out and do some research in the 'real' world of the public services
Key points	a list summarising the key topics covered in that section
Case studies	examples of real scenarios to help explain a concept or help to link the theory with real practice
Assessment activities	activities designed to support achievement in relation to learning outcomes
In summary	a feature summarising what you have just learnt in the unit

Many of these features will help you to compile the evidence needed for your assessments. In addition, you should try to carry out the following on a regular basis:

- watch the television and listen to the radio for items and articles on the public services
- read both the local and national newspapers
- keep a scrapbook of important news stories on a range of issues connected with the public services.

All of this will keep you up to date with what is happening in the world of the public services. This is very important as some of the grading criteria require you to complete tasks independently – this is with little or no help from your tutor. The more aware you are of what is going on, the easier this will be for you!

What else do you need to do?

Always make sure you complete the pass criteria for each unit to ensure you succeed. Many assessment points follow on through pass, merit and distinction grades. Pass criteria generally ask you to list, define or describe. For merit, you will need to compare (what is the same and what is different?) or explain (give reasons for something). For a distinction, you will have to analyse (examine in detail the reasons for or the organisation of).

Finally **Good Luck!** We hope this student book helps you to reach great success in your course.

Acknowledgements

Alamy, cover

Alamy, page 288

Alamy/Janine, page 292

John Birdsall, page 286, 352

Gareth Boden, pages 164, 199

Bromley-by-Bow Centre, page 2*

The Countryside Agency, page 388

Crown Copyright, image from www.photos.mod.uk. Reproduced with the permission of the Controller of Her Majesty's Stationery Office, page 39

Crown Copyright, image from www.photos.mod.uk. Reproduced with the permission of the Controller of Her Majesty's Stationery Office/photograph by Stuart Bingham, page 32*

Crown Copyright, image from www.photos.mod.uk. Reproduced with the permission of the Controller of Her Majesty's Stationery Office/photograph by Cpl Dave Liddle, page 63

Crown Copyright, image from www.photos.mod.uk. Reproduced with the permission of the Controller of Her Majesty's Stationery Office/photograph by W02 Giles Penfound, page 69

Crown Copyright, image from www.photos.mod.uk. Reproduced with the permission of the Controller of Her Majesty's Stationery Office/photograph by Sgt Jack Pritchard, page 54

Getty/Stu Foster, page 115

Girl Guides Association, page 256

London Borough of Tower Hamlets/ Andy Wood pages, 5*, 9*, 18*

Jeff Moore (jeff@jmal.co.uk), page 3*

Network, pages 8, 276, 284

PA News Photos/European Press Agency, page 24

Photodisc, page 181

Photofusion/Jack Chapman, page 14*

Rex Features/-, page 62

Rex Features/Adrian Dennis, page 327

Rex Features/DPPI, page 273

Rex Features/GPU, page 24*

Rex Features/Philippe Hays, page 16

Rex Features/Nils Jorgensen, page 21

Rex Features/MCY/NAP, page 79

Rex Features/RESO, page 307

Rex Features/ULANDER, page 312

RNLI, page 245

South Yorkshire Police, page 6

Topham/Chapman/PA, page 324

Topham/Firepix, pages 11, 227

Topham/The Image Works, page 316

Topham/Ian Murno, page 238

Topham/National Pictures, page 57

Topham/PA, pages 27*, 81, 305, 345, 349

Topham/PA/ESC, pages 11, 14, 64

Topham/PA/ESCD, page 19

Topham/Picturepoint, page 3*

* These photographs are in Unit 12 which appears on the Heinemann website.

Every effort has been made to contact copyright holders of material reproduced in this book. Any omissions will be rectified in subsequent printings if notice is given to the publishers.

The public services

Introduction

This is one of the most important units you will study on your First Diploma course. It informs you of a wide variety of possible career options and helps you decide which career options might be right for you. Even if you already have a clear idea of which service you want to join you still need to know as much as you can about the other services. More and more the services are working together in cooperation and partnership to deliver the best service to the public, so an understanding of all of the services will help you see how they can work together and impact upon each other. It is also important to understand the roles and responsibilities of the services because of their power to affect people's lives and influence society and the government. They are also often the nation's largest and most stable employers, and a career with them will normally be reasonably well paid, give numerous opportunities for promotion and be varied and challenging. For this reason competition for employment opportunities in the services can be fierce, particularly for highly sought after posts such as those of police officer, firefighter and certain roles in the armed services.

This unit will help you prepare for applying to the public services for jobs and will help you make informed career choices. This in turn will make you more attractive as a prospective employee to the public services which are looking for people who are well informed and realistic about what life in a public service means.

How you will be assessed

This unit is assessed via an integrated vocational assignment (IVA). The IVA is an externally set assignment which your tutors should give to you at the beginning of the academic year and collect from you no later than around mid-March. The IVA section in this book, which you will find in the Appendix, will provide you with more guidance.

After completing this unit, you should be able to achieve the following outcomes:
1 Examine the purpose, roles and responsibilities of a range of public services.

2 Examine a range of jobs within the public services.
3 Investigate the application and selection process for a given public service.
4 Investigate the entry requirements and opportunities for career development within a given public service.

The public services

The term 'public service' means different things to different people.

Think about it

What do you think the term 'public service' means? Come up with a definition that you can discuss with your colleagues.

Put simply, doing something described as a 'public service' is any act that contributes to the well-being of society or individuals. Even small acts like picking up litter or checking on elderly neighbours, could be regarded as a public service. We all perform a public service at some time in our daily lives, such as helping out a fellow student who doesn't understand a topic, making sure we leave a classroom as we found it, or saving energy by turning the light out in rooms as we leave. All these actions improve the lives of individuals or society as a whole and can therefore be considered a public service.

Let's do it!

Make a diary of your actions over the last seven days. Highlight how many of your actions could be considered to be a service to the public. What does your diary show you? How does it compare to the diaries of your fellow students?

In most societies there are organisations which provide professional services to the public and which are collectively called 'the public services'. In thinking about public service organisations you probably think about those that are uniformed such as the police and the army, however there are many that do not involve wearing a uniform.

The following are a list of uniformed and non-uniformed public services.

Uniformed	Non-uniformed
Police service	Probation service
Fire service	Social services
Ambulance service	Education service
Army	Local government
Royal Navy	Youth and community services
Royal Marines	Mountain/Cave rescue
Royal Air Force	Victim support
Coastguard	Civil service
Prison service	MI5/MI6
Customs and excise	Trade unions
National Health Service	Refuse collection services

Table 1.1

Each public service listed above performs a different role in society, however their roles should fit together and complement each other so that they help as many people as possible, without overlapping, which would be costly and wasteful. Imagine the public services as a large jigsaw with all of the different services fitting together to make a better society.

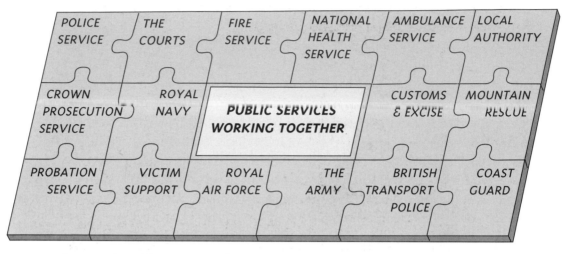

Figure 1.1 *The public services working together*

Most public services are funded by the government, with money from the taxes the public pays.

Let's do it!

Look at the public services listed in Table 1.1 and see if you can guess which ones are funded by the government and which ones are not.

Public services fall into two categories: statutory and non-statutory. Statutory public services are required to exist by law and are funded by the government. Non-statutory public services are not required to exist by law and are often charities or self-funded. See the table below for some examples.

Statutory public services	Non-statutory public services
Police service	Victim Support
Fire service	Help the Aged
Ambulance service	Trade unions
RAF	Alcoholics Anonymous
Royal Navy	Samaritans
Education service	NSPCC
NHS	Salvation Army
Probation service	Church groups

Table 1.2

As you can see, some of the services funded by the government do not involve wearing a uniform, such as the probation service, and some services not funded by the government do wear a uniform, such as the Salvation Army.

It is not possible in this unit to cover all the public service organisations mentioned so far, but we will cover five of the most common ones that public services students tend to seek a career in.

- Police service
- Fire service
- Army
- Prison service
- Customs and excise.

Police service

The origins of modern law enforcement in the UK can be traced back to the 13th century, to the locally appointed magistrates and petty constables whose job was to maintain the peace and deal with those who broke the law. However, the modern police service in England and Wales was not formed until 1829, by the then Home Secretary Sir Robert Peel who created the Metropolitan Police Act. Police services in counties outside of the London metropolitan area were created by the County Police Act 1839. The roles and responsibilities of the police service have been changed by many other Acts since those early days, among them the Police and Criminal Evidence Act 1984, the Crime and Disorder Act 1998 and the Police Act 1997.

 Key point

The name Robert is often shortened to Bob or Bobby and this is why police officers are sometimes referred to as Bobbies – after their founder Sir Robert Peel.

Roles and responsibilities of the police service

There are 43 police services in England and Wales, all of them sharing a common purpose and common values. These are to

- uphold the law fairly and firmly
- pursue and bring to justice those who break the law
- keep the Queen's peace
- protect, help and reassure the community
- operate with integrity, common sense and sound judgement.

These are the roles and responsibilities the police are required to fulfil, however many police services also set local priorities which largely depend on the needs of their particular area. Most services also have individual mission statements, which are summaries of the aims of the particular constabulary, and each will also have individual performance indicators which tell the public and government how well a particular police service is performing. The best way to examine this information is by looking at real examples of how the police services present this information.

The following are the aims, priorities and mission of the South Yorkshire police service.

THE SOUTH YORKSHIRE STRATEGIC POLICING PLAN 2003–2005

OUR VISION

To help make South Yorkshire a safer and more just society

The Police Authority will achieve this by working with and on behalf of all our communities, in partnership with the Chief Constable, to ensure there is efficient and effective policing.

In particular by:

- Consulting with all stakeholders to shape policing
- Determining budgets and monitoring the effective use of resources
- Holding the Chief Constable to account

The Chief Constable promises to focus the efforts of South Yorkshire Police on:

- Providing public reassurance
- Tackling anti-social behaviour and disorder
- Reducing volume, street, drug, violent and gun crime
- Combating serious and organised crime
- Increasing the number of offenders brought to justice
- Improving road safety

OUR PRIORITIES

To reduce crime, improve performance, increase visibility and reassure the public

In order to achieve these we will:

- Make full use of consultation results and improve communications
- Maintain high standards of corporate governance, continually improve our processes and embrace diversity
- Align our activity within the three key areas of People, Resources and Service Delivery

PEOPLE

Creating and maintaining a professional workforce capable of delivering an effective and efficient service

RESOURCES

Making best use of available resources to meet our priorities and the demands placed upon us

SERVICE DELIVERY

Implementing a Reassurance and Visibility Strategy

Implementing the South Yorkshire Policing Model

Figure 1.2 *South Yorkshire policing plan*

As you can see, South Yorkshire police services has a particular vision for policing in their area that includes information on their mission, priorities and resources. Most police services have something like this on their websites. You can access this information to find out more about which particular police service you would like to join. You can also use information like this to make comparisons between police service areas.

Let's do it!

Find the mission and priorities of three more police constabularies and compare them with the information from South Yorkshire detailed on page 6. Identify all the differences and similarities.

What do the police actually do?

The police do a great deal more work than we are often aware of. Most of us think of police work as responding to emergency calls. This is true, but it doesn't cover half what the police are expected to do. Other duties include

- responding to non-emergency calls such as noise nuisance, abandoned vehicles and dealing with stray animals
- completing a huge amount of paperwork
- improving community relations
- reducing the fear of crime by maintaining a visible presence on the streets
- working in partnership with other services to reduce crime
- crime prevention
- giving evidence in court
- crime investigation
- educational visits to schools and colleges
- firearms licensing
- the licensing of pubs and clubs
- regulating door supervisors
- referring victims of crime to support agencies
- overseeing the procedure for licensing betting offices
- underwater search
- missing persons' reports
- providing advice and information on personal safety and protection of property
- providing the government with information and statistics
- escorting of abnormal loads
- holding people in police custody.

These are only some of the jobs that the police must do in order to fulfil what the public and government require of them.

Figure 1.3 *One of the duties of police officers is to give educational talks to children and young people*

 Think about it

Can you think of anything else the police deal with in the course of their work?

Table 1.3 lists some of the positive and negative aspects of working in the police service.

Positive	Negative
○ It is an interesting and varied job ○ There are plenty of opportunities for career development and progression ○ You will work as part of a team and make friends ○ You will meet different people every day ○ You have the opportunity to change job roles throughout your career ○ Good rates of pay compared with other services ○ Excellent pension and benefits ○ You get to retire at 55 ○ Secure employment ○ Ongoing training	○ Unsocial hours/shift work interfering with personal and family life ○ Risk to personal safety ○ Unpleasant nature of some of the work such as dealing with child abuse cases ○ Public attitudes towards the police are not always positive ○ Not just a 9–5 job, you must uphold the standards of the police service in your off-duty hours too ○ Responsibility for people's safety is in your hands, you can't afford an 'off' day

Table 1.3

Think about it

You are a police recruitment officer who is giving a talk to a local college about opportunities in the police service. The students ask you the following questions, and you must answer them as fully as you can.

1 What is the purpose of the police?
2 What kind of priorities do the police set?
3 What kind of work do they do?
4 What are the good and bad things about being a police officer?

Fire service

The history of the fire service in the UK can be traced back to the great fire of London in 1666. This fire blazed for three days and made over 200,000 people homeless. As a result, London was divided into quarters and each quarter was allocated fire fighting equipment. This was one of the first organised attempts to prevent fire. The first formal fire brigade did not exist until 1824, when 80 men were recruited for the specific purpose of fighting fire in Edinburgh. The Fire Services Act 1947 is the legal basis for the existence of the fire service, although laws have been passed since then which have modified the role and responsibilities of the fire service. Today there are 50 separate fire brigades in England and Wales employing around 33,400 full-time firefighters and around 12,000 retained (part-time) firefighters.

Roles and responsibilities of the fire service

Like the police service, the fire service is required to set aims, objectives and priorities. Since there is no national fire service to which you can go to find what these are, you must research individual fire brigades for their priorities and mission statements. The examples below give an indication of what some brigades are doing.

Cleveland Fire Brigade

Mission statement:
Working with others to build a safer environment

Objectives:
1 Act to reduce the number of fires occurring and work with others to reduce risk to life, property and the environment from fire and other emergencies.

2 Provide and maintain an efficient and valued fire and rescue service, which is responsive to the needs of our community.

3 Maintain a well equipped, skilful and highly motivated workforce who are able to work safely and reflect the diverse communities we serve.

4 Continuously improve performance in order to deliver best value.

5 To develop partnerships with a range of agencies in the public, private and voluntary sectors to support the achievement of these objectives.

North Wales Fire and Rescue Service

Mission statement:

To make North Wales a safer place to live, work and visit

Objectives:

1 To prevent accidental and malicious fires.

2 To protect people from being killed or injured by fire and other hazards.

3 To protect the community, businesses and the environment from being harmed by fire and other hazards.

4 To find ways to improve in order to meet the expectations of the community.

5 To operate as effectively and efficiently as we can, making the best use of the resources we have available.

Although these targets give an indication of what the fire service does at an organisational level they do not actually specify the tasks and roles the fire service may engage in. Some of these roles are detailed below.

What does the fire service actually do?

Apart from responding to emergency calls in the case of fire or serious road traffic incidents, there are other roles the fire service is required to do, such as

- promoting fire safety
- animal rescue
- hazardous materials incidents
- fire prevention
- disaster management
- fitting smoke detectors
- chemical spillages
- recovering objects
- educating children
- industrial accidents
- working in partnership with other services
- protecting the environment
- flooding incidents
- industrial fire training
- first aid
- releasing people trapped in lifts
- checking that business premises comply with fire regulations
- giving evidence in court
- preserving evidence at the scene of a deliberate fire (arson)
- fire safety advice in the home
- dealing with terrorist incidents.

Figure 1.4 *Fighting fire is the most important part of a firefighter's job*

 Think about it

Does the fire service have more roles and responsibilities than you thought?

Let's do it!

List the five most important roles that the fire service fulfils.

Table 1.4 lists some of the positive and negative aspects of working in the fire service.

Positive	Negative
Secure employment	Unsocial hours/shift work
Variety of work	Dangerous nature of the work
Retirement at 55	Poor pay in relation to some other careers
Opportunity for progression and promotion	Disturbing nature of some of the work, particularly when deaths are involved
Ongoing training	Physically demanding work at incidents
Excellent pension and benefits	
Part of a close-knit rescue team	
Saving lives	

Table 1.4

The army

The British Army has a long and distinguished history. It was formed by royal warrant on the 26 January 1661. It is one of the few modern armies to be based on the 'regimental system', which makes it difficult to discuss the army's history as a whole because each regiment has its own history and traditions. A soldier or an officer will normally serve in the same regiment throughout their career, a system which has the advantage of creating pride and loyalty in a regiment and which boosts fighting spirit and leads to a committed and motivated fighting force. Some regiments have had long histories, such as the Honourable Artillery Company, founded in 1537, the Royal Monmouthshire Engineers, founded in 1539, and the Coldstream Guards, founded in 1650, to name a few.

Of course the army has faced many major reforms since 1661, particularly in the 19th and 20th centuries. After the Crimean War against the Russians there were major calls for army reform as many soldiers had died from disease and neglect and poor administration. Although the Crimean War was a successful endeavour for the British Army, the loss of many soldiers to non-battle conditions was disturbing and triggered the 'Cardwell reforms', which improved conditions for those in the army and changed the rules for commissioning officers. Other conflicts which changed the way the army operated included the Boer War at the end of the 19th century. This brought about a major rethink in army tactics and strategy as the army was not used to dealing with fast moving and covert militia groups like the Boers. As a result the British Army that fought in the First World War (1914–18) was better trained than any previous one.

Legislation sets out the parameters the army must work within, such as the Army Act 1955 and the Armed Forces Discipline Act 2000. The army is currently under strength in several areas, but has a total strength of around 100,000 and is the largest single UK employer.

Let's do it!

Carry out research into the Crimean War or Boer War, to find out what conditions the British Army fought under, what was learned from this and what changes were made to the army as a result. Discuss this as a class.

Let's do it!

Carry out research on the internet into various regiments of the British Army. When you have finished gather the information together as a class, and produce a wall display on your findings.

Roles and responsibilities of the army

The army is part of the Ministry of Defence (MOD), which has a strategic mission which includes all aspects of the defence of the nation. This mission and the army's objectives are described below.

Ministry of Defence and Armed Forces

Mission statement:

The purpose of the Ministry of Defence, and the armed forces, is to:

- Defend the United Kingdom and Overseas Territories, our people and interests.
- Act as a force for good by strengthening international peace and security.

Objectives:

- Make a vital contribution to Britain's security policy and its promotion at home and abroad.
- Direct and provide a defence effort that meets the needs of the present, prepares for the future and ensures against the unpredictable.
- Generate modern, battle-winning forces and other defence capabilities to help
  - prevent conflicts and build stability
  - resolve crises and respond to emergencies
  - protect and further UK interests
  - meet our commitments and responsibilities
  - work with Allies and partners to strengthen international security relationships.

These objectives give you an idea of how the army sees its role in terms of the wider issues of defence, however they do not really describe what the army actually does day to day.

What does the army actually do?

This is difficult to answer because of the huge variety of individual roles within the army. What the average soldier or officer does varies depending on the regiment they belong to. The main elements of the army are described below, along with the roles they are likely to fulfil.

- *Household Cavalry and Royal Armoured Division* – armoured reconnaissance, ceremonial duties, mobile combat.
- *Army Air Corps* – airborne combat, reconnaissance, directing artillery, moving troops and stores, airborne command.
- *Royal Regiment of Artillery* – surveillance, target acquisition, armed defence of troops and equipment via projectile weaponry.
- *Royal Corps of Engineers* – building bridges, destroying bridges, clearing and laying mines, surveys and map production, camp construction, power generation, airstrip building, ordnance destruction.

Figure 1.5 *A soldier's duties will depend on what regiment they belong to*

- *Royal Corps of Signals* – communications.
- *Intelligence Corps* – information gathering, spying, counter-intelligence.
- *Royal Army Chaplain's Department* – support for soldiers and officers.
- *Royal Logistics Corps* – provision and distribution of all equipment and stores to army personnel.
- *Royal Army Medical Corps* – wartime responsibility for sick and wounded of both sides in battlefield conditions and peacetime care of soldiers and their families' medical needs.
- *Royal Electrical and Mechanical Engineers* – maintenance of all army equipment to ensure it is safe and fit for purpose.

The British Army has a guide for the behaviour of all soldiers and officers regardless of which regiment they may be in, which promotes putting others before yourself, facing up to danger, high standards of discipline, loyalty to the service and respect for others. If you are unable to follow these rules then the army is probably not the place for you.

Table 1.5 lists some of the positive and negative aspects of working in the army.

Positive	Negative
Varied and interesting role	Very disciplined environment
Wide variety of job opportunities	Lack of freedom to do as you please
Opportunities for advancement and promotion	Dangerous nature of work
Stable and secure employment	Very poor pay in comparison with other services
Opportunities for travel and living abroad	Postings abroad can harm personal relationships
Sense of belonging/camaraderie	Promotion is difficult to achieve without good qualifications
Early retirement	
Ongoing training	
Lots of opportunities for sports or developing new skills	
Provision of food and lodgings	
Make lots of friends	

Table 1.5

Think about it

What skills would you need to develop if you were considering a career in a particular section of the army?

HM Customs and Excise

Her Majesty's Customs and Excise is one of the oldest public services and has developed greatly over time, however its essential function has not substantially changed.

Let's do it!

List five things you associate with customs and excise. Compare your list with the rest of the class.

Roles and responsibilities of customs and excise

Customs employs over 22,000 staff in the UK and its primary role is to collect taxes and duties from the public. These taxes help fund the running of our society, by helping to pay for the public services such as education, health care and the police. Customs collect around £100 billion every year in taxes such as VAT and duties on tobacco, alcohol and petrol. It also protects the interests of British and international business by monitoring the import and export of goods, including the seizure of counterfeit goods, such as fake designer clothes or copied DVDs. Customs also has a large role to play in the fight against crime, in that it

- detects and investigates individuals and companies who evade their taxes
- works in partnership with other services to prevent the import of drugs into the UK – this is mainly done through shipping ports and airports

Figure 1.6 *The collection of taxes and duties by the Customs and Excise service helps to pay for the public services of this country*

- works with other services to prevent the importation of offensive and illegal material such as child pornography
- works to prevent the trade in endangered plant and animal species.

Customs is a very successful service. In 2000–2001 it prevented drugs worth over £1.5 billion reaching the UK and intercepted hundreds of millions of pounds worth of smuggled goods such as tobacco and alcohol, which otherwise would have lost the government many millions of pounds in taxes.

Like the other services we have examined, customs and excise is required to produce aims and objectives. Its aims and objectives for 2003–2006 are as follows:

HM Customs and Excise

Aims:

To administer the indirect tax and customs control systems fairly and make it as easy as possible for individuals and businesses to understand and comply with their obligations.

Objectives:

Objective 1: Collect the right revenue at the right time from indirect taxes and to improve the level of compliance with customs and statistical requirements.

By 31 March 2006 reduce illicit market share within the excise regime to no more than

- 2% for oils in England, Scotland and Wales
- 17% for tobacco

and implement a strategy for reducing the scale of the VAT losses from March 2003.

Improve customer service by

- ensuring by 2005 that 100% of services are offered electronically, wherever possible through a common government portal, and take-up for key services of at least 50% by March 2006, and
- delivering reductions in the costs of compliance for businesses.

Objective 2: Reduce crime and drug dependency by detecting and deterring the smuggling of illegal drugs and other prohibited and restricted goods.

Reduce the availability of illegal drugs by increasing

- the proportion of heroin and cocaine targeted on the UK which is taken out
- the disruption/dismantling of those criminal groups responsible for supplying substantial quantities of class A drugs to the UK market
- the recovery of drug-related criminal assets.

Table 1.6 lists some of the positive and negative aspects of working within the customs and excise service.

Positive	Negative
- Variety of work undertaken - Variety of entry levels depending on experience and qualifications - Various sites round the UK to be attached to - Safer than many other public service jobs	- Low rates of pay in comparison with other services, particularly at lower grades - No automatic early retirement - Aspects of the work may be routine and lack excitement

Table 1.6

Think about it

Why do you think the customs and excise service has chosen the particular targets detailed above? Explain your reasons.

HM Prison Service

Prisons have a very long history in the UK, however other methods of punishment have been used in preference to prison, such as hanging or transportation to convict colonies in America and Australia. Transportation ceased to be an option after the American War of Independence in 1776 and when sending offenders to Australia was halted in 1857, although this was not officially abolished until 1868. These changes meant that more prisons needed to be built in this country. A rapid prison building programme in the 1840s resulted in 54 new prisons being built between 1842 and 1848, many of them still in service today. The prison service used to be run by local authorities, but the 1877 Prison Act brought all prisons under the control of central government, which is still the case today. The prison service currently employs 44,000 staff who deal with approximately 72,000 inmates in 138 prisons.

Roles and responsibilities of the prison service

The roles and responsibilities of the prison service are stated very clearly in its mission statement and strategic objectives which are outlined below.

HM Prison Service

Mission statement:
To build a safe, just, and tolerant society in which the rights and responsibilites of individuals, families, and communities are properly balanced, and the protection and security of the public are maintained.

Objectives:
- To protect the public by holding those committed by the courts in a safe, decent, and healthy environment.
- To reduce crime by providing constructive regimes which address offending behaviour, improve educational and work skills, and promote law-abiding behaviour in custody and after release.

Principles:

- To deal fairly, openly, and humanely with prisoners and all others who come into contact with us.
- To encourage prisoners to address offending behaviour and respect others.
- To value and support each other's contribution.
- To promote equality of opportunity for all and combat discrimination wherever it occurs.
- To work constructively with criminal justice agencies and other organisations.
- To obtain best value from the resources available.

Of course these are the aims of the prison service overall, but what are the usual roles and responsibilities of an individual prison officer? The description below highlights the tasks that a prison officer may have to fulfil in the course of their duties.

What does a prison officer actually do?

A prison officer's duties include

- ensuring the security of the prison by conducting searches of prisoners and visitors and general security checks of property and locations

Figure 1.7 *Prison officers play a vital role in keeping the public safe and secure*

- maintaining order in the prison environment
- supervising prisoners and keeping a count of prisoners in the prison or the wing where an officer might work
- taking care of prisoners and their property
- promoting human rights
- administrative duties
- ensuring prisoners do not commit self-harm
- preventing bullying and victimisation of prisoners by other prisoners
- the rehabilitation of prisoners
- writing reports on prisoners
- using appropriate restraint techniques.

Table 1.7 lists some of the positive and negative aspects of working in the prison service.

Positive	Negative
- Early retirement - Stable and secure employment - Good opportunities for promotion - Graduate fast-track scheme - Rewarding job which is a service to the community - Large variety of roles within the job - A public service job which offers direct and sustained contact with the public - Fast-track entry for experienced managers - Opportunities for professional development and innovation - Opportunities to develop teamwork skills	- Poor salary in comparison with other careers - Shift work - Confined working environment - Lack of opportunity to work outdoors - Prison can be a tense and intimidating environment - No guarantee of a posting of your choice - Prison can be a dangerous environment

Table 1.7

Assessment activity

To achieve a *pass* grade (P1), you need to identify and explain the primary role, purpose and responsibilities of at least two public services.

Different jobs within the public services

You have now found out about a variety of public services, but within each public service there are numerous roles to be fulfilled. We will now examine three different roles in the police service.

Roles within the police service

There are many possible roles you could perform in the police service, such as police officer, special constable and administrative officer, to name a few. In a well-organised service each role works to support each other role and they are all as important to the operational effectiveness of the service as each other. The three roles we will compare for this service are police constable, civilian support staff and police community support officer.

I Police constable

All police officers must spend two years on probation as a patrol constable before they can specialise in a particular area of police work. Many police officers choose to remain as patrol constables for all their career. The role of patrol constable involves many of the following tasks.

- *Foot patrol* This involves the walking of a specific route (or beat) to act as a visible uniformed presence. It can act as a deterrent to criminals who are operating in the area and reduces fear of crime in the general public. Although it is rare that a beat officer will come across a crime in progress, the general public often express their opinion in polls that they would like to see more officers on the beat.

Figure 1.8 *Police constables on the beat*

○ *Working in schools to talk about safety and crime* Patrol constables are often called upon by local schools to talk to children about issues as diverse as personal safety, making hoax 999 calls, drug awareness and paedophiles on internet chat rooms. This means that they must be well-informed about such issues and confident enough to speak about them. This kind of role can help build police–community relations in younger generations and is therefore very important.

○ *Assisting in the event of accidents, fights and fires* Patrol officers are often called upon to attend unexpected incidents in which they might have to intervene in a public order incident, such as a pub fight or a domestic violence incident. They may also have to attend a local accident where a person has been injured and possibly administer first aid until assistance arrives.

○ *Road safety initiatives* Patrol constables may often be called upon to participate in road safety initiatives. This may include visiting schools to educate children on the dangers of traffic, or it may include taking part in initiatives such as exhaust emissions testing, documents checks, and roadside car safety checks such as tyre depth.

○ *House-to-house enquiries* During the investigation of serious crimes, such as murder or abduction, officers are often called upon to go door to door on a particular estate to gather information that householders may have about a particular crime in their area. This can be time-consuming but is a necessary task and a valuable investigation technique.

○ *Policing major public events* Patrol officers are often asked to ensure public safety at events such as football matches and public demonstrations such as political rallies. When large crowds gather there is always the risk of fighting breaking out or people being hurt in crushes. Police officers plan for contingencies at such events to make sure everyone is safe.

○ *Giving evidence in court* Police patrol officers are often called upon to give evidence in court as to a crime or an incident. They may have information relevant to a case which may affect the outcome of the trial.

○ *Reducing crime initiatives* Police patrol officers also take part in very specific crime reduction operations which target problem crimes such as underage drinking or youth nuisance behaviour which may be causing problems in a particular area. They also offer crime reduction information on protecting your property and neighbourhood watch.

Once the probation period is over a police constable can apply for a role other than that of a patrol officer. Some of the roles they may choose to apply for are described in Table 1.8.

Police constable roles	Brief job description
Dog handler	Dog handlers and their dogs work as a team. The dogs assist with catching criminals, searching buildings and policing large crowds, such as those at football matches. They are often trained to find drugs or explosives.
Traffic police	All forces have officers deployed on road policing. Part of their duties involves tackling vehicle crime. They ensure road safety by enforcing traffic laws such as those relating to speeding and drink driving. They also deal with road accidents and help road users.
Criminal Investigation Department (CID)	Officers engaged in detective work account for about 1 in 8 of all police staff. They receive intensive training to enable them to work effectively in this field. The day-to-day work of detectives is busy and demanding. Their core role is to investigate serious crime and to act upon intelligence which can lead to the arrest and prosecution of hardened or 'career' criminals.
Special Branch	Special Branch officers combat terrorism. They work at airports and seaports, providing armed bodyguards for politicians and public figures and investigating firearms and explosives offences that may be connected to national security matters.
Firearms units	These are specialist teams trained in the use of firearms who assist with dangerous operations.
Drugs Squad	The growth in the misuse of drugs in the UK is a major cause for concern. These specialist officers work with operational officers and other agencies to target drug dealers and tackle the drugs problem. They play a very important role in combating this area of organised crime
Fraud Squad	We all bear the cost of fraud in our insurance premiums or in the higher cost of products. The police service has a specialised Fraud Squad, run jointly by the Metropolitan Police and the City of London Police. Other forces also have Fraud Squads and they assist each other in investigating fraud. Fraud Squad officers also work with the Serious Fraud Office, a government department set up to investigate large-scale fraud.
Mounted units	Police horses work under the guidance of very skilled riders and play a vital role at events where there are large crowds, such as football matches, race meetings and demonstrations. They are also used to provide high visibility policing at a local level, often in parkland and open spaces.

Table 1.8   Note: Information taken from www.policecouldyou.co.uk

2 Civilian support staff

The civilian support staff employed by the police service play a very important role in ensuring the police service runs smoothly and that uniformed officers are not so tied up in administrative duties that they cannot police the streets.

The variety of support roles for civilians includes crime researcher/analyst, a role involving gathering crime intelligence and analysing it for patterns which can then be addressed by uniformed officers. Researchers/analysts also gather information on police force effectiveness in order to ensure that the force is meeting its Home Office targets. More common support roles involving contact with the public are call handlers and front-counter personnel. These are usually the first people the public will come into contact with when reporting a crime or contacting the police. They handle general non-emergency telephone enquiries as well as 999 calls and prioritise the response of the uniformed officers. The front-of-house staff deal with general enquiries by the public as well as dealing with people who are called to attend the police station for other reasons, such as surrendering themselves for arrest. They are the public face of the police and need to be very aware of creating a good impression in order to improve and build upon police–community relations. One of the best known civilian aspects of the police service are of course traffic wardens, whose job is to police parking and static traffic violations. They help maintain a smooth flow of traffic and help to ensure that illegal parking is punished, as such behaviour could create danger for other motorists and for pedestrians.

Figure 1.9 *The civilians employed by the police service play a crucial role in helping the service to run smoothly*

3 Police community support officer

A community support officer (PCSO) is a civilian who acts as a visible presence on the streets of local areas where anti-social behaviour is a problem. They perform some of the same duties as a patrol constable in that they reduce fear of crime among the public in such troubled areas. Their role is relatively new and may involve any or all of the following duties:

- dealing with anti-social behaviour, such as graffiti, truancy, litter and youth nuisance

- supporting victims of crime
- protecting the public from security threats
- assisting with house-to-house enquiries
- detaining a suspect until a police constable arrives
- directing traffic and removing vehicles.

PCSOs complement the work of the traditional police constable by focusing on lower level crime, so that the police can respond more effectively to more serious crime. Support officers are uniformed, and many police services have introduced a uniform which is very similar to the uniform of a police constable. This is to give the role credibility with the public.

Think about it

Do you think one of the above police roles is more important than the others? Explain your reasons.

Conditions of service in the public services

Conditions of service in the public services covers the information you need to make a reasoned career choice about which service would suit you best. Conditions of service include factors such as

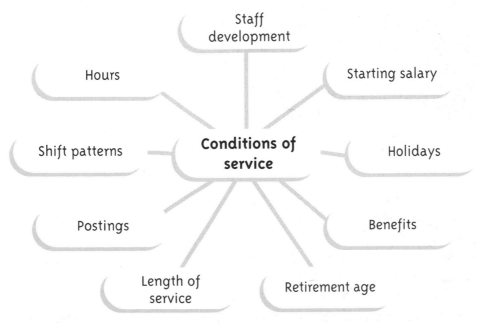

Figure 1.10 *Some of the conditions of service you find in the public services*

Table 1.9 below shows a comparison of the conditions of service in several public services.

	Police service – constable	Fire service – firefighter	Prison service – prison officer	The army – soldier
Starting salary	£19,227	£16,563 for first 6 months	£16,725	£13,080
Holidays	21 days for first 5 years	25 days	22 days on entry	30 days per year
Retirement age	55 years old	55 years old	55 if employed before 1987, otherwise 60	22 years after joining
Length of service	No set length	No set length	No set length	Minimum of four years
Postings	Anywhere within a police constabulary area	Any fire station in brigade area	Any prison in England and Wales	Home and abroad at any British or Allied military base
Shift patterns	Varies between forces	Two day shifts of 9 hours followed by two 15-hour night shifts followed by four days off	Various: day, evening, night and weekend	Variable depending on regiment, location and situation
Hours	40 hours per week	42 hours per week including lunch breaks	39 hours per week	Depends on operational needs

Table 1.9

Assessment activity

To achieve a *pass* (P2, P3), you need to describe the type of work done by at least three different personnel from within a public service and explain in detail the conditions of service for one of these roles.

Key points

- Primary research involves you going out and interviewing people or collecting information from them directly via a questionnaire or survey.
- Secondary research involves using books, journals and the internet to discover information other people have already drawn together.

Assessment activity

If you are aiming to achieve a *merit* (M1), you will have to show in-depth primary and secondary research for jobs in a chosen public service, for example three jobs in the fire service:

- Firefighter
- Watch manager
- Station manager.

Primary research may involve going to a fire station to ask questions about the different roles and secondary research can be done on the internet, in books or from your class notes in college time.

Application and selection procedures

You need to know about the application and selection procedure for a given public service. Here we will examine one of the most popular public services that people wish to join – the police service.

Entry requirements specify the minimum personal and professional achievements that you should have before applying to a public service. The more specialised and difficult the role the more entry requirements will be asked for. If you do not meet the entry requirements for your chosen public service, you will have to consider what you can do to develop your skills and abilities to meet or even exceed the requirements. Of course in some cases it may just be a case of waiting until you are old enough to join, even so you could be doing things which make you more attractive to a public service, such as getting additional qualifications at college or taking up some voluntary work in the community. Whenever you consider applying to a public service you should remember that there are many other people who want that particular job, and these may be people with more experience and qualifications than you. As you can imagine this can be difficult, but the key is good preparation. If you have researched your chosen career and you have made the most of the opportunities you have been given in your life so far you will have a distinct advantage over the competition.

Joining the police service

The police service is a rewarding and challenging career, and you need to be the sort of person to ensure that the roles and responsibilities, as described earlier, are fulfilled to a high standard

Entry requirements

Table 1.10 shows the entry requirements needed to join the police service.

Police officer entry requirements	
Age	You must be 18 years old to apply, but if you are successful you will not be appointed until you are $18\frac{1}{2}$.
Height	There is no height requirement for this service.
Health	You are required to undergo a physical examination so you should be in a good physical and mental state of health. The police service may reject applicants who are obese, diabetic, asthmatic, have a history of mental health difficulties or who have any other condition which may affect their ability to perform the duties required of them.
Fitness	You do not need to be super-fit, but you will be expected to show a good level of fitness which will include stamina, agility and strength, which will be assessed in a job-related fitness test which you will find detailed in the public service fitness unit.
Qualifications	The police service does not require any formal qualifications, but you must demonstrate a good standard of English, which will be tested during your application procedure. However it is important to remember that although you may not need any formal qualifications to join, they will certainly help you appear more attractive as a potential new employee and help with your promotion prospects.
Eyesight	The current vision requirements are not less than 6/36 vision unaided in each eye (this is the second line down on an optician's chart) but you should have 6/6 vision (the seventh line down on an optician's chart) when using both eyes, however you may be aided by glasses or contact lenses. You should also be able to distinguish primary colours which may rule out some forms of colour blindness.
Nationality	You must be a British citizen, a member of the Commonwealth or EU and have no restrictions placed on your residence in the UK.
Criminal convictions	You should declare all criminal convictions in your application. Having a criminal record will not necessarily prevent you from becoming a police officer as many convictions are judged on an individual basis, but there are some offences which will automatically rule you out. These are offences such as: murder, manslaughter, rape, kidnapping, terrorism, hi-jacking and death by reckless driving. In general you will be excluded if you have served a prison sentence or if you have committed crimes of violence.

Table 1.10

Just because you meet these requirements doesn't mean you will be a good police officer. In addition to these you need to possess the following skills and qualities:

- Self-confidence
- Interest in the community
- Excellent communication skills
- Tact and diplomacy
- Teamwork skills
- Ability to work on own initiative
- Problem-solving ability.

The application process

If you meet all of the entry requirements and you think you would make a good police officer then the next stage of the process is to get an application form. This can be obtained from your local constabulary recruiting department or from the police recruitment website at www.policecouldyou.co.uk . Some constabularies require you to send in a CV so that they can assess you for suitability before they send you an application form, but this can vary from force to force so it is always wise to check first. Once you receive an application form you will usually have to address the following:

- Personal details
- Name
- Address
- Date of birth
- Contact details
- Forces you wish to apply for (only applies if you are using the internet form)
- Do you wish to apply for the High Potential Development Scheme
- Nationality
- Convictions and cautions
- Tattoos
- Health and eyesight
- Business interests
- Financial position
- Previous addresses
- Details about your immediate family
- Employment details and references
- Education, qualifications and training
- A competence assessment which asks you about situations you have been involved in and how you reacted, including equality and diversity situations
- Why you want to be a police officer
- What do you expect the job to be like
- How have you prepared for your job application
- An equal opportunities questionnaire
- A personal statement.

Completing the form takes time and effort. If you complete it incorrectly or it shows you in a poor light, you will be weeded out in what is called a 'paper sift'.

Key point

A paper sift is a way of getting rid of unsuitable applications and it is used by many public services as well as many other employers. It involves checking application forms and weeding out any that are incomplete, do not show a reasonable standard of English or where the form demonstrates that an individual is clearly unsuitable for the job or doesn't meet the entry requirements.

Hints and tips to complete your police application form

1 Read the form thoroughly and ensure you understand every question.
2 Read the guidance notes thoroughly, they give you specific advice on what you need to do.
3 Photocopy the form several times so that you can practise filling it in and get it checked through before you complete the original.
4 Be honest, if you are not it will be found out and you will ruin your chances of the career you want.
5 Be meticulous about your spelling and grammar.
6 Ensure the things you write do not breach the principles of equality and diversity.
7 Take guidance from your local careers office or your college lecturers on how best to present yourself.
8 Use the appropriate style of writing. If it says black ink and block capitals then this is what you must do. In addition, your handwriting should be clear and legible.

The police recruitment procedure is becoming increasingly standardised across all 43 police services in England and Wales. This means that the procedure for becoming a police officer will be more or less the same wherever you apply. However you should still check for regional variations with your local force.

Personal statements

When you are competing your police application form, or indeed any application form, the most difficult type of question to answer is often the personal statement or the supporting information that is required. You should pay particular attention to this part as it is your opportunity to tell the service of your choice why they should take you on as a new recruit. It should be relevant and specific to the requirements of the job you are applying for. Examples of good practice in giving answers can sometimes be found on police recruitment websites such as www.policecouldyou.co.uk.

Let's do it!

Write a 200-word personal statement which summarises the achievements in your life so far.

Police selection procedure

The list below assumes you are successful at every stage.

1 On receipt of a full application form your details will be checked to make sure you meet the entry requirements.
2 If you meet the requirements your application form will have a competency-based questionnaire review.
3 If you are successful at the competency-based questionnaire review your medical form will be forwarded to the occupational health unit.
4 If your form is approved by the occupational health unit you will attend a recruit assessment centre.
5 If you are successful at the assessment centre you have to complete a medical questionnaire confirmed by your GP and forwarded to the occupational health unit.
6 Background checks and references will be taken up.
7 You will attend for a medical examination.
8 You will attend for the physical fitness test.
9 A joining date will be agreed.

Police assessment centre

One of the most important parts of the police application procedure is the assessment centre which each constabulary runs for its potential recruits. The assessment centre will have a variety of exercises such as:

- Written communication exercises such as memos, reports or letters which are marked on spelling, grammar, appropriateness and respect for diversity.
- Interactive role plays such as dealing with difficult members of the public in a customer service situation.
- Formal interview for the position of constable which includes a certain number of set questions.
- Police Initial Recruitment Test (PIRT), which is a series of tests designed to check your maths and verbal logical reasoning.

Assessment activity

To gain a *pass* (P4), you will have to accurately describe the current entry and selection stages for a given public service.

Curriculum vitae (CV)

You may be asked to produce a CV at some point in your application procedure for any service so it is important that your CV is up to date and relevant to your application. At one time a CV was just a list of your personal information, but the presentation of CVs has moved on and you should be aware of this. The examples below show two CVs with identical information, the first one is an example of how not to do it, the second one is an example of good practice.

CV Example 1

Name: David Smith jnr

Address: 32 East Way Close, Botheringham, B32 7AJ

Telephone Number: 01742 112112

E-maoil: daveyboy@lovemachine.co.uk

Date of Birth: 1/1/1987

Marital status: Single, but have a girlfreind

Driving Lisense: I do not drive, but I am taking lessons

School: Botheringham Compreensive I passed 5 GCSE's

- Maths E
- Endlish F
- Geography C
- PE A
- French F

I have also completed a Btec Fitst Diploma in Public services at Botheringham College

Work experiences: I have woked in a pizza shop and done a paper round. I also do some roofing with my dad and help at a local youth club

References:

David Smith Snr   Fat Garrys Piza shop

Botheringham Roofing Co   101 high Street

Botherningham   Botheringham

Let's do it!

Look at the CV above and list as many things as you can that are wrong with it.

CV Example 2

Curriculum Vitae

David Smith

A hard working and energetic young man, well able to cope with working in a high pressure environment under specific time constraints. Excellent interpersonal skills and a high level of experience in working with the public in a variety of situations. Excels in a variety of sports and has a high level of commitment to working with the community.

Contact Details:

Address: 32 East Way Close, Botheringham, B32 7AJ
Telephone: 01742 112112 (Home) 07967 11231123 (Mobile)
E-mail: d.smith@both-coll.ac.uk
Date of Birth: 1/1/87

Educational Achievements:

1998–2003   Botheringham Comprehensive School, Main Street, Botheringham, B23 4EW

- Physical Education A
- Geography C
- Maths E
- English F
- French F

I also achieved 100% attendance certificates for every year I attended Botheringham Comprehensive and I won The Arthur Wenden Award for excellence in sporting achievement in 1998, 1999 and 2000.

2003–2004   Botheringham College of Further Education, Lower Vale, Botheringham, B45 4TY

BTEC First Diploma in Public Services (6 units)

- The Public Services   Distinction
- Public Service Skills   Distinction
- Public Service Fitness   Distinction
- Crime and Its Effects   Merit
- Expedition Skills   Merit
- Workplace Welfare   Distinction

Career Achievements:

Sept 2000–June 2001   Newspaper Delivery Operative
This position involved the delivery of early morning and evening newspapers on a set route. I developed my time management skills and self-discipline in fulfilling this role as I had to be very conscious of making sure I delivered all of the goods regardless of external conditions such as the weather.

July 2001–May 2002   Pizza Chef
Working to fulfil food orders with speed and efficiency. I interacted with the public on an ongoing basis providing a friendly and reliable front of house service as well as observing health and hygiene regulations with diligence.

June 2002–Sept 2003   Builders Labourer

In this position I worked as part of an interconnected team of roofers and builders adhering to strict deadlines and producing high quality work. My teamwork skills were enhanced and I developed an appreciation of how people working together can achieve more than individuals working alone

Sept 2000–Present   Volunteer Youth Worker

I volunteer three evenings a week to help at a youth club in my local area. This involves coordinating and running sporting events for young people aged 11-14, improving their sporting skills and ensuring that health and safety guidelines are followed. I enjoy this type of work very much and like to think that I act as a positive role model for the young people I train.

Additional Information:

I have played football and cricket for the county under-18s teams and I enjoy a variety of other sporting and adventurous activities such as skiiing, climbing and canoeing. I like to go to the cinema, particularly to see science fiction films, and socialise with my friends. I have recently started to attend ju-jitsu classes and I hope this will enhance my physical coordination and sense of self-discipline even further. I am looking for a career opportunity where I can work with people in a community environment as I feel that this is what my skills and inclination best suit me for.

References:

Ms Alison Court	Mr A J Singh
Lecturer in Public Services	Youth Services Manager
Botheringham College of FE	Botheringham Youth Club
Lower Vale	Murray Road
Botheringham	Botheringham
B45 4TY	B17 9LU

 Think about it

How do the two CV's compare? What are their differences and similarities.

Let's do it!

Create your own CV.

Assessment activity

For a *pass* (P5) and *merit* (M2), complete a simulated application and selection procedure accurately and within a three-week period. This procedure will be as follows:

Week 1   Submit a CV and letter of application to your tutor for a specific public service job.

Week 2   Submit an application form for the same job.

Week 3   Prepare for and arrange and attend for a mock interview with your tutor.

Additional recruitment information

The following highlights some common factors you might have to deal with during any public service application and selection procedure.

Psychometric tests	These are tests designed to assess your capabilities in maths, English, problem solving, spatial awareness and mental agility. Not all services use them but many do. They give the service in question a reasonably accurate picture of your abilities.
Fitness tests	These are self-explanatory and you will find several of them detailed in the unit on public service fitness (Unit 3). They show the service of your choice that you are fit enough to complete the duties required of you.
Simulations	Role plays and simulations are becoming more common in public service selection as they give an idea of how people react when put in difficult situations. They can be used to assess the potential recruit's interpersonal skills and problem-solving ability.
Presentations	Many services require you to give a presentation of around 10 minutes on a particular public service topic. It highlights your ability to speak in public and communicate information effectively to others, which as you can imagine is a key skill in the public services.
Types of interview	There are many kinds of interview that you might come to face in applying to a public service. These might include formal interviews, group interviews, and panel interviews. It is your responsibility to find out what you are likely to face and prepare for it.
Dress code	Generally you should always be smart and professional at interview, unless you are attending for a fitness test or other task which requires specific dress. This means suits for both men and women.

Assessment activity

If you are aiming to achieve a *distinction* (D1), you will need to provide a detailed analysis of the roles, jobs and selection process of a chosen public service such as the police force.

Career development in the public services

Once you have been successful in your application and selection procedure you must remember you are only at the beginning of a public service career that will hopefully last many years and be very rewarding. It is highly unlikely that you will want to do the same thing for the next thirty years or so, and the public services offer a variety of opportunities to change your role regularly and move through the ranks. We will now investigate what happens during your initial training in a public service and what you might choose to do after you have completed your probationary period.

Basic training

Most public services have a period of basic training for new recruits. This is designed to equip them with the skills and abilities essential for successful completion of their initial duties. This is often followed by a probationary period where a new recruit has the opportunity to put these skills into practice in a supportive environment until they are fully qualified members of a public service. These periods of initial training and probation vary between services and are often dependent on the complexity of the job you would be required to do. Table 1.11 shows you the differences.

Public service	Initial training	Probationary period
Police	15 weeks	2 years
Fire service	16 weeks	1 year
Royal Navy	8 weeks	Depends on specialisation, could be up to six years to train as a nuclear engineer

Table 1.11

Initial training for Royal Navy rating

Initial training for Royal Navy ratings is conducted at *HMS Raleigh* and lasts eight weeks. It involves intensive study and testing, and requires you to take in a great deal of information in a relatively short time.

The process is as follows:

> **Week 1**
> You need to complete an enrolment form which commits you to spend the next four weeks at *HMS Raleigh*. After four weeks if the service is not for you, then you may leave. Medical and dental checks are conducted to ensure you are in a good state of health to perform your duties. You are taught how to take care of your kit and equipment. In addition you will begin to learn naval drill and work on increasing your fitness.
>
> **Weeks 2–8**
> For naval ratings this is when training begins in earnest and continues throughout the next seven weeks. It involves the following activities:
>
> - *Parade training drill* This involves learning how to perform naval drill, which is slightly different to army and police drill. Learning drill is a team task and it promotes teamwork, coordination and discipline.
> - *Education* You have to sit the basic English and maths tests for the navy and be taught how to keep a ship seaworthy and safe.
> - *Kit inspection* This involves keeping your kit clean and tidy. Ships are very cramped environments and space is at a premium, so it is very important that each rating learns how to respect others by maintaining kit.
> - *Firefighting and first-aid training* These are important skills in a naval environment and you will be taught the basics of both.
> - *Ship's damage control* It is important that ratings understand the design of the ships they serve on. This is because they may be called upon to repair damage caused by enemy weapons. This includes becoming familiar with the repair equipment used on board your ship.

Physical training

Fitness tests must be completed before passing into the Royal Navy. These are conducted in the eight-week basic training period and are as follows:

- *Raleigh fitness test* A 2.4-km run (to be completed within a set time), a 300-m shuttle run, press-ups and sit-ups.
- *Swimming* This involves swimming 40 metres in naval overalls, followed by treading water for three minutes. You will also practise life-raft drills dressed in a life jacket and survival suit.
- *Outward-bound activities* This involves an adventure training weekend where you will learn how to use a map and compass, complete practical teamwork exercises and an expedition (with back-pack) across Dartmoor.
- *Military training* You will learn how to carry out drills and firings.

As we have already discussed, you may decide you have the potential to progress further in your career and decide that you wish to consider promotion. It should be noted that starting at the bottom as a rating will mean it will take you much longer to progress up the career ladder; only 20% of officers start as naval ratings, the majority of them get additional education such as a degree and enter the service as an officer. The promotional structure in the navy follows.

Ranks in the Royal Navy

Able rate	The starting point.
Leading rate	The Royal Navy suggests that an able rate who is capable should be able to become a leading rate by the age of about 22.
Petty officer	A capable leading rate who works hard and shows an aptitude for leadership should be able to make petty officer by the age of around 27.
Chief petty officer	The average age of a member of the service who started as an able rate to reach this rank is early to mid-thirties.

Warrant officer

Sub-lieutenant

Lieutenant

Lieutenant commander

Commander

Captain

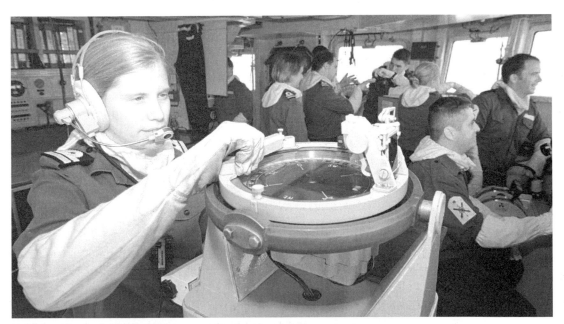

Figure 1.11 *Ranks in the Royal Navy – ratings and a captain*

Case study

Joining the Royal Navy

Aysha is 17 and just about to complete her First Diploma in Public Services. She wants to join the navy but is unsure whether to join now or get more qualifications so she can join as an officer. She needs some career advice and she has asked you to help her.

1 Do you think Aysha should join the navy as a rating or as an officer?
2 What preparation should she do to help her during her eight-week basic training?
3 If Aysha joins as a rating how long would it take her to get to the rank of chief petty officer?
4 Give Aysha a 150-word summary on what she can expect from her basic training.

Initial training for police officers

The two-year probationer training programme is made up of a number of stages each of which are equally important and all of which must be completed if a recruit is going to become a fully fledged police constable.

Stage 1 (minimum of two weeks)

You will be introduced to policing to

- gain a basic understanding of the role of a police officer
- learn how to deliver the best service to the public.

Stage 2 (15 weeks)

You will study the law and learn the core skills needed to deal effectively and professionally with a range of duties the police are expected to attend to.

Stage 3 (2 weeks)

You will

- be prepared for accompanied patrol
- learn about local procedures, force priorities and the communities you will serve.

Stage 4 (10 weeks)

You will work with a trained tutor constable as you put everything you have learned into practice on patrol under his or her guidance.

Stage 5 (2 weeks)

You will

- be assessed for suitability for independent police patrol
- learn more about local procedures and local policing plans for your own constabulary.

Stage 6 (Remainder of probation including a further 30 days' minimum training)

- You will complete the rest of your probation with your own constabulary, with a minimum of 30 days dedicated to further training.
- Your performance will be assessed in terms of competence, skills and knowledge and if you are found to have been successful in your probationer training after this two-year period you will be confirmed as a regular police officer.

All police officers must complete these two years on probation regardless of their qualifications or ambition. After the two years are up a recruit can seriously consider how they would like to progress in the service. The promotional structure for the police service is as follows:

Figure 1.12 *The epaulettes of ranks in the police service*

Promotion in the police service is not easy, automatic or dependent on length of service. Officers are promoted according to their individual performance, skills and abilities, and they must pass further exams and interviews. These exams are Objective Structured Performance Related Examinations (OSPRE) and they come in two parts: part one tests the officer's knowledge of the law, and part two tests their management and supervisory skills. This is important because as an officer moves through the ranks they also take on more and more management responsibility.

Think about it

Do you think that a two-year probation period for all police officers is a good idea? Explain your reasons.

Initial fire service training period

The basic training of a firefighter begins with 80 working days (16 weeks) at the fire service training school, which involves learning the skills in the use of firefighting equipment, fire safety legislation, rescue techniques, first aid and fire extinction. There is also a strong emphasis on maintaining the high standards of fitness needed in the service. The initial training of firefighters is very intensive and trainees are expected to undertake revision and study in their own time as well as in class. The one-year training probationary period of a firefighter is conducted at a fire station in the area they have chosen to join in. This is effectively a year of on-the-job training where a recruit's performance is continually assessed for ability and competency. However, a firefighter is not considered fully qualified until they have completed two more years of active service in an operational fire station.

Promotion in the fire service

Currently there are no advanced routes into the fire service as there are in the police and the Royal Navy. All recruits join as a firefighter and all have an equal chance of promotion to senior positions. The ranks in the fire service are:

Chief
Fire Officer

Deputy Chief
Fire Officer

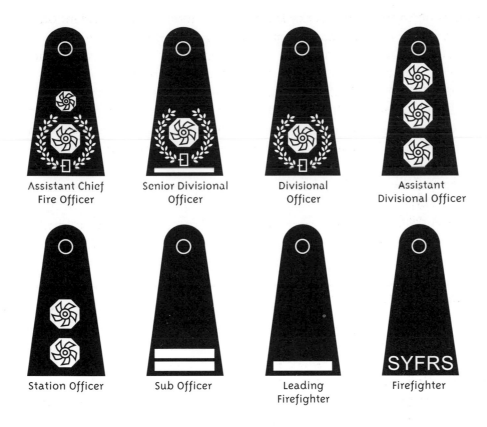

Figure 1.13 *The epaulettes of ranks in the South Yorkshire fire service*

In theory it is possible to reach the rank of station officer with five years experience, but generally it will take much longer than this. Promotions above this level do not crop up very often and you may be required to move brigades if you want to advance your career further.

Assessment activity

For a *pass* grade (P6), you will have to describe in detail the initial training programme for a given public service.

Your own career development

You must now consider your own career development and assess your suitability for a career in your chosen service. Many services can assist you with this by providing a self-selection questionnaire (SSQ) which asks you questions to help you decide whether you would be suitable for the role you have chosen. The example below is used by South Yorkshire Fire and Rescue Service.

Wholetime Firefighter SSQ

Are you?

- ○ Over 18 with 20/20 vision
- ○ Interested in people
- ○ Able to get on with people from different backgrounds
- ○ A good team player
- ○ Able to work under pressure
- ○ Able to think on your feet
- ○ A problem solver
- ○ Sensitive to others' needs
- ○ Able to handle people who may be distressed, confused or obstructive
- ○ Committed to developing your skills
- ○ Prepared to study beyond the working day
- ○ Able to follow orders
- ○ Committed to keeping physically fit
- ○ Prepared to work day and night shifts, evenings, weekends and public holidays
- ○ Interested in working with your hands
- ○ A practical person
- ○ Able to cope with routine
- ○ Prepared to work outside in all types of weather
- ○ Prepared to commit up to 55 days to your initial training

Assessment activity

For a *merit* (M3), you need to find the SSQ for the particular public service you wish to join and complete it. On the basis of the questionnaire, consider how suitable you would be to complete basic training.

Another good way of assessing how suitable you would be for a career in the public services is to draw up a SWOT analysis. SWOT stands for **S**trengths, **W**eaknesses, **O**pportunities, **T**hreats. Below is an example of a SWOT analysis for a public service student.

Name: Kassim Hussain

Background: Kassim has just completed his First Diploma in Public Services with mainly merits and is considering his future career options.

Strengths	Weaknesses
• Good academic record • Likes learning • Prepared to undergo further training • Supportive family • Confident • Good communication skills • Physically fit • Good state of health • No ties or commitments	• Not old enough for the police • Lack of work experience • Lack of life experience
Opportunities	**Threats**
• To complete the National Diploma in Public Services • To join the army straight away • To do an IT course • To take a year out to travel • Work in a civilian job to get some experience	• Other candidates with more experience • Join a service too young and may regret it

Let's do it!

Draw up a SWOT analysis for yourself.

Another method of assessing your suitability for a chosen career is a skills audit. This is a way of measuring and recording an individual's skills and abilities and comparing them to what they need for a certain job. There are many methods of evaluating your skills and abilities both on the internet and in self-development books. Consider the audit below.

Answer the following questions as honestly as you can on the following scale

1 Very Poor
2 Poor
3 Average
4 Good
5 Very Good

Skills	1	2	3	4	5
Confidence					
Public speaking					
Coping with new situations					
Making friends					
Talking to strangers					
Making eye contact with others					
Communication					
Vocabulary					
Clear speech					
Body language					
Respect for diversity					
Honesty and directness					
Teamwork					
Ability to work with others					
Ability to take orders					
Ability to listen and respond to others					
Respect for the opinions of others					
Ability to participate in discussions and offer suggestions					
Interpersonal skills					
Sensitivity to others					
Ability to cope with the distress of others					
Diplomacy					
Ability to be fair and impartial					
Ability to read body language of others					
Conflict management					
Ability to keep your temper					
Ability to calm others					
Ability to resolve a situation without shouting or violence					
Confidence to step in to help others who are in conflict					
Ability to liaise with different kinds of people					

Assessing your results:

Each section has a maximum of 25 points available. Fill in your results below:

Skills	Points
Confidence	
Communication	
Teamwork	
Interpersonal skills	
Conflict management	

In areas where you have received less than 15 points you need to consider how you will address these areas of weakness so that you can improve the core skills needed for career development in the public services.

In order to address the areas for development that you have, you should consider the use of an action plan. An action plan is a method to help you turn areas of weakness into areas of strength and help you monitor the process so that you know how far you have progressed towards your goals. For example, if your area of weakness was a failure to resolve conflict, then your objective would be to become effective in that skill, and the way of achieving this would include going on training courses.

There are several things which ought to be present in a personal development action plan. These are:

- Identify the problem
- Set an objective to achieve
- Detail how you intend to meet your objectives
- Describe the support you need from others
- List any resources you might need access to
- Dates for review or completion.

You may be familiar with many of the above points from your own college's tutorial procedure, which is designed for similar purposes.

The following is an example of a personal action plan.

Personal Action Plan

Area/s for development:

My interpersonal communication skills are weak and I find myself misreading situations because I don't have the confidence to clarify what is going on. This is going to disadvantage me if I decide to join the police service.

Targets to achieve:

1 To improve my understanding of body language

2 To become more conscious of my own body language

3 To develop the confidence to ask for clarification in situations if I don't understand what is going on

4 To find out what interpersonal skills the police require in a potential recruit

Actions required by you:

- Ask a close friend to monitor my body language to see if I am communicating in a friendly manner

- Make a diary of body language that I see and use a good quality body language book to see what it means

- Consider going on a course on interpersonal communication to improve my skills

- Research the interpersonal skills needed by the police

Actions required by others:

- Friends to help me by monitoring my actions and giving me the benefit of their advice

Resources:

College prospectus

Police application information

Good quality body language book

Dates for review/completion

I will review the situation every two weeks to see the progress I have made and change the action plan if needed. Dates: 30th Jan, 15th Feb, 1st Mar, 15th Mar.

By the 15th March I should have achieved my targets completely.

Assessment activity

To gain a *pass* (P7), you need to produce an action plan for your own career development.

Assessment activity

If you are aiming for a *distinction* (D2), you will have to provide an evaluation of your own potential and limitations for career development within your chosen public service.

CHECK WHAT YOU KNOW

1 What does PIRT stand for?
2 When was the police service formed?
3 What does CV stand for?
4 What is the role of the fire service?
5 What is the role of the prison service?
6 What is the starting salary of an army soldier?
7 What is the retirement age of a police officer?
8 What are the main elements of a CV?
9 What is the rank structure for the fire service?
10 What is an action plan used for?

Resources

Websites

www.edexcel.org.uk This site contains your IVA assignment and learner's instructions on how to complete it. In addition it contains the full details of this unit for you to examine.

www.mod.uk This is the website for the Ministry of Defence. It contains lots of information on working in the armed services and what the services do.

www.army.mod.uk This is the site for the British Army. It contains details on careers in the army both as a soldier and as an officer.

www.royal-navy.mod.uk This site contains careers information for both the navy and the Royal Marines, as well as lots of information on what the navy is currently doing.

www.raf.mod.uk The website of the Royal Air Force.

www.ta.mod.uk This contains lots of information on the UK's Territorial Army, including careers information.

www.policecouldyou.co.uk This is a really good site which will help you find out anything you ever wanted to know about becoming a police officer or working as a civilian in the police service. It also contains several really useful case studies which will help you assess if you have what it takes to be a police officer. Once you are on the website go to 'What would you do?' to access them.

www.careers.ed.ac.uk This is a general careers website, but it contains lots of information about the emergency and armed services.

www.hmce.gov.uk This site contains information about HM Customs and Excise, including what they do and how you could join.

www.hmprisonservice.gov.uk This site contains information on the prison service in the UK.

Each fire, ambulance and police service will have its own website. The best way to find information which relates to your area is to use an internet search facility, such as Google, and key in your chosen service and the county you live in. For example, if you lived in South Yorkshire you would key in 'Police – South Yorkshire' (or fire or ambulance service) and the following websites would pop up:

www.southyorks.police.uk South Yorkshire Police Service

www.syfire.org.uk South Yorkshire Fire and Rescue Service

www.syas.nhs.uk South Yorkshire Ambulance Service.

Public service skills

Introduction

This unit will help you identify and develop a range of teamwork and personal skills that are very important for anyone considering a career in any of the public services. You will also be able to use these in other areas of employment.

You will look at some of the different qualities that are essential for effective teamwork and the different types of teams that exist in the public services. When you participate in a range of different activities you will have the opportunity to identify your own existing teamwork skills and how to develop these.

You will also examine a range of interpersonal and personal communication skills, which are important for working in the public services, as well for your personal life.

How you will be assessed

Throughout the unit the activities and tasks will help you learn and remember information. There are some case studies to add industry relevance to the topics and what you have to learn.

At the end of the unit, there are questions to test your knowledge and assessment tasks outline the evidence requirements for assessment in order to obtain a pass, merit or distinction, as well as suggesting ways of providing assessment evidence. This unit is internally assessed.

After completing this unit, you should be able to achieve the following outcomes:
1   Investigate the purpose and importance of teamwork in the public services.
2   Develop a range of teamwork skills.
3   Identify and demonstrate a range of interpersonal skills and personal effectiveness skills.
4   Develop a range of communication skills.

Teamwork

What is a team?

The word 'team' means a group of people working together to achieve a certain goal or objective. We usually associate the word with sport, as in the case of a football team. However we use the term in various other contexts, as in business where we talk about management teams and in the public services where we have rescue teams, lifeboat teams, paramedic teams, firefighting teams. It is also used in the context of groups of animals being used to pull objects: for example a team of oxen pulls a cart, a team of horses pulls a plough and a team of dogs pulls a sled. It was thought at one time that a group of animals of the same family worked better together.

For a team to succeed it has to have

- good communication
- positive leadership
- motivation
- discipline.

Remember

Together

    Everyone

        Achieves

            More

The aims of a team are to

- achieve the task in the most efficient way
- complete the task in the quickest possible time
- use the correct systems at the right place and at the right time to minimise injury
- maintain the team's effectiveness by supporting each other.

There are many different types of teams in the public services and they are essential for

- maintaining the professional operation of the armed forces and the emergency services that make up the uniformed public services
- maintaining the well-being of all who are employed by the armed forces, the emergency services and all other areas of the public services such as the prison service and coastguard.

In the public services it is essential that you are able to work and operate as part of a team.

The following are needed to achieve effective teamwork:

- Those in the public services need to work very closely with all types of people in society, and to deal with stressful situations which require swift, well-thought-out action in order to save life and to maintain public order and safety.
- They make use of teamwork so that their work is carried out efficiently and quickly. An effective team of people will have more strengths than weaknesses and all the individual team members will be supported by each other when they are carrying out a task.
- All emergency services and the armed forces have to deal with people who are in situations when they are frightened, in pain, confused, shocked or obstructive. Many accidents and incidents do not discriminate; there is not a particular type of victim. You will have to learn how to deal with all types of people when they and you are in very difficult circumstances.

You will find that teams come in many different forms in the public services:

- They may be very large and made up of smaller teams working together. An example is a large police force with smaller specialisation teams working within it. These could be traffic police or dog handlers.
- They will be identified by the tasks they carry out and their role. An example is an ambulance crew which will be clearly identified by their clothing, their equipment and their ambulance, as well as the tasks that they carry out, such as emergency life-saving skills and the rapid transportation of injured people either by ambulance or by air ambulance.

The teams that exist within the public services are mainly uniformed. They not only work as individuals within their own service, they also work as part of teams, such as a combined emergency service, in many situations and incidents.

Types of teams in the public services

Crew

This is a group of people who work together as a team. This team is known as 'the crew' whilst they are working together, for example on a civilian aircraft they are known as 'cabin crew'. The term is used in the case of the following teams in the public services.

An aircrew

In the Royal Air Force an air crew will consist of the people who are flying and navigating the aircraft and any others who carry out tasks on board the aircraft. A fighter jet such as the Harrier Jump Jet will only have one or two crew in it. A larger aircraft such as a Hercules transporter plane will have more people in its crew. This is because of space and also the tasks that the aeroplane has to carry out. The fighter jet needs to be light and its role is to strategically attack or defend. The transporter plane is very large and will need a crew who will pilot, navigate and ensure the safety of its cargo and passenger troops during the flight and landing.

There are also helicopter crews. These can be used in all the armed forces, the police, ambulance service and other rescue services such as the mountain rescue service or the coastguard. The size of the crew depends on the size of the helicopter and what role it has. For example, a Lynx helicopter in the Royal Navy will have an aircrew of two. The larger Sea King helicopter is operated by the pilot but there will be other crew on board, especially if it is operating on a search and rescue mission.

Figure 2.1 *A Sea King helicopter on a rescue mission*

A submarine crew

That submarines are crewed by males only is because of the conditions they live and work under and because of the scarcity of the space needed for the separation of sexes, as in matters such as sleeping quarters. Cramped space and long periods of time spent on active duty at sea means that a submarine crew has to work and live in close quarters for long periods of time. Other problems may also arise with men and women living and working so close together. The closeness of a crew is reflected in the submarine captain being known as 'the father' of the crew.

Shift work

The work of the uniformed public services goes on all day long. The police, fire and ambulance services, for example, don't simply close down at the end of a normal day of work or at the weekend. The service must go on all day, every day. To make this possible the services have to operate a shift system of work. A shift is a specific period of work carried out by a group or team of personnel. The shift system is a continuous series of separate periods of work, each one comprising a group of personnel who carry on the work of the previous group until the end of their shift, when they in turn hand over to another group. The shift patterns however will vary in each of these services.

Some people like working on a shift, even during the night, as it means they have the increased flexibility of having concentrated periods of time off. Those with families are then able to spend more time with them than a nine to five working pattern allows. The fire service uses their shift pattern as a positive aspect of a career in the service, as it enables parents to combine a more flexible type of career with having a family.

Since the Working Time Regulations of 1998, all uniformed services which have shift patterns have to produce shift schedules that seek to minimise the adverse effects of shift work on staff. All personnel also have an obligation to be aware of the potential adverse effects of shift work on their own health and safety and that of others. Plenty of information is now available on how to cope with working in shifts.

The hours of a shift will vary and change on a weekly or monthly basis. All shifts are put up on a noticeboard and logged on a computer system so that everyone knows who is at work and who is not. This is for efficiency and safety so that it is known how many people are on the shift and whether it has a complete team. If it is not a complete team, then there is a procedure to get extra cover so that health and safety standards are maintained. The fire service works a 42-hour week with two day shifts and two night shifts followed by four days off.

When asked about why he liked shift work, a firefighter said

'You work two days and two nights on. I'm using the four days off to go to college on a computer course. Your brain is always buzzing and the fire services will always sponsor or support more learning.'

Case study

Shift work

John is a leading firefighter and has been in the fire service for 10 years. He combines the demands and challenges of the job with helping to bring up his two-year-old son. His wife is a nurse and they both work in shift patterns so that they both are able to care for their child.

John works a 42-hour-week on 'Red Watch'. His shift is two days from 9 am to 5 pm and this is followed by two nights from 5 pm to 9 am. He then has four days off. John likes working a shift pattern for several reasons:

- It gives him the chance to spend quality time with his two-year-old son.
- It gives him varied time off – sometimes during the week and sometimes at the weekend.
- He and his wife don't have to pay for expensive child care outside the home.
- He has the chance to participate in sport and leisure activities in off-peak times.

John says that for him there are no real negative aspects to shift work apart from how busy he and his team get during the night shift attending incidents.

Watches

A shift system is traditionally known as a 'watch' in the Royal Navy and in the fire service.

In the fire service there are a number of watches at each station which will be named after colours, such as the 'White Watch' or 'Blue Watch'. The number of watches depends on the size of the fire station.

Those on a watch will work very closely together and develop a close bond. This is part of the identity of their team and it will ensure the team is effective and can support each member of it.

Someone with a problem can usually work it out within the team, however sometimes there will be friction even in a close team, especially in stressful circumstances. So, if there is any problem the watch cannot work out themselves, then they can take it to a more senior fire officer.

The Royal Navy has its own watch system, which originates from the days of sailing ships when there would be a 'watch' to navigate and steer the ship manually. Even though modern technology now does most of these tasks, you still need to have people! The Royal Navy's watch system operates so that there is continuous cover to ensure that the ship's essential facilities and equipment are maintained 24 hours a day. The watch system also develops close-knit teams that work well together. If there are any problems within a watch, the Royal Navy encourages its men and women to ask for help if a situation is affecting them. The personnel system in the Royal Navy is called the 'Divisional System', as each group of personnel is known as a 'division', and it ensures that every person is part of a chain of command. From the bottom to the top of the chain the divisional system looks after each link to ensure an effective team. This ethos is emphasised in the advertising slogan for the Royal Navy, which is 'The team works'.

Regiment

This is a unit of soldiers in the army and is often described as being like a very large 'family'. It has its own traditions and battle honours that are celebrated to remember past glories and these are part of the spirit and ethos of the regiment.

A regiment is one of the most important units in the army and consists of about 650 soldiers who are commanded by a colonel. When a regiment consists of several of these units it is called a battalion. These have the

same structure as a regiment and are numbered in ascending order, for example the First Battalion Parachute Regiment and the Second Battalion Parachute Regiment.

A regiment usually represents a certain geographical area in the country, so many who join a particular regiment are from the same area and even the same family, which reinforces the closeness of the 'family' team. Every regiment has its own badge and role.

Figure 2.2 *Soldiers form a strong bond with their regiment which continues even after they have left the army*

Multi-agency team

This is a team made up of other teams from different services to work together on a particular project or incident.

In the case of a major traffic incident, several emergency services will be involved, including the police, fire service and ambulance service. These emergency services train together on special exercises so that they become experienced in working together to deal with a variety of incidents, such as traffic accidents and terrorist attacks.

Multi-agency planning of incident

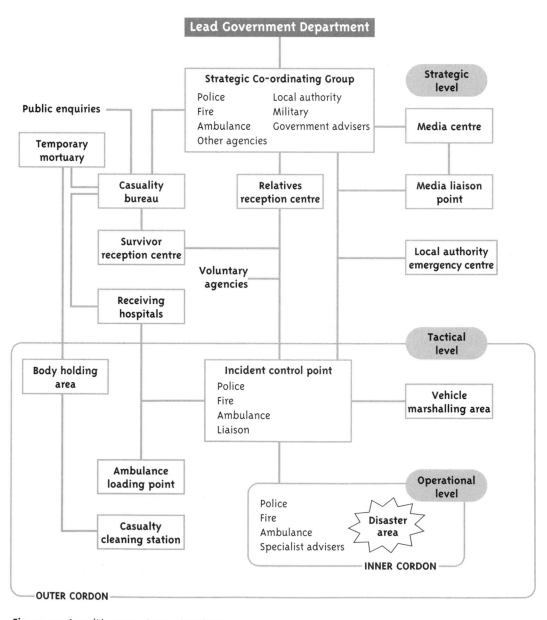

Figure 2.3 *A multi-agency team structure*

The fire service has been selected by the government to lead the new multi-agency plan called 'New Dimensions', which has been instigated to cover any conventional biological or chemical attack on a public area in this country. The fire service will lead the other emergency services in such an incident as they have the appropriate equipment, the necessary protective biological and chemical defence suits and the experience to work with the other emergency services in such an incident.

Specialist teams

These are teams set up for a particular purpose for which they have special knowledge, training and skills. An example of a specialist team is the Emergency Planning Unit (EPU) in a police force. This is a dedicated specialist unit of officers and support staff within the specialist operations of the force.

The Emergency Planning Unit works with other emergency agencies to ensure that the force is prepared to respond to any critical incident or major emergency by producing emergency and contingency plans for

- unknown incidents at unknown locations, such as a plane crash
- unknown incidents at known locations, such as sports and football stadiums
- known incidents at known locations, such as chemical plants.

The role of the police is to coordinate the overall emergency service response.

The training and preparedness of such emergency response units has always been a priority. However, since the terrorist attacks on the World Trade Centre in New York on 11 September 2001 and the following anthrax attacks worldwide, it has a particularly high priority. Emergency services train together on exercises designed to test the plans and to raise awareness of emergency procedures to enable staff to deal with and respond to major incidents.

Let's do it!

Think about 11 September 2001 and as a group find out what each of the emergency services in New York did to deal with the crisis.

In the event of a critical incident or emergency the EPU staff provide the necessary support to the overall incident commander.

Project teams

A project team is one that is formed to carry out a particular task. This is usually carried out over a period of time. Project teams exist in the private sector, for example in business, and in the public sector, for example in the uniformed services and the civil service.

An example of one in the public sector is an organisation which has been given the task of carrying out the recommendations of a public enquiry. When there has been a major disaster or incident there is usually a public enquiry set up by the government. A detailed report is produced about what has happened and what action should be taken. Proposed improvements are organised by a central project team at a very senior level of government and there will be smaller teams working with the main team.

An example was the enquiry set up after the murder of the black teenager Stephen Lawrence in 1993 and the subsequent non-arrest of his suspected murderers by the Metropolitan Police. The public outrage that followed this failure of the police led to the enquiry to discover what went wrong and to recommend what should be done to avoid something like it happening again. The enquiry was headed by Sir William Macpherson and its findings was called the Macpherson Report, which was published in 1999. It criticised the policing methods of the Metropolitan Police and called for the continuous monitoring and initiation of new policies.

The Report found the Metropolitan Police in London to be 'institutionally racist' in their policing of a multi-cultural environment. As a result many committees and project teams have come to work together at the main police headquarters and also in the various areas of the Metropolitan Police. The aim is to improve the abilities and attitudes of the police officers at all levels through updated training and constant support so that they are able to carry out their role of policing communities and keeping law and order in a modern, diverse society.

The Macpherson Report led to the amendment of the 1976 Racial Equality Act in 2000, so that there is now considerable legal responsibility on the public sector to have in place anti-racism legislation and to take immediate action should any behaviour in an organisation be perceived as a form of racism.

 Think about it

What kinds of people would be involved in an enquiry such as the one into the death of Stephen Lawrence?

The importance of teamwork

When you see the flashing blue lights and hear the sirens of the emergency services, do you think of them as a 'team' rushing to deal with an emergency? One person of course doesn't make a team and it is impossible to carry out most emergency tasks without one. Remember, 'There is no "I" in team!'

Every person in the uniformed services has a role to play in their team. Some have more than one role. A fire brigade has firefighters who are trained to drive the fire engine. Police officers will have a specialist role and a general role, for example a beat officer may also be involved with community outreach to young people.

In the armed forces, teamwork is essential for carrying out tasks in peace time and in times of operational requirements when the armed forces is under the command of a commander-in-chief in an area of war – called the 'theatre of war'. Every person under command of the commander-in-chief is part of his team, and all of them know how important it is to work together. It's like having a chain. Each person is a link in the chain and it remains strong as long as there is no break in it. Everyone has to make sure the chain doesn't break, even under pressure.

Achieving organisational objectives

Every organisation has an 'objective'. This is the purpose of the organisation and what it sets out to achieve. The role of the armed forces is to defend the territories of the United Kingdom and its overseas territories and to strengthen international peace and security. The role of the police is uphold the law, to cut crime and to make communities safer. The role of the fire service is to fight fires, to take part in other rescue missions and to promote fire safety in the community.

The organisational objective can also be known as the 'mission'.

Mission of the fire service

The mission of the fire service is to
- preserve saveable life
- promote fire safety within the locality
- deal with all incidents with professional competence
- minimise the effects on the environment.

Everyone in an organisation needs to know and understand what part they play in the organisation and what the aims and objectives of that organisation are. Knowing this is particularly important if personnel are going to face very stressful and dangerous situations in carrying out their work. Speak to anyone in the uniformed services about the dangers they face, and they say, 'This is my job … this is what I am trained to do.' Many have been involved in life-threatening situations and have seen their colleagues injured, and in some cases die. However they know they have to do their jobs as professionals.

Mission of the ambulance service

Each ambulance brigade has a different mission statement but the role is the same. It is about working as part of the emergency services and providing help and care to patients by dedicated, trained staff. The mission statement of the London Ambulance Service is

'A world-class ambulance service staffed by well trained and proud people who are recognised for contributing to the provision of high-quality patient care.'

Case study

Christopher Finney

An eighteen-year-old soldier, Christopher Finney, won one Britain's highest military honours when he was in Iraq as part of Operation Telic in 2003. It was for rescuing a comrade who got trapped in their burning armoured car which had been hit by 'friendly fire' (this is when the same side mistakenly attacks their own soldiers as enemy forces). He was composed enough to radio for help despite his wounds.

Figure 2.4 *Trooper Christopher Finney was awarded the George Cross for bravery in rescuing a colleague under fire during the Iraq war*

The soldier describes what happened to him…

> 'I was driving a Scimitar (armoured car) near a small village when we were hit on top. (The armoured car had been hit by cannon fire and ammunition started to explode in the turret.) I didn't know what had happened and I thought we were under attack from a rocket-propelled grenade.'

The solider found cover from the explosions but came back to rescue the gunner who was trapped in the hatch.

> 'I could see that he was trapped half out of his hatch and got him to the ground and started first aid. His headset was hanging off the side of the turret so I used it to send a report.'

Both men survived but received serious shrapnel wounds. They were rescued and treated by other soldiers who had moved up to where the attack had happened to provide medical aid to them and weapon support against oncoming Iraqi forces.

The soldier's award was one of the honours awarded to these soldiers during this intense action. The British forces commander said,

> 'This young man who was only eighteen at the time and had been in the army for less than a year showed outstanding courage … his clear-headed courage and devotion to his comrades was out of all proportion to his age and experience.'

What qualities of teamwork do you think are shown in this case study?

Camaraderie

This means 'team spirit', which is the loyalty and support that comes from working closely with other people in a small or large team under stressful and sometimes dangerous circumstances. This requires absolute loyalty to each member of the team, leadership of the team and awareness of the strengths and weaknesses of the team. A female firefighter explains what she thinks camaraderie means to her:

> *'Teamwork means someone will help you if your flat wants decorating. If your car's making a funny noise someone will look at it. If I come in not smiling I guarantee that within 10 minutes at least three people will ask if I'm OK. They make jokes, but they really care.'*

Command and control

In the uniformed services you carry out tasks that are physically and mentally demanding, and which can be extremely unpredictable and potentially dangerous.

An effective team is one which has a leader who communicates with the team as well as being in communication with people outside the team. This is called 'command'. The higher someone's rank in any of the

Figure 2.5 *An army staff exercise involves working closely as a team*

uniformed services, the more command they have of a large number of people, however each person has their own role in any situation. For example, in the armed forces there is a chain of command from the commanding officer of a battalion downwards and back up again. There is a mission command within the armed forces, with everyone taking part understanding what the commander's (leader's) intent is and what the main effort of an operation is, from the lowest ranking soldier to the colonel, and up to the staff level.

The commander-in-chief of the British forces in Iraq holds a very senior rank. This role is to have an informed overview of what is going on and be able to manage and command how to deal with this and any circumstances that arise. However, they will rely on intelligence information and the views and opinions of other colleagues in other parts of the armed forces, who will be of lower rank. Nevertheless, their various skills and knowledge are vital to the planning and success of carrying out such an operation.

Command and control of an incident

There needs to be command and control of personnel when there is a major incident which involves police, fire and ambulance, such as a major traffic accident, major fire or other major rescue incident.

Many personnel from different emergency services will attend such an incident and it is important that all of them are accounted for. The fire service has 'identification tally tags' that hook onto the incident board on their appliance (fire engine) so that there is a record of who is there and where they are at all times. If it is a major incident and there needs to be more than five fire appliances, then there is a command support unit, which is a communications unit coordinating the incident.

Let's do it!

Look at the fire strike in 2003 and discuss the different services that were involved and what their roles were.

Problem solving

Good teamwork is about making the best of what every member has to offer in order to achieve your aim as quickly and effectively as possible.

It is very important to look at a situation and come up with an idea of how to complete a task or how to solve a problem. Imagine you are a police officer and have been called to someone's house as they are locked out!! What do you do? You could decide it's easier to 'pop the locks' with a piece of plastic than call out the fire service to break the door down!

Being able to solve problems is crucial in all the uniformed services. This is why there are many different types of written and practical command tasks during your selection procedure and at every stage of your training. Being able to think quickly, even when you are tired and under extreme pressure, makes you able to do this more effectively in 'real life', when other people's lives may depend on you making the most effective decision.

Sometimes there is no 'right' decision, as when you are faced with a constantly changing situation. In such as case you have to be flexible in your plans and carry out the task as effectively as possible. This is called 'managing risk'. This is important and you cannot do it through strength and bravery alone – you need skill and teamwork.

Support

When the armed forces are in the front line of operations on active duty or when the emergency services are at a major incident, they do not get there by themselves; they need support to carry out their job.

A team can be supported by
- logistics, such as the supply of clothing and equipment
- maintenance of equipment
- communication to other units or forces, especially if extra help is necessary
- morale and emotional support.

The armed forces have most of their equipment provided by their 'logistics units'. These provide the essentials for operational effectiveness, sometimes in difficult situations. This could be a war zone where there is no electricity, water or even proper roads and bridges! These units specialise in 'making something out of nothing', and they generally manage to supply most of the needs of the armed forces, as well as humanitarian aid to countries at war.

Backing up the emergency services is also very important. Each service has operators who control the communications between the emergency services. When you call 999 this is relayed straight to a communications headquarters for the area and the appropriate services are sent out. Sometimes other emergency services are alerted, either from the communications centre or via radio at the actual incident if they are needed.

Support is not just about equipment, food and manpower. It is also about the emotional support that members of a team can give each other, such as being able to talk about things that affect them in either their professional or private lives. Team members support each other, which is particularly vital when operating in an area where the risk of losing your life is very high.

Figure 2.6 *One of the roles of the modern soldier is providing humanitarian aid to people whose lives have been shattered by war or conflict*

A firefighter was asked how he managed to combat stress when he had a bad experience. 'Tea round the mess table' was the answer! He and his colleagues found it more beneficial to talk about their experiences over a cup of tea than to have a more formal counselling session. If you are dealing with uncertainty, stress, danger, injury and violence it is important to try to keep all of this in perspective, and your team mates can help.

Combining individual skills

A member of the emergency services describes what they think of this:

> 'It's all about teamwork and pulling in the same direction … you need the thinkers, the problem solvers, the people who are clever with their hands, all different strengths. You get together and the results come out of that.'

Professional skills are combined in all the uniformed services. For example, the organisation of the army is such that each part of it supports the other in a battle situation and in the logistics of supply and communication.

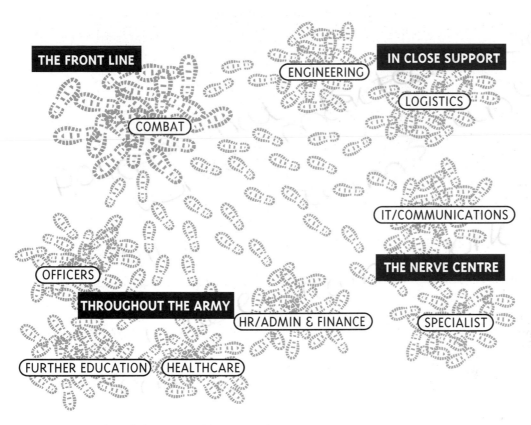

Figure 2.7 *A plan of the army and how it works*

All the uniformed services are taught how to combine their own individual skills with those of other people so that you are able to select the best person for a particular job and the other team members will support them.

Assessment activity

To achieve a *pass* (P1) you need to show that you understand and can explain the importance of teamwork in two different public services.

Working together in small groups, research the importance of teamwork in at least two different public services. You can look for information on the internet, in careers literature and also speak to people who work in the public services. As a group, produce a presentation of your findings. Make your own detailed research notes and keep them for part of your assessment.

In doing your research, think about the following:

- What type of team is it?
- What are the roles and responsibilities of the team?

- How do members work together?
- Why is teamwork important in what they do?
- What does teamwork achieve?
- How does teamwork make the task easier?
- How does this type of team help society?

Qualities for effective teamwork

Discipline of yourself and of a group

What is discipline?

In all the uniformed services success depends on teamwork, which comes from demanding training, strong leadership, comradeship and trust. Trust is based on shared values, the maintenance of high standards and the commitment of everyone to their task, to their organisation and, particularly in the armed forces, to their nation.

The uniformed services need discipline to be effective, and so you must obey all lawful orders that are given. Self-discipline is the best form of discipline, as it earns the respect and trust of colleagues and equips you to cope with the difficult individual decisions you will have to take at any time in your career.

An instructor in the armed forces explains what discipline means in training:

> 'Training now is not about shouting at you for getting something wrong. It is about motivating and explaining because that's how you learn to solve problems and you have to adapt all of your knowledge to different circumstances.'

 Think about it

Why do you think discipline is necessary in the public services?

Think about a recent major event, such as the terrorist attack in Madrid, and what the consequences might have been if there was a lack of discipline in dealing with the event.

Leadership

What is leadership?

Leadership is about more than holding a certain rank and giving orders! It is about leading a team so that it achieves. A team without leadership will achieve little, a team that is well led and motivated will achieve whatever it wants.

All of us have the potential to be leaders. It comes naturally to some, but most of us have to learn the art of leadership, and we can learn to do this by practising a number of basic principles.

- Take a genuine interest in other people and show them that you have their interests at heart.
- Be concerned with your team's training, their welfare and their responsibilities.
- Be confident in yourself and your team that you will reach the highest standards.
- Be approachable and learn how to communicate well so that you can help and encourage your team.
- Always remember that you are all part of the same team and without each other you are just one person!

Creating morale is a very important part of leadership. A healthy team spirit is essential to the success of the team. Morale is a combination of enthusiasm, determination and a happy working environment. If the team is low on morale, then efficiency and professionalism decreases and this will result in a very unhappy and ineffective workforce.

A recent example of good leadership was the rousing speech by a British Army colonel, Tim Collins, to his troops in Iraq. The speech was seen as a reflection of a tough compassionate leader.

> '…We go to liberate, not to conquer. We will not fly our flags in their country. We are entering Iraq to free a people and the only flag which will be flown in that ancient land is their own.'

Figure 2.8 *Colonel Tim Collins inspiring his troops*

What qualities should a leader have?

There are different styles of leadership and there are different kinds of leaders. However, we are all a leader in our own way and the uniformed services are looking at that *potential* for leadership. When taking part in selection and training, you are being observed and marked for the potential leadership you show during training and how you react to the challenges of your new experiences.

In the table below write down five situations in which you have shown leadership qualities. This could be when you helped someone or when you had a problem and managed to work out a solution. An example has been done to start you off.

My leadership qualities	What happened?	How can I improve this quality?
1 Good communication Ability to motivate someone	I helped another student who was having difficulty in doing an assignment and who needed help and confidence in their ability	Being aware of what other people may be feeling and what their circumstances are
2		
3		
4		
5		

Table 2.1

Commitment

Personal commitment is the foundation of the uniformed services. You must be prepared to carry out your role whenever and wherever you are required and to do your best at all times. This means that you must put the needs of the objective and your team ahead of your own interests.

Loyalty and trust

These are important qualities in life as well as in the uniformed services. Your loyalty to your colleagues and your service must be unquestioned. You must always carry out an order to the best of your ability; if you disagree with it or think that it is wrong, you can always make your point to the appropriate person afterwards. However, it is important to understand that whilst you are being trained and are inexperienced it may be better to accept that the decisions and orders of those who are more senior are based on much more experience than you have.

Trust is closely connected to loyalty. You have to trust your colleagues and the service you are in. They will help you achieve your tasks and help you remain safe in dangerous situations. Trust is also about knowing that every person in the uniformed services is highly trained and that you can rely on their knowledge, expertise and skills at all times.

Cooperation

Team members need to cooperate with each other in the uniformed services. You could be faced with situations that are uncertain and dangerous and with a society that is diverse and varied. The emergency services mainly deal with situations in our own society, but the armed forces deal with many more diverse situations in other countries with very different societies to ours and which are under the additional strains of war and terrorism.

Team members have to cooperate with each other physically and mentally in order to do a task quickly, particularly when someone's life depends on it.

Identity

The identity of a team depends on such things as the regiment they belong to, the special job they do, and the particular uniformed service they are part of. Your uniform marks you out as a member of a particular team and you will be trained to wear that uniform with pride and professional confidence. However, you will also be part of a very large team that serves the general public. When in uniform you are identified as a person who is trained to help people, possibly only when they are in need of emergency help.

In the uniformed services a friendly rivalry takes place between teams within the services, such as the messes in the armed forces and the watches in the emergency services. Plenty of jokes are made about each of the armed forces and their so called 'identitities', but it's mostly good humoured and part of the 'identity' – that is, sharing a certain mode of behaviour and a set of beliefs that are reflected in the way that you behave. For example, your behaviour in your private life has some bearing on your professional life. You would not expect a firefighter to cause fires or a police officer to break the law!

A person's identity is also their professional reputation. However, sometimes people in the uniformed services damage the reputation of the service, but thankfully they are a minority.

 Think about it

What characteristics of behaviour would you expect people in the uniformed services to have?

Norms

Members in a team often share types of behaviour which are the norms of the team. These can be good qualities if the team works well, and can include determination, enthusiasm and skill. However, if the team does not work well then the norms of behaviour may be more negative, such as laziness, untidiness and a lack of motivation.

The standard and behaviour of any team has a lot to do with the leader. Most team members look for the sort of leadership that tells them what they have to do and when they have to do it. It is up to the leader to harness the enthusiasm of the team and to create a motivated team spirit which will increase their professionalism in their job.

Teams in the uniformed services rarely lack motivation and fall below the standards required, but it can happen when the pressure is not intense. In such cases it is very important to ensure that a team is motivated and proud of itself so that the equipment is maintained in good order and, more importantly, safe to use.

Communication

Good communication skills are vital to working in the uniformed services. You are taught these skills from the moment you start basic training.

Communication can be

- verbal, for example an order from one person to another
- direct speech and the use of speech via equipment, for example using a radio
- visual, for example writing and drawing pictures
- non-verbal, for example body language and sign language.

When you are a member of the uniformed services it is very important that you have a natural ability to communicate with a huge variety of people in routine activities and in emergency scenarios. As the uniformed public services deal very closely with the general public, it is vital that their attitudes should reflect the society they serve. In communities where there is a high proportion of people who do not have English as a first language, the uniformed services make every effort to communicate and work with the local community. They achieve this through interpreters and the service's own community officers who run local outreach projects. These projects help inform and educate the local community about fire prevention and crime prevention. There is also continuing recruitment from ethnic minorities in order to reflect modern day society.

The uniformed services expect very high standards of communication as it is a vital part of teamwork. However, you will never be expected to deal with a situation that can't be managed effectively by yourself. You will learn to assess a situation before dealing with it so that your involvement is effective. You will be able to call for backup as this is part of the communication system of the uniformed services.

Sometimes communication and teamwork does go wrong. This may be in exceptionally dangerous circumstances that become uncontrollable, such as in warfare operations or if a person is working 'undercover' during a surveillance operation in the police or in the armed forces.

However, no one in the uniformed services is sent to do a task that they are not fully trained to do and in circumstances that could be beyond their capabilities. This is part of an effective risk assessment of a situation so that any type of operation can be carried out as efficiently as possible. Potential injury or loss of life is part of any risk assessment but senior personnel in any uniformed service have a 'duty of care' to those who they command and this includes giving orders that may put the lives of their personnel in unnecessary danger.

Case study

The police

A beat officer is walking outside a pub one evening and hears what appears to be sounds of a disturbance going on inside the pub.

What do they do?

They are by themselves and it would be not be a sensible option to go and investigate further because

- they are alone
- their presence in uniform may aggravate the situation and cause panic among the people who are there
- in a group situation there is a need for manpower backup.

The police officer needs to radio for assistance and they need to give the following information:

- Where they are
- What they have heard and observed so far
- What backup they may need, e.g. medical assistance
- Any other relevant information.

Let's do it!

Form into small groups, each one making up 15 questions for a quiz on the quality of effective teamwork and how this applies to the public services. Each group then hands out their questions to the other groups in the class. The team with the most correct answers wins.

Assessment activity

To achieve a *pass* (P2) you have to describe at least five qualities of effective teamwork in two different public services.

Below are tables showing five qualities that are found in two different public services, the fire service and the army.

As well as using the information from the tables, make arrangements for a member of a uniformed service to give a presentation to your group. This will give you the information that you need to produce a detailed account for this outcome and you will also gain a lot of information from their individual experiences.

Most of the uniformed services need the same qualities for effective teamwork as well as other qualities needed for each particular service.

Five qualities for effective teamwork in the fire service	How would you use these?
Courage This can be mental and physical courage	Leading other members of your team and other members of the general public in a potentially dangerous situation
Confidence in your mental and physical abilities and skills This can be confidence that you naturally have or that has increased through training and experience	Constant training and assessment of your abilities and skills so that you are confident at all times in your ability to carry out a task as effectively and as safely as possible
Mental and physical stamina This can be your natural stamina or what you have built up through the appropriate training and experience	Coping with the physical activity of your tasks and being mentally 'robust' so that you can avoid any unnecessary stress that may affect your ability to carry out your job To be as supportive as possible to your team and the people that you are saving whilst in difficult and dangerous circumstances

Communication that is effective, relevant and suitable for a particular situation	Relaying important information so that this can be acted upon, e.g. calling for backup of equipment or manpower
	Warning team members and others of potential dangers when you are on a 'call out'
	Communicating with people or even animals who are in pain and danger in order to help them survive
	Problem-solving skills especially when you are under pressure
	Breaking down barriers that may exist between the general public and your service, e.g. community outreach
Problem-solving skills when you are under pressure	Being able to remember the layout of a building and access points to water
	Thinking of the best and most effective way to tackle a problem so that you and your team are able to deal with it in the quickest amount of time and with the least possible danger to the team and other people

Table 2.2

Five qualities for effective teamwork in the army	How would you use these?
Courage and self-confidence	When you are under pressure to achieve a task and it is dangerous, e.g. on active service or when other people's lives are in danger and you are rescuing them
	If you have self-confidence other people will believe in you and this will help you be an effective leader and team member
	Remember! Self-confidence is something that you improve by training and experience

Communication	Effective communication to your team when you are in a dangerous situation
	Relevant reporting of information to your team and chain of command for manpower, equipment or reporting intelligence information
Self-discipline	Being able to look after yourself so that you are not a liability to other members of your team.
	Being aware of how all your actions may affect other people and possibly endanger their lives
Observational powers	Remembering facts and what you have seen. Being able to assess the risk factors of a situation from your observations
Leadership	Carrying out tasks to the best of your ability as a team member and also being able to take charge of people in a variety of different situations and circumstances even when you are exhausted and in discomfort

Table 2.3

Teamwork skills

You will actively participate in teamwork skills during your course. This will include:

- Classroom activities such as
  - discussions
  - debates
  - role play
  - presentations
  - group research.
- Physical activities such as
  - personal activity days with the armed forces
  - outdoor activities and expedition skills.

As the course progresses you will see a difference in your teamwork skills. You may also be able to improve on your teamwork skills by using them in any job that you may do outside college, such as voluntary work or work experience.

Development of teamwork skills

During this course you will strengthen your skills in all areas, but particularly in teamwork. You will discover how to improve your weaknesses and you will be given help to do this. By working with your class and tutors as a team regarding your work and practical activities, you are already demonstrating determination, communication and time management!

The uniformed services do respect the effort that you are making and the challenges that you face during your course as you are already practising the skills that will result in successful entry into the uniformed services.

Problem-solving strategies

It is important to use your knowledge and experience of command tasks on the personal development activity days with the armed forces, and also on similar activities that you may have carried out as a class, as this will help you in selection for the public services when you have to take part in similar tests.

An example is when you have to take instructions from an army staff team and then communicate these to your team and lead them in carrying out a physical task under certain conditions. For example, you could be leading your team in building a raft that can float and your team having to row it to a certain point on the water and back to shore.

Problem solving can be either physical or mental and is normally carried out as a test when you are under pressure to simulate a situation that reflects a real-life scenario.

Observation, communication, determination and teamwork are all assessed as part of problem solving. You are assessed on the way you handle the situation as an individual and as a team, not that you solve the problem as there is sometimes more than one solution!

Case study

Coastguard, Royal Navy, police, ambulance multi-agency incident

The coastguard service is part of the Maritime and Coastguard Agency (MCS), which is part of the Department of Transport. It is responsible for safeguarding 10,500 miles of coastline and thousands of square miles of sea.

Its role is to be responsible for the initiation and coordination of all civil maritime search and rescue within the United Kingdom area and it is the authority that responds to incidents at sea or along the coastline.

The following incident is a good example of a multi-agency incident. It also attracted a lot of public interest as it was a tragic incident that may have been avoided. The deaths of 23 Chinese cockle pickers on the treacherous mudflats of Morecombe Bay illustrates a human tragedy and a very large-scale emergency operation that had to be mounted in order to save lives and then recover those who had lost theirs.

This situation also illustrates the need for further investigation as there were deaths and probably negligence in allowing these people to be there in the first place. The emergency services had to hold an enquiry into this situation and review their communications and plans of action, and make improvements if required. For example, there may need to be more warnings about the dangers of the fast incoming tides so that people are very aware of the risks of the area.

The national and international publicity that this incident attracted also exerted more pressure on the uniformed services involved, as their actions were scrutinised publicly. The further questions of who these people were and their status as illegal immigrants are outside the roles of the emergency services, however questions such as 'How do you ensure that people are not forced to take risks that are potentially life threatening, as these people did?' may be asked.

The teamwork that took place would have included:

- The coastguard searching the area by sea and by air. Liaison with the Royal Navy for equipment and manpower backup.
- Communication with the medical services to treat or transport the recovered bodies. An autopsy on each of the bodies to establish the cause of death.

Identification of the bodies. This would involve teamwork between the police and the medical services.

The coastguard ensured the joint safety of the emergency services who were working in the dark and with the added danger of the continual fast-flowing tides that flow into the bay at 10 km per hour; faster than the average person can walk or run.

An emergency plan for the area was put into action, but this would have been flexible to include any new developments. The continued media presence would have had to be organised so that the work of the emergency services was not hampered during the immediate rescue operation and also in the following days.

What other teamwork skills does this incident illustrate?

Figure 2.9 *Multi-agency rescue team on Morecombe Bay*

Cooperation

Members of the uniformed services need to cooperate with one another to carry out the tasks that have to be done, and to do them as effectively as possible with the minimum of effort and with the minimum casualties in a team. Professionalism must be maintained in any situation, and even if people do not get on with each other they have to train together and work together to achieve the objectives of their team.

 Think about it

Can you think of a situation when cooperation is essential?

Let's do it!

Take a situation that requires cooperation to deal with it and discuss what would happen if there is a lack of cooperation.

Conflict management

The uniformed services often have to deal with people who are frightened, traumatised, aggressive and sometimes without hope. These emotions can easily lead to conflict. Imagine peace-keeping troops having to carry out their tasks in the face of an aggressive population after a war, when those people have lost family, property and are just surviving without much hope. This happened in the Kosovo conflict in 1999 and is now happening in Iraq.

Using listening and speaking techniques to calm a situation usually works. You don't need to have the local language. If the situation requires it members of the uniformed services can use necessary force or unarmed combat skills to restrain people or quell aggressive behaviour. This may involve applying force to certain physical pressure points on a body in order to decrease aggressive behaviour.

Assessment activity

For a *pass* (P3) you will actively participate in at least five different teamwork activities. These activities should be varied and not be just about sport. You will need to have witness statements from a sports coach or your tutor if they are observing you. You must ensure that you are active in your participation and that you demonstrate teamwork skills during the course of these activities.

Suggestions for these activities include
- a sponsored event for charity
- a sports event or training course such as a 'Community Sports Leadership Award'
- team training for a sport
- a community project that is in the college or in your community.

It is important that you provide the appropriate evidence to backup what you taking part in. This can include
- photos/videos and tape recordings
- a PowerPoint presentation about your activities
- a written assignment work by yourself
- reports and witness statements that are signed by an assessor or your tutor.

Assessment activity

To gain a *merit* (M2) you will have to demonstrate responsibility within roles during team activities. In all your team activities and any classroom activities you need to demonstrate
- enthusiasm and a positive attitude at all times during these activities
- motivation as a team player and also leadership qualities when called upon
- an awareness of safety with relevance to the particular activity.

Interpersonal skills and personal effectiveness

Interpersonal skills

Assertiveness

You can be assertive without using force. Wearing of a uniform requires a certain amount of assertiveness in order to convey a message of ability and confidence. The general public expects that of anyone in uniform as each of them should be trained to the best of their ability before carrying out any tasks with the general public or taking part in any armed forces operations.

Speech has to be assertive as well as your general attitude. When you are talking be relevant, positive and keep to the point. Always ask a question in a manner that will get you a 'Yes' and not a 'No' answer. Use realistic information as to what the consequences may be if you do not get the answer you want!

The uniformed services need to be assertive to maintain order and the respect of the people who are relying on them, especially when dealing with the general public, whether on a routine matter or in an emergency scenario.

Body language

Body language can be used against you. This is a visual form of communication that can be interpreted by others in ways that are different from what you intended. So you have to be very careful about what messages you convey through your physical expressions.

Members of the uniformed services in dealing with different people in different situations need to be flexible. Soldiers on a peacekeeping mission or helping in a disaster area, may play games with

Figure 2.10 *A British soldier responding to Iraqi children shows another side of soldiering – that of caring*

local children. This sends out a message of cooperation, of caring and that they too are part of a family somewhere.

Personal effectiveness

These skills are very important in communicating with people in a variety of circumstances. In the uniformed services it is very rare not to be dealing directly with people in a wide range of situations. During selection for any of the uniformed services, you will be assessed for your potential in personal effectiveness. You can be trained in these skills, however if you are already able to communicate, solve problems and get on with other people without too much effort, then you will have a better start to your training.

Most of those on public service courses will already have acquired these skills from doing a college course and the tasks they had to carry out. Your tutors will be able to help you assess your potential as well as your strengths and weaknesses. None of us are perfect and it is very much to our advantage to go on gaining experience and knowledge, even those who hold a senior rank!

Problem-solving strategies

You need to be able to initiate solving a problem even if you are under stress and have the pressure of a team relying on you. During a team command task, you may be using a plank of wood to simulate building a bridge, however you may at some time be faced with having to actually build a bridge over a river that is of strategic importance, and in enemy territory!

Using your skills and knowledge to assess a situation is also very important and this becomes easier with experience. As a team leader you will have to have the confidence to make decisions based on facts. These decisions may not be popular with your team, so you need to have the confidence and determination to persuade them to carry out whatever task in the most effective way possible.

Decision-making

A decision may need to be made for immediate action or it may be made for a planned action. Once it is made it is rare to withdraw it as this will cause confusion in an emergency scenario or in a warfare situation.

If you are the leader of a team you have to base your decision-making on facts and realistic possibilities. These decisions may not be popular with your team, however you need to have the confidence and determination to persuade your team to carry out your decisions as effectively as possible. In the armed forces it will also be backed up by up-to-date intelligence gathered by specialists and also by using the local knowledge of civilians and your own team.

Even if a decision is unpopular with a team they will have less respect for a leader who shows indecision about making the decision and then apologises for making it, especially in a time of crisis!

Goal-setting

This is about motivating yourself and having some control over what you do and when. If you are on a long march and have become exhausted, cold and want to stop, you should set yourself a goal of pressing on and passing a certain point, and once you have reached that point, set yourself another goal for reaching an even further point, and go on doing this until you feel a sense of achievement that will motivate you to complete the rest of the march. The uniformed services need people who are motivated and determined. Having goals they can look forward to achieving, whether realistic promotion goals or physically stretching goals, helps people stick with a career, even in difficult times, and helps them become better leaders.

Stress management

Appropriate facilities and support needs to be in place to help those in the uniformed services deal with the various stresses of their jobs. In the armed forces the padres are not just there for religious reasons, they are also there to help people by listening to their problems and helping them deal with those. The command system of any force imposes discipline, but it is also a human resource machine that functions 24 hours a day. The most senior officer down to the most junior rank have the same rights to a listening ear, friendly support and practical medical help if they are suffering in any way because of their job.

Managing stress is important. It costs a lot in terms of time and money to train members of the uniformed services, and so retaining them is vital to having a well-trained and manned force. The uniformed services take stress management very seriously, and have introduced various strategies to prevent stress occurring, such as providing sporting and social facilities, even in a war zone, communication where possible with friends and family and pro-active associations that deal with families of those serving in the uniformed services. The communications within organisations are now much more transparent.

The Second Sea Lord of the Royal Navy recently stated that the Royal Navy of the future needed to be flexible, responsive and technology driven, but all of these things would not replace its most important asset … its people.

Time management

There is a saying that military time is five minutes before civilian time. During basic training in any of the uniformed services it is not practical to do everything asked of you in 24 hours, so you learn very quickly how to do things in a certain way that requires a minimum of effort while maintaining high standards. When you are on call in the fire service or in the ambulance service you have to get ready within minutes, so you must always be alert physically and mentally and ready to switch quickly into professional mode.

The more training and experience you have, the easier time management is. Time is a precious commodity when you are dealing with disasters and saving people's lives, so it is important to respect it and not waste it.

Assessment activity

To gain a *pass* (P4), you need to be able to describe the importance of interpersonal skills and personal effectiveness for public service work.

Complete the following appraisal form on a classmate, describing their interpersonal skills and personal effectiveness, giving examples of when these skills have been displayed. Include comments on the importance of these skills and how the classmate might improve on them.

Public Service Appraisal Form

Student name _____   Date _____

Appraised by _____

Interpersonal skills	Comments	How you might improve
Dealing with conflict		
Use of body language		
Communication skills – verbal		
Body language: Own Others		

Personal effectiveness	Comments	How you might improve
Problem solving		
Decision making		
Goal setting		
Stress management		
Time management		

Assessment activity

To gain a *distinction* (D1), you need to be able to demonstrate exceptional teamwork, interpersonal skills, personal effectiveness and communication skills.

During all the exercises and presentations that you take part in for the outcomes of this unit, make sure that you demonstrate

- motivating your colleagues
- bringing your colleagues into the discussions so that no one is left out
- encouraging people to join in an activity
- making helpful comments when necessary on the performance of others so that they are motivated to improve their performance.

Communication skills

Communication is the cement that binds all the other skills of the uniformed services together. It is central to the aims, objectives and achievements of every person who wears a uniform.

The communication skills used in the uniformed services require you to digest information as effectively as possible in as little time as possible and then relay it to the appropriate units or agencies, especially if there is an emergency.

Reading

In reading information here are certain techniques to use.

Skimming and scanning

These are skills in picking out information quickly from written documents and then selecting the most relevant information to use.

Detailed reading of service documents

Officers or other people in charge of personnel will be responsible for this. These may be references used for policy issues or to check facts in a disciplinary case. In the Royal Navy the reference books are known as 'BRs' (Books of Reference). They are mostly classified and cannot be removed from a base or a ship. They have to be continually updated and this is the responsibility of the Writer branch.

Reports

These can be factual evidence or people's records. Both are important, as they may be required as evidence in the case of someone charged with a crime they have committed. A report on someone is part of their career promotion, so it is important for anyone involved in making such a report to read very carefully their previous reports so that they have as complete picture of the person as possible. It is their promotion and this should be respected.

In the Royal Navy the annual reports are known as RORRS reports. Most reports are now computerised but the rules of security still apply.

Writing

It is a general rule in the armed forces that you do not write a formal letter when a conversation face to face, a telephone call or an email will suffice. There is enough paperwork as it is, so don't create any more if you don't have to!

The structure and format of letters to senior officers varies from service to service, but you should always check their rank and any decorations that they may hold, as well as their title. Some very senior officers also have a knighthood or hold a peerage so check out your facts first! During training you are always shown how to compose a variety of letters so that your ignorance does not embarrass you either professionally or socially.

Writing reports

This also varies from service to service in layout and content, however as a general rule a report should consist of relevant information with any references at the back and appendices if you need to put in the extra information that you have referred to in the main content of the report.

It is also important to categorise the security of the report and look after it accordingly. There is always advice on this no matter which uniformed service you are in. It is generally the Administration branch that will help you with this information.

Note-taking

This needs to be quick and easily understood. There is no point in taking notes if you cannot read them back when you are transcribing them!

It is also important if you are required to take notes, that this paperwork is looked after as it may contain vital information.

It was unfortunate during the Soham murder investigation in 2003 that notes on evidence were lost. This held up some of the factual information in the investigation and influenced the evidence given at the trial.

Verbal communication

The voice is a powerful weapon. It can question, motivate and comfort depending on its tone. Questioning skills are very important. If you ask a closed question it is designed to have the answer of 'Yes' or 'No'. If you ask an open question the answer will need more explanation from the person who is answering. There are various reasons for using different types of questions for different scenarios. Closed questions are used for brief responses and open questions are an aid to putting people at ease.

Discussions

You would not have a discussion about an order as it is important to obey one unless it is unlawful. However, it is important for anyone in the uniformed services to be able to organise their thoughts on paper as well as verbally, and at selection you will be given the chance to discuss anything, not because the assessors want to test your knowledge but because they want to assess your power of speech and how you would work with others in a working situation.

Verbal presentation of information

The information you give a team verbally needs to be factually correct, relevant and brief because of the limits of time, especially in an emergency situation. You need to give as many necessary facts as possible, then make a decision and act on it immediately before you lose the team's motivation.

Barriers to verbal communication in operational situations

The media needs to be given certain information in a conflict situation, however they cannot be given intelligence information that can be passed on to the enemy. After all even the enemy watches CNN! This is one of the problems of satellite TV and the continuous coverage of world events. In the case of military action too much information can give away the positions and activities of troops.

In the case of military patrols in a conflict zone there may be a need to restrict communication to military sign language so that the enemy is not warned of your presence.

Attention	I am ready or are you ready?	I don't understand	Join me	Follow me
Halt or stop	Enemy in sight	Prepare for action	Turn right (left)	Disregard previous command

Figure 2.11 *Sign language used by the military*

Barriers to communication in non-operational situations

It is important to ensure safety and security of information and communications even in non-operational situations. For example, a mobile phone can be used as a tracking device even if it is switched off. To prevent this the SIM card must be removed from these phones on board a ship, as the signal can be picked up and used to track the ship's movements.

When it is important that the right message is conveyed by a particular uniformed service, you need to select the relevant information and to give a balanced view. If at a press conference a senior police officer states a negative opinion or makes a negative comment about a situation then it can take a long time to repair the damage. It is better to be positive about a negative situation so that people are motivated to improve it.

Language is another barrier to communication, one which is present in operational and non-operational situations. If there are various non-English-speaking people in an emergency situation, such as a fire or an accident, it is very difficult to help them and work with them if they are unable to understand your commands or questions. It is possible to call in interpreters, however it is still a problem for many uniformed services. To help deal with this more people who do speak other languages as well as English are being recruited. These people are used for outreach projects to help communication with minority groups who may be disengaged from the emergency services because of language difficulties.

Listening

Effective listening skills

Information can be picked up by overhearing what people are saying. So it is important that no one in the uniformed services talks about their role and responsibilities in public, or even on a phone, as it is possible for information to be used and circulated in a way that may put others in danger.

Listening to someone's views can help calm them and encourage them to cooperate with you and your team, because you are paying attention to them and giving importance to their views. So they become a kind of extension of your team. This is what is happening in Iraq as the views of the people are being listened to and there are plans for handing over to them political power and control of law and order. This is a long-term plan but the people are now involved in the process.

Barriers to effective listening

The language used and the interpretation of what people say can be a barrier to effective listening. You also need to understand local customs and how people think and why they act in the way that they do, otherwise you will not understand in their terms what they say to you. If you are dealing with the general public, in this country or abroad, you will have to deal with people who are very young, old, in distress and who are very scared of you, especially if you are wearing a uniform. You need to listen to what they are saying in order to gain their trust in you and to show that you are doing a job, that it is lawful and that you are following the high ethical standards of your service.

Technical skills

It is important to use technology and not for technology to use you. The technology of communication, such as emails, is now highly advanced and has spread throughout the world. However, it is not always secure, so steps are needed to ensure that security is tight, even in the case of emails between members of the uniformed services and their families. Using the telephone, fax and email has to be secure and relevant to the job you are doing. The use of radios and mobile phones has changed the way the uniformed services communicate. Mobile phone records are now also used as evidence in any investigation, as are emails and internet access records.

The relationship to the public services

Entry requirements

When you go for selection to any of the uniformed services you are being assessed on your potential to achieve certain targets after your training. Your attitude and the effort that you put into selection are your most important skills. However, it is also important to have good verbal skills at interview and also in dealing with the team tasks that you are expected to do. If you do not voice an opinion or make a suggestion then the staff will have nothing to mark you on. Remember, no one will tell you to be quiet!

Basic skills needed for entry

Being able to read and write are vital as computers will not always be accessible to help you.

If a person scores highly on an entry test then they will be given a choice of trades to choose from in the armed forces. However, if you do not score highly this will be your standard to start with. If you are accepted for the service you want to join, you will then be trained to reach a higher standard. The training and skills that you receive in the uniformed services means that you are able to learn and get paid for it at the same time! If you have potential in anything, the uniformed services will help you realise it.

In-service training

This is all about the goals, education and continuous professional development which is relevant to your career, specialisation and interests. You are fully supported in any training you do and any course that is either relevant or useful to you as a person. You may need to improve on your study skills if you are taking exams that require a lot of study, but you will be helped at every stage to achieve this.

Operational activities

You are required to be flexible, aware, able to make instant decisions, and to preserve life and maintain law and order at all times. This is a challenge for any of the uniformed services. As soon as you are on duty you will not know what you are going to face, so you have to be physically and mentally prepared at all times. However, as this unit has illustrated, it is not just you who has to be prepared. You are just part of a team and if you are not prepared then the team has a weakness in its effectiveness. If you have more strengths than weaknesses then the team will reflect that as well.

Assessment activity

To achieve a *pass* (P5), you have to describe the importance of effective communication skills in the public services.

Select about five scenarios from information that you have on the uniformed services and describe how the communication used in them made a difference to what happened.

Assessment activity

To achieve a *merit* (M3), you have to explain the importance of effective communication skills in the public services.

When you are presenting information in your assignments, ensure that you do this in a detailed and unambiguous format so that it can be clearly understood by a third party.

Use five scenarios from your notes that demonstrate the importance of effective communication skills in each scenario.

Assessment activity

For a *distinction* (D2, D3), you have to evaluate the use of teamwork and communication skills in public services. You will also have to critically analyse the importance of effective communication skills in the public services.

Using the five scenarios that you have chosen, give detailed examples of how teamwork and communication skills were used to good or bad effect. Analyse this and decide if they could be improved and if so how.

CHECK WHAT YOU KNOW

1 Can you describe what the word 'team' means?
2 What are the characteristics of an effective team?
3 What are the characteristics of a non-effective team?
4 What sort of characteristics does a good team leader have?
5 Name *two* types of teams in the uniformed services.
6 What is a regiment?
7 What is a specialist team?
8 Give an example of verbal communication.
9 Give an example of non-verbal communication.
10 Give two reasons why communication is important.

Resources

Journals

Fire
Navy News
Police News
RAF News
Soldier

Websites

Army – www.army.mod.uk
Fire service recruitment – www.homeofficegov.uk/fepd/cifs.htm
HM Customs and Excise – www.hmce.gov.uk
London Ambulance Service – www.lond-amb.sthames.nhs.uk
Police – www.policecouldyou.co.uk
Royal Air Force – www.raf.mod.uk
Royal Marines – www.royal-marines.mod.uk
Royal Navy – www.royal-navy.mod.uk

Public service fitness

Introduction

Being physically fit is important for anyone working in the public services because of the physical demands of the various jobs within the services, for example firefighters. If you access the www.royal-navy.mod.uk website, you will find a list of the positive benefits of being physically fit to do the jobs in the Royal Navy. These benefits are

- improved fitness to fight and ability to cope with the demands of life at sea
- improved confidence in your own capabilities
- improved physical ability, which in turn maximises resistance to injury
- improved ability to recover more quickly from injury and physical stress
- improved alertness and reduced levels of psychological stress
- improved good health, now and later in life.

This is a core unit for your BTEC Level 2 First Diploma in Public Services course. It introduces you to the concepts of public service fitness. The unit will provide you with the necessary understanding of fitness in the context of the public services and the specific fitness requirements.

How you will be assessed

For your assessment of this unit you will need to complete a number of activities (known as assessment activities) to meet the assessment criteria. You should remember that as with all your units on the public service course you can achieve a pass, merit or a distinction grade. The assessment activities in this unit are designed so that you can meet all the criteria required to pass the unit. In addition, if you wish to do the extra work you will also be able to meet the merit and distinction criteria, through the assessment activities. However your tutor may set you activities other than the assessment activities, which in this unit will also allow you to meet the assessment criteria.

As the assessment criteria can be met through a variety of methods you will have to complete a number of activities, ranging from a presentation to designing your own fitness programme. Generally speaking, in your assessments you will have to

- plan and implement a personal fitness programme
- undertake a fitness test
- explain the use of repeated fitness tests
- describe the major body systems
- explain the importance of good nutrition
- plan a dietary programme.

After completing the unit, you should be able to achieve the following outcomes:

- Develop a personal fitness programme.
- Actively explore the requirements of the public service fitness tests.
- Examine the major body systems in relation to health and fitness.
- Demonstrate an understanding of nutrition and its impact on health and fitness.

You will also have an increased knowledge of health, nutrition and the human body. Most importantly, this unit will allow you to improve and maintain your fitness levels so you meet the entry requirements for your chosen public service.

Fitness programme

To improve your fitness so that you can meet the entry requirements of a fitness test at your interview it is important you have a fitness programme. A fitness programme is basically a plan, which you should use to improve your fitness over a period of time, for example eight weeks. When you are planning your fitness programme it is of vital importance that you consider your health and safety at all times. When you implement your fitness programme it is important that you do not injure yourself or cause yourself or others any harm. This section will look at different training methods (different styles of training), for example long-distance running and the importance of health and safety.

Fitness is linked to health and we will now discuss what this means but they are clearly different. A good level of fitness should allow the individual to perform an activity, task or sport. In the case of a soldier a good level of fitness will enable them to complete an activity such as marching for 10 miles. The fitness a soldier has is based on stamina, which is a part of fitness.

When we say that someone is healthy, we usually mean that they are fit and well, however it is more complex than this. For a start being healthy also involves our state of mind and our ability to interact socially with the people we live with in our community. This is what the World Health Organisation says:

'Health is a state of complete physical, mental and social well-being, not merely the absence of disease.'

From this you can see that if someone had a chest infection or a broken leg they would be classed as not being healthy.

Before you start to plan and implement your fitness programme it is important that you identify which fitness tests you need to pass at your interview. Once you have done this it is important that you perform the fitness tests to get a baseline score. The baseline score tells you how much you will need to improve. You can see this from the following case study.

Case study

Fitness tests for public services

Joe

Sadie

Tariq

The above three people want to apply for the public services when their Diploma in Public Services course finishes in the summer. To do this they will have to undergo a number of fitness tests. Below are some of the fitness tests for each of the services Joe, Sadie and Tariq want to join.

	Joe	Sadie	Tariq
Age	17	18	20
Public service	Army	Police	Police
Public service fitness test	2.4 km (1.5 mile run)	Grip strength test	Multi-stage fitness test (bleep test)
Target	Best effort	32 kg	Level 8 shuttle 1
Results	18 minutes 32 seconds	20 kg	Level 9 shuttle 5

Table 3.1

1 What do you think is meant by the term best effort?
2 Why is it important for all three applicants to have a fitness test before they start their training?
3 Why do you think the police force has different fitness tests?
4 Which two applicants need to improve their fitness levels and why?
5 If you have a good level of fitness like Tariq why is it important to still follow a fitness programme?

Training methods

As you will be aware there are different ways of training your body. For example, some of your friends in your group will prefer to go for a run, while others prefer to go to the gym and lift weights.

Planning

When you are planning your fitness programme it is important you consider a number of aspects. These are

- the length of the fitness programme (e.g. 3 months)
- the time, equipment and facilities available to you
- the training method which is best for you
- how to maintain health and safety
- the entry requirements of your public service, for example the fitness tests – how many press-ups you need to do in a minute.

Let's do it!

By yourself but as part of a group, conduct research into the fitness tests you will have to pass for your chosen public service. For this you should consider using

- your application pack
- the internet
- journals, for example *Police News*
- the local careers connexions office
- the local recruiting office
- a guest speaker who may visit your school or college
- your tutor.

Once you have done this, compare and contrast your findings with another group member who is interested in another public service.

Figure 3.1 *You need to test how fit you are for the job*

Strength, stamina and muscular endurance

When you are planning your fitness programme it is important to base it on one or more of the following components of fitness:

- strength
- stamina
- muscular endurance.

The fitness tests you will need to pass for the public services will involve these components, therefore you need to know what they mean.

- *Strength* This is also known as muscular strength. Strength can be defined as 'the ability of a specific muscle or muscle group to exert a force in a single maximal contraction to overcome some form of resistance'. An example of this resistance would be the hose a firefighter has to carry, which is heavy and requires strength.

- *Stamina* This is also known as aerobic fitness. It is defined as the ability of the body to supply the exercising muscles with oxygen to maintain the aerobic exercise for a long period of time, for example 10 minutes. Aerobic fitness is important for most exercises because good levels of such fitness will supply the muscles with the oxygen required for exercise. Examples of stamina exercises are jogging, swimming and cycling.

- *Muscular endurance* Unlike strength, which involves the muscle performing one action, muscular endurance involves the muscle making a number of continuous movements. Muscular endurance can be defined as 'specific muscle or muscle groups, such as the biceps, making repeated contractions over a significant period of time (possibly over a number of minutes)'. Press-ups and sit-ups require a good level of muscular endurance.

FITT

When designing a fitness programme you should use the concept of FITT to aid you. This stands for

- Frequency
- Intensity
- Time
- Type

Frequency

The frequency of a fitness programme relates to the number of training sessions you do each week you exercise. However it also may be the number of exercises you perform at one time, for example 20 press-ups.

 Key point

The number of sessions a week you exercise should not exceed five, so as to avoid the risk of burn out.

Figure 3.2 *The number of press-ups you do at any one time is an example of the frequency of exercising*

When developing a fitness programme a beginner should not exceed 2–3 sessions a week. However, after an increase in fitness over a long period (3 months and more) you should increase the frequency.

When performing your fitness programme it is important you increase the frequency of the exercises as this helps you improve your fitness. This can be seen in the following case study.

Case study

A fitness programme

The local recruiting officer told Amir who wants to enter the fire service that he should incorporate press-ups into his fitness programme. After four weeks he has followed this plan (along with other exercises):

Week 1	2 × 15 press-ups (twice a week)
Week 2	2 × 20 press-ups (twice a week)
Week 3	3 × 17 press-ups (three times a week)
Week 4	3 × 20 press-ups (three times a week)

1 What do you notice about the frequency of the exercises performed by Amir?
2 Please identify the three ways in which Amir increased the frequency of exercises.
3 Why do you think it is important from a health and safety perspective to have a gradual increase in frequency?
4 Briefly draft out week 5 and week 6 for Amir, showing an increase in frequency.
5 Do you think this fitness programme will improve Amir's muscular endurance?

Intensity

Intensity is the most important factor to consider when planning and implementing a fitness programme.

Key point

The term 'intensity' relates to how hard you are working.

Figure 3.3 *How hard you have to work depends on what you have to do*

Remember, you do not always have to be working at 100% of your maximum heart rate (MHR) to increase your fitness levels.

Key point

Your maximum heart rate is calculated using the following equation.

Maximum heart rate = 220 – age

However, if you work near to 60% (MHR) you are likely to improve your stamina (aerobic fitness) over a long period of time. Furthermore, for some individuals, such as an athlete recovering from injury, there are health benefits to exercising below 60% (MHR).

Let's do it!

As a group devise and carry out a basic stamina workout which includes four clear levels of intensity. To assess the intensity levels you may want to measure the heart rate (beats per minute) against your maximum heart rate (220 – age). Once you have collected the raw data this can be plotted on a line graph as the heart rate or as a percentage against your maximum heart rate. On completion of the graph you should be able to evaluate whether your chosen exercises had four clear intensity levels.

The concept of intensity within a fitness programme is closely linked with the principle of overload.

Key point

Overload is a principle which relates to exercising against intensity greater than that which you normally exercise at.

For example, if you swim 10 lengths in a training session you should aim to swim 12 in the next. The extra two lengths makes it harder (increased intensity) for your body because it is overloaded. As the body is overloaded it will change and you become fitter. Therefore it is important that you increase the intensity on a regular basis in your fitness programme.

Time

Time is also known as the duration of exercise, for example 45 minutes.

Generally, it is suggested that the exercise time should exceed 20 minutes at the correct intensity level to allow for improvements in your stamina. This is because after 20 minutes at the correct intensity the body will be in a state of overload. It is important to remember that overload is required to improve our fitness. However, if you currently train for 30 minutes then you should increase this to 40 minutes to allow for overload.

Key point

Stamina can be improved by high intensity/low duration or low intensity/high duration exercise.

Type

The type of exercise you do will often depend on your choice, for example it may be running, swimming or cycling.

The choice of exercise method may be based on your access to facilities and equipment, given that not all of you may have regular access to a swimming pool, for example. If you are a runner then you should concentrate a large percentage of your training on running, as swimming, for example, trains different muscles.

When choosing the type of exercise you should consider
- the equipment/facilities available
- time available
- the fitness required for the public service you want to join.

Generally, it is recommend that you

- exercise 3 to 5 days each week
- warm up for 5 to 10 minutes before aerobic activity
- maintain your exercise intensity for 30 to 45 minutes
- gradually decrease the intensity of your workout, then stretch to cool down during the last 5 to 10 minutes.

Diagnosis of personal fitness needs

In planning your fitness programme you need to make sure it suits you because you will have different

- *needs* – e.g. to pass the police force entry test
- *abilities* – e.g. good level of stamina but poor strength
- *goals* – e.g. to run the 1.5 miles in 13 minutes.

It is important that your training matches the fitness tests which you will be doing at the selection process. In the army you have to do as many pull-ups (heaves) as you can before you fatigue.

Therefore it is important for those training to go into the army that they should perform upper body strength exercises in their fitness programme.

Figure 3.4 *Pull-ups are a test of your upper body strength and muscular endurance*

In the next section we will discuss the fitness tests which you will need to pass to enter the public services. It is paramount for you to know that certain local areas, for example North Yorkshire, have slightly different fitness tests for the fire service. Therefore you should research your local area. However most services have to meet the national standards.

Key point

A fitness programme should be tailor-made for you. If your friend has to do sit-ups in their test whereas you need to do a 1.5 mile run, then you will need a different fitness programme to your friend.

Case study

Getting fit for the ambulance service

Leroy, aged 23, has been working in his local supermarket stacking shelves for five years. He has decided to apply for the ambulance service now because he has passed the entry age of 21. After some research he has discovered that there is no fitness test at the interview stage, however he will need a good level of fitness and health. Leroy has good upper body strength through his job and training at the gym, however he has poor flexibility, especially in his back. He has discovered that his interview is in three months' time.

1 Why is it important for Leroy to have a good overall level of fitness for the ambulance service?

2 How do you think Leroy could find out (diagnose) what levels of fitness he needs for the ambulance service?

3 Why will Leroy need strength and flexibility for the job?

4 Leroy has been told by a friend who works at the local gym that he should complete a number of fitness tests. What do you think a fitness test is and can you name one?

5 Why do you think it will be important for Leroy to take the fitness tests now rather than in three months' time, when his interview takes place?

6 Leroy has started a fitness programme to improve his stamina. Why do you think he should test his fitness every four weeks?

7 Would you advise Leroy to have a medical check by his doctor prior to the interview?

It is also important not to overlook your preference for exercise. If you wish to improve your stamina using a treadmill rather than a bike then this is acceptable as both should allow you to meet your goal. However, running on a treadmill would be better if you have to pass the 1.5 mile run.

Assessment activity

After you have discovered which fitness tests you will be expected to do, you should complete the following form to achieve a *pass* (P1) grade.

Name:		
Student number:		Date:
Public service:		
Fitness test 1:	Level	

Fitness test 2:	
Fitness test 3:	
Fitness test 4:	
Fitness test 5:	
Fitness test 6:	
Estimated date of fitness tests (if you have applied for a job).	

This form will allow you to start your assessment, which asks you to plan and implement a personal fitness programme because you will have now identified your personal fitness needs. You will need to complete this assessment activity regardless of the grade you are working towards.

Instigating and following a fitness programme

When you start and follow a fitness programme you need to understand a number of issues. It is important you follow these eight golden rules:

The eight golden rules of training

1 Before starting you should have a clear goal – for example 45 sit-ups in a minute.

2 Make sure your training plan is training the correct components of fitness – for example running will improve your stamina, weightlifting will not.

3 At the start of your training it will be hard but after two weeks it will get easier because you are getting fitter.

4 If you have an injury or illness do not exercise as this will make it worse in the long run.

5 Make sure you warm up and cool down to avoid injury in all your sessions.

6 Ensure at all times you have water with you to avoid dehydration and help the recovery process.

7 Have rest days because they help you improve your fitness – you must avoid over-training.

8 On some days you will not feel like training – so a training partner or group will really help to meet your goals.

Rest periods

After a period of exercise it is important to give your body time to recover through rest. While resting, your body has the time required to repair and heal itself. For example, during strength training muscle fibres break. Therefore the rest period allows your fibres to repair themselves and then eventually become stronger and so improve your strength.

Rest periods incorporated into your fitness programme will reduce the chance of over-training. Over-training syndrome is a dangerous result of too many workouts without adequate rest. There are a number of symptoms associated with over-training, which can affect your health. These are

- loss of appetite
- loss of muscle
- lack of sleep
- injuries – e.g. shin splints
- increased number of infections and illnesses.

 Key point

You should try to have rest periods (days off) between your training sessions to avoid burn out and to allow time for your body to recover.

Routines and variation of training methods

Although it is good to get into a routine with your training because this helps you improve your fitness, sometimes you will need to include some variation. Variation in your programme helps you overcome or avoid boredom.

Once in a while you may want to change your training method, for example from circuit training to cross training (a mixture of training methods), which will be discussed later.

Weights

To improve your strength and muscular endurance you can use free weights, also known barbells or dumbbells. The use of free weights will allow you to exercise in your home.

The use of free weights has certain advantages. These are

- increased strength in the short term (4 weeks)
- a greater range of movement
- being able to specialise on certain movements or muscle groups
- aiding the training of balance and coordination.

Key point

Using free weights increases the risk of injury and using larger weights requires helpers to oversee (spot) you while exercising, for the sake of your health and safety.

Fixed resistance machines

Your local fitness centre should have fixed resistance machines, such as those made by Nautilus®, which allows you to change the load based on the fitness programme schedule.

These types of machines allow variable resistance (load) ranging from 0 to 100 kg (on most machines). However, they are expensive and unsuitable for the home. On the positive side, they are safer than free weights and you can change the range of movement by readjusting the settings.

When comparing which method of training produces the best results in terms of improvements in strength, there seems to be no clear advantage in using fixed resistance machines or free weights. You will probably have your own preference.

Circuits

In a circuit training session a number of exercises (or stations) is organised in rotations for you to do, usually under some time constraint, for example 1 minute per station. Between the stations there should be a designated rest period. The rest period should be between 15 to 30 seconds.

The circuit can be specifically designed to improve your stamina, muscular endurance, strength or a combination of these. To avoid fatigue the stations should be structured in a way that consecutive exercises use different muscle groups, for example shuttle runs (legs) may be followed by press-ups (upper body). To improve your fitness you may want to

- decrease the rest period
- increase the number of stations
- increase the number of circuits
- increase the duration spent at each station
- increase the number of circuit sessions per week.

Let's do it!

Using the session planner or one similar, design a 30-minute session (to include warm up and cool down periods) to improve a combination of stamina, muscular endurance and strength.

Training session planner

Date _____ Individual/Group name _____ Time of session _____

Aims _____ Session location _____

Equipment required _____

	Time	Content
Warm up		
Main		
Cool down		

Once you have reached a good level of fitness the rest periods may become light work periods, such as jogging on the spot or skipping. Circuit training offers you the following benefits. It

- adds fun and variety to the training
- allows training of a combination of fitness components, for example stamina, muscular endurance and strength
- allows you to specialise on a specific movement pattern or muscle group
- requires minimal equipment
- can involve a number of people, which helps you make it fun.

10-station circuit

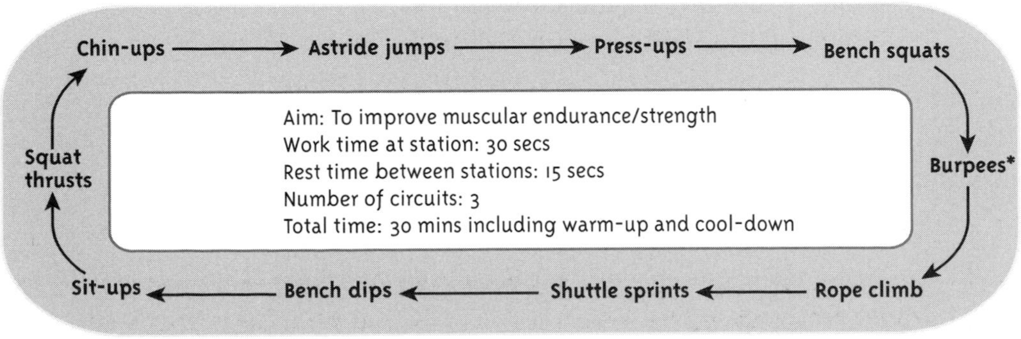

Chin-ups ⟶ Astride jumps ⟶ Press-ups ⟶ Bench squats

Squat thrusts

Burpees*

Aim: To improve muscular endurance/strength
Work time at station: 30 secs
Rest time between stations: 15 secs
Number of circuits: 3
Total time: 30 mins including warm-up and cool-down

Sit-ups ⟵ Bench dips ⟵ Shuttle sprints ⟵ Rope climb

*A burpee is a squat thrust combined with a star jump

Figure 3.5 *A circuit session offers a range of benefits*

Cardiovascular training

To improve your stamina you will need to perform some type of cardiovascular training (cardiovascular means the use of your heart and lungs). There are five main types of cardiovascular training. These are

- steady state
- interval
- Fartlek
- circuit (see the previous section)
- cross.

Steady state training

Steady state training is also known as continuous or long slow distance training. It involves you training at a steady pace over a long distance. The intensity of steady state training should be moderate to high (60% to 80% MHR) over a long distance and time.

Due to the level of intensity in this type of training, you are able to train for a considerable time. This method of training at a lower intensity is ideal for

- beginners to exercise
- athletes recovering from injury
- special population athletes – children, OAPs etc.

To increase your level of stamina you should increase the distance or time of training.

Interval training

In this kind of training you perform an exercise bout (work period), followed by a rest or recovery period before completing another work period.

Interval training can be used to improve your stamina by varying the intensity and length of the work periods. The following is an example of one interval for improving your stamina.

> Stamina – run for 2 minutes (60% MHR) – rest for 30 seconds – run for 2 minutes (60% MHR)

It is possible to improve your stamina by

- increasing the intensity of the work periods
- increasing the number of intervals
- decreasing the rest period (time)
- making the rest period more intense – for example slow jog rather than brisk walk.

When designing the programme it is important that you consider

- the number of intervals (rest and work periods)
- the intensity of the work interval
- the duration of the work interval
- the duration of the rest interval
- the intensity of the rest interval.

In using internal training for your fitness programme it is important that the rest intervals should be the same or greater than the work periods. However, as you have already discovered, the rest period can be shortened if you have a good level of stamina. The intervals should exceed 1 minute in length with an intensity level that exceeds 80% of MHR.

Fartlek training

Fartlek training is another method of improving your stamina. Here you vary the intensity of work while you are running. The intensity of the training is changed through the terrain that you are running over. You may run over

- sand
- hills
- undulations
- soft grassland
- wooded area.

Fartlek training is suited to outside training intensity, where the intensity can be varied. There are no rest periods, however you have more control and are able to decrease the intensity at any given time to have informal rest periods. The benefits of Fartlek training are

- you control the pacing
- you can reduce the boredom of conventional training
- it is suitable for off-season training to maintain your stamina.

Cross training

You can also reduce the boredom of training by varying the type of exercise. You could combine running, rowing and swimming in your fitness programme. This method of training would benefit a beginner by adding variety to their programme. The main disadvantage is that you train different muscle groups. This may be important if you have to take the 1.5-mile run test, because you should really concentrate on running.

Health and safety

When you are planning and implementing your fitness programme it is important to maintain health and safety at all times. If you ignore health and safety this will lead to injury, illness, or possibly death.

Let's do it!

With the aid of your tutor, draw up a list on the whiteboard or flip chart of the injuries you have experienced. You will probably list a wide range of injuries. When you have done this have a group discussion on the causes of these injuries, for example lack of warm up.

We will now discuss the factors you need to consider when you are fitness training.

Safe practice

From a health and safety point of view it is paramount that you consider

- the exercise environment
- previous physical injury
- age
- weight
- other personal factors, for example being asthmatic.

The exercise environment

If exercising in a fitness suite or gym, there are a number of things you have to think about. These are

- exercise machines should be well spaced out and in working order
- any loose equipment, for example free weights, should be stored correctly when not in use
- whether there are sufficient fluids available to stop you dehydrating
- it should not be too warm in the room
- there should be suitable ventilation to aid the cooling process.

Assessment activity

One way of reducing your chance of injury or illness while you are exercising is to perform a risk assessment on your exercise environment. You are now to perform a risk assessment on your exercise environment. An example has been done. If you need more information on risk assessments please read Unit 5 on workplace welfare.

Hazard	Risk (low/med/high)	Possible outcome	Control measure
Lack of warm up	medium	Pulled muscle	Warm up before starting main workout

Figure 3.6 *A risk assessment sheet*

You tutor should show you how to complete the risk assessment form.

If you are exercising outside it is important to consider

- the appropriateness of your footwear for the surface – Should you wear boots rather than trainers?
- the temperature – Do you need to do a longer warm up to avoid injury if it is cold?
- the traffic – If running on the road are there more safe options, for example running around the park?

You need to complete this assessment activity regardless of the grade you are working towards.

Physical injury

If you have not trained for some time, for example six months, due to injury, you need to start on a lower intensity fitness programme. The fitness programme should be increased slowly in terms of intensity, frequency and time so you don't get injured or demotivated. However the fitness programme should still place enough stress on your body so that your fitness improves.

When you exercise, train or play sport there are a number of injuries which you may pick up.

Injuries range from something as simple as a small bruise to death. Here are some of the common injuries you could receive when exercising, training or playing sport:

- *Abrasion* This is also called a graze. It can be caused by a fall on the floor, for example when you fall when playing basketball.
- *Bruise* A discoloured area underneath the skin caused by contact with another object or person such as a squash ball or a tackle in football.
- *Fracture* A break in the bone, of which there are different types, an example being a compound fracture. As with a bruise, these are normally caused by impact with an object or a person.
- *Sprain* A tearing or stretching of the ligaments caused by a sudden pull (due to a lack of a warm up or poor technique).
- *Strain* This is a tearing or stretching of the muscle fibres caused by suddenly pulling them too far (due to a lack of a warm up or poor technique).
- *Stress fracture* A fracture of the bone often caused by doing too many exercises over a period of time, for example shin splints are caused by running on concrete.

The general causes of injuries are illustrated in the diagram below.

Figure 3.7 *Some causes of injuries while exercising*

Being injured can have certain consequences, including

- time off work – this can lead to a reduction in pay
- change in job role – if you are a police officer you may have to do administration work for a couple of weeks
- decreased fitness levels
- removal from a sporting team
- reduction in exercise time
- change to fitness programme
- loss of time and money – costs of taxis and time spent at the hospital or the doctor's
- emotional – feeling down because you are not exercising.

Age

Older people can benefit greatly from the changes brought about by fitness training, for example lower blood pressure. However, these changes take longer to achieve than in a younger person. Planning a fitness programme for an older person needs to take into account the intensity of the programme at the start. The programme should start with low intensity exercises, for example a brisk walk rather than jog over a reduced distance.

Planning a fitness programme for a child also needs special consideration. More children are now taking part in structured fitness programmes in this country, in sports such as basketball, football, rugby and cricket. However, it is important not to treat children as if they were small adults when planning a programme, as their skeletal and muscular system is still going through changes. Therefore, it is important the child does not

- train or play in excessive heat or a cold environment
- perform an extensive and long workout
- over-train or compete in too many competitions.

Adolescents (aged 13–18) should not do too much strength training, for example lifting heavy weights, because their bodies are still developing. Too much strength training can damage the bones, ligaments, tendons and muscles. Therefore strength training should be kept at a low intensity and increased gradually as they mature physically.

Weight

People often start to exercise because they think they are overweight, and they believe exercise will help reduce their body weight, which it can.

If you are overweight due to excessive body fat you need to consider your training plan before you start to exercise. You should start at a lower intensity of exercise to maintain your health and safety. If your plan is to exercise by running, then your heart rate should not exceed 60% MHR.

Furthermore, you should only train twice a week and plan to increase the frequency after one month.

Other personal factors

Other factors need to be considered when planning and implementing your fitness programme. These are

- finance
- current fitness level
- gender
- medical conditions.

Finance The cost of exercising or training can discourage people. It can be expensive because you may have to pay for

- kit – shorts, trainers, etc.
- training equipment – free weights, bicycle, etc.
- facilities – cost of using the local gym or badminton court.

However, you do not need to spend a small fortune to enjoy the benefits of exercise and training. Here are few tips to help you:

- Use the outdoors for exercise, for example go jogging around the local park, but always be safety conscious.
- Use everyday household equipment for training, for example a 2-litre bottle of water provides an ideal load for strength and muscular endurance exercises.
- Borrow a book on exercising from your local library which provides you with a variety of simple cost-free exercises.

Current fitness level Your current fitness level will have an influence of the type of training you can do. You may have a good level of fitness and simply train to maintain that level of fitness. However, if your fitness level is fairly low then you should start at a lower level of exercising so that you can build a base level of fitness. This level of fitness can be added to later when you increase the intensity of the exercises.

Gender Women are capable of performing the same exercises as men. However, there are special circumstances, such as pregnancy, which need to be considered when planning a fitness programme. If you are pregnant you will still be able to train, however you should avoid high intensity exercises. Swimming is a very low impact exercise and is ideal for maintaining your stamina. As a precautionary note you should check with your GP before starting exercise if you are pregnant.

Medical conditions There are a number of medical conditions, for example asthma, which will not stop you exercising, however they do require a good level of health and safety.

Figure 3.8 *Women can perform the same exercises as men*

If you suffer conditions such as asthma and diabetes you need to have your medication with you when you are exercising. You may also need your GP to examine you before you start your fitness programme, to advise you on which types of exercises could make your medical condition worse and which ones will not.

These are some of the medical conditions which require a GP consultation prior to exercise:

● *Asthma* This causes shortness or breath, wheezing and coughing due to narrowing of the airways.

- *Diabetes* This is caused by a lack of or insufficient amounts of insulin (hormone), which regulates glucose. It can lead to weight loss, hunger and fatigue.
- *Eczema* This is an inflammation of the skin which causing itching and sometimes scaling or blisters. This can be affected by excessive amounts of sweat, therefore you should use clothing which allows your skin to breathe.
- *Injury* An old or current injury will have an influence on the type of training you can do.

Preparation before activities

Warming up before the main exercise period is vital for your health and safety. It prepares you for the intense training session. You need to warm up to

- increase heart rate
- reduce the chance of injury – pulls or strains
- increase the blood flow to the working muscles
- increase the muscle temperature
- prepare you for the environment
- improve the stretchiness of the tendons and muscles.

Warm ups consist of two clear stages. You start with a general warm up consisting of jogging, stretching and other general related exercises. The specific warm up is related to the exercises you will do in the main workout. The time for this should range between 5 and 20 minutes.

- Gentle loosing exercise – e.g. heel raises
- Aerobic phase – low intensity, e.g. light jogging, walking, cycling, etc.
- Stretching programme – specific stretches for the main activity.

Safe equipment and practice

In training to improve fitness you are likely to use equipment such as a treadmill. When using equipment it is important that you

- have an induction on how to use the equipment before you start training
- use the equipment in an appropriate and professional manner
- report any damages to the equipment to an appropriate supervisor
- work in pairs to avoid any injuries
- never work in the fitness suite or gym on your own
- have first-aider and kit present at all times.

Let's do it!

In small groups produce a two-minute video, or an audiotape for radio, which focuses on health and safety while training in a fitness suite. The aim is to advise people who are exercising on how they can reduce the risk of injury.

Clothing

What you wear for exercising needs to be appropriate for doing the exercises themselves and for your own health and safety.

- Always wear the appropriate clothing for the exercise – e.g. tracksuit bottoms not jeans.
- Always wear the correct footwear – e.g. running shoes for running; otherwise you could injure yourself. Avoid wearing flat-footed trainers.
- Always wear bright reflective clothing if running on the street in the dark, to make sure oncoming traffic can see you.

Personal safety

For your own safety

- inform someone you are going out to exercise, so that at least someone knows where you are
- avoid taking valuables with you – such as money or jewellery
- run with a dog or running partner, if possible
- don't wear headsets as these can distract you
- run against the on-coming vehicles as this allows you to view the traffic
- try to vary your route so that you don't develop a recognisable pattern
- make sure you know the route that you are going to take
- if running at night, only run in well-lit areas.

Cool down

You need to cool down after the main workout exercise. This tends to be shorter than the warm-up period and involves low intensity exercises. The main aim of the cool down is to return the body to its resting state. The reasons for cooling down are to

- remove waste products through the working muscles, which are still receiving the oxygenated blood
- decrease the chance of stiffness, by doing stretching exercises
- reduce the chance of muscle soreness after the session has finished
- reduce the chances of fainting after an intense session.

Communication dangers and risks

During training you need good communication between yourself and your tutor or fitness instructor. Your tutor should inform you of the many aspects of your training, such as

- how to use the equipment – e.g. the resistance machines
- the warm up and cool down exercises
- the correct technique for exercises – e.g. press-ups.

Communication can break down if the tutor fails to give you the proper instructions or if you don't listen to what the tutor is telling you. You could then injure yourself or others who are exercising alongside you. For example, if you are exercising on a treadmill and don't know how to stop it, you could fall off and injure yourself, and maybe also the person on the adjacent treadmill.

 Key point

If you are unsure about any of the exercises you have to do, for example using the correct technique, it is important to ask your tutor or fitness instructor for clarification to avoid the risk of injury.

Joe, Sadie and Tariq previously performed a number of fitness tests (see page 96). Based on these fitness tests, they have now decided to plan and implement their own fitness programmes. As an example, Joe's fitness programme for the next six weeks is set out on page 119.

 Think about it

1 What do you notice about the frequency and intensity of the exercises over the weeks?
2 Why do you think the exercises will help Joe pass his test?
3 What other types of exercises could Joe do to reduce the chance of boredom?

CHECK WHAT YOU KNOW

1 What does FITT stand for?
2 What is the difference between interval training and Fartlek training?
3 Which components of fitness do free weights train?
4 Name *three* safety features you could take when running on the road?
5 Why is it important to have a cool down after training?

TRAINING PROGRAMME

WEEK ONE

DAILY
a. Warm up (all warm-ups to be 6–10 mins)
b. Upper body/abdominal exercises 5–8 mins
c. Steady jog/walk 10 mins
d. Cool down

Start by doing five repetitions of each of the upper body exercises until the 5–8 mins are up. These repetitions can be increased to 10, 15 or 20 in later weeks.

WEEK TWO

DAILY
a. Warm up
b. Upper body/abdominal exercises 5 mins
c. Jog 15 mins
d. Cool down

During the jogging phase aim to achieve about 1.5 miles.

WEEK THREE

MON – THURS
a. Warm up
b. Upper body/abdominal exercises 5 mins
c. Mark out 20 m distance. Sprint for 20 m then jog back. Maintain for 5 mins.
d. Jog 10 mins
e. Cool down

FRI – SUN
a. Warm up
b. Upper body/abdominal exercises 5 mins
c. Run 18–20 mins
d. Cool down

Run should cover at least 2 miles.

WEEK FOUR

Repeat week 1 programme but increase upper body/abdominal repetitions to 15–20 and run time 18–20 mins.

WEEK FIVE

Repeat week 2 programme but either increase upper body/abdominal exercise repetitions or decrease rest time between each exercise. Run time 20 mins.

WEEK SIX

MON/TUES
a. Warm up
b. Upper body/abdominal exercises 5 mins
c. Run 20 mins
d. Cool down

THURS/SAT
a. Warm up
b. Upper body/abdominal exercises 5 mins
c. 2 miles best effort
d. Cool down

Wed/Fri/Sun – rest days

Figure 3.9 *Joe's training programme*

In summary

- It is important to plan a fitness programme which is suited to your needs and goals.
- Rest periods whilst training are vital to avoid over-training and to allow the body time to recover and repair itself.
- When exercising you must ensure you have a safe environment at all times to avoid injury and illness.
- When planning the fitness programme you must consider the age, weight, previous injury, fitness level and medical conditions of the individual.

Assessment activity

As you are now aware, it is important you are fit enough to pass the fitness tests at your interview. You can improve and maintain your fitness through a clear structured personal fitness programme. At the start of your programme, which will be for more than three months (depending on your timetable), you may need the support of your tutor. Your tutor should identify the facilities and equipment you can use during your fitness programme.

You need to do the following tasks. You should make sure you have completed the assessment activities 1 and 2 because they will help you with these tasks.

1 You are to plan and start a personal fitness programme using one or more of the training methods we have discussed. Remember, you should aim to train the correct fitness component – stamina, strength, muscular endurance or a combination of these. You could use the following planner:

Weekly Training Log

Week number _____ Athlete's name _____ Date _____

Day	Morning	Afternoon	Evening
Monday	F I T T	F I T T	F I T T
Tuesday	F I T T	F I T T	F I T T
Wednesday	F I T T	F I T T	F I T T

Thursday	F I T T	F I T T	F I T T
Friday	F I T T	F I T T	F I T T
Saturday	F I T T	F I T T	F I T T
Sunday	F I T T	F I T T	F I T T

Figure 3.10 *A weekly planner*

You should attach your sheet from the first assessment activity to the front of your fitness programme. This planner could be used as a log book of your training sessions.

2   You are to produce a one-page summary sheet of how you are going to take into account your health and safety whilst you are training, for example what kit are you going to wear? You should attach the risk assessment (the second assessment activity on pages 110–111) to your one-page summary sheet.

You will need to complete this assessment activity regardless of the grade you are working towards.

Fitness tests

At your interview for the public service you have chosen you may have to pass

- a medical
- a number of fitness tests
- an interview
- a written test
- a computer-based test.

As each public service has different fitness tests, you need to know which ones you need to pass for your public service. This section will highlight the different fitness tests.

Fitness tests

Fitness testing has become more popular due to the recognition of the importance of fitness to physical performance and health. It is used to measure and then evaluate a component of fitness, for example strength. If you are selected for a public service you will be tested to make sure you are fit enough to start its training programme.

Used by the public services for entry purposes

It is important that you meet the fitness standards set by the public service you have chosen. However, it will also be looking at your attitude, which is just as important.

 Key point

For the public services you will be expected to produce your 'best effort'.

Let's do it!

In a group, discuss what is meant by the term 'best effort'. You should then discuss why it is important to produce your best effort for the public services.

Army

Apart from physical fitness, the army will also be looking for potential, drive, determination and the desire to succeed. If you have these qualities they need to be allied to your physical fitness for you to succeed. Therefore you must be relatively fit before you do the following tests, which are very demanding.

- *Carry* This test evaluates your upper arm and shoulder strength. You have to carry two jerry cans (20 kg each) across a set course at a constant speed of 5.4 kph. The test measures how far you can carry the jerry cans for.

- *Dynamic lift* This measures how much weight you can lift from the floor to a height of 1.45 m. The test uses an Incremental Lift Machine.

  You start with a load of 10 kg and this is increased every time by 5 kg until you can longer lift the weight.

- *Run* To measure your stamina you have to do a run. Firstly, you do a warm up run and walk in a squad for 6 minutes carrying 0.8 kg. You then have to run a set distance of 2.4 km and produce your best effort. If you want to go for a specific job in the army you will have achieve a certain time in this test.

- *Heaves* (pull-ups) You will have to perform as many heaves as possible until you fatigue and cannot do any more. Your chin should be clear of the top of the beam. You must also ensure that after you lower yourself your arms are fully extended.

- *Body mass index* This looks at the relationship between your height and weight and is discussed later in this section.

- *Body fat (%) and Fat free mass (kg)* This is measured using a Bodystat 1500 machine and is discussed later under the heading 'bioelectrical impedance'.

- *Static lift* Using a machine called a dynamometer you are asked to produce as much force as possible in one lift.

  When you do this test make sure that your feet are shoulder-width apart, your back straight and your legs are bent.

- *Back extension* To test your ability to carry loads using your back muscles you have to perform this back extension test. The test uses a device called a Back Extension Rig.

  A digital reading is given based on how much you can extend your back against a resistance.

Figure 3.11 *A back dynamometer*

Royal Navy

You will have to pass a Pre-Joining Fitness Test (PJFT) before being accepted for training by the Royal Navy. Your stamina is tested through a 1.5 mile run on a treadmill in a civilian fitness centre. This is to make sure you are ready for phase 1 of the training. You will be expected to meet the following standards:

Age	Male	Female
	PJFT	PJFT
15–24	12 min 20 secs	14 min 35 secs
25–29	12 min 48 secs	15 min 13 secs
30–34	13 min 18 secs	15 min 55 secs
35–39	13 min 49 secs	16 min 40 secs

Table 3.2

You will also be asked to perform the test again during your induction phase at your training at *HMS Raleigh*. However the standards are more demanding:

Age	New Entry Fitness Standard (Rating)	
	Male	Female
15–24	11 min 13 secs	13 min 15 secs
25–29	11 min 38 secs	13 min 50 secs
30–34	12 min 05 secs	14 min 28 secs
35–39	12 min 34 secs	15 min 09 secs

Table 3.3

In addition to the run you will also need to pass the Royal Navy swimming and strength/muscular endurance tests. In the swimming test you must swim 40 metres and then tread water for three minutes in overalls, then leave the pool without help.

You will have to meet these standards:

Physical Fitness Test			
Men	Time	Women	Time
23–26 press-ups	2 mins	17–19 press-ups (Knees to be kept on the ground at all times)	2 mins
39–53 sit-ups	2 mins	29–43 sit-ups	2 mins
5 × 50-m shuttle run	53–59 secs	5 × 50-m shuttle run	66–72 secs

Table 3.4

Royal Marines

Becoming a Royal Marine is very challenging and requires a higher level of fitness than other parts of the Royal Navy (the Royal Marines are part of the Royal Navy).

'Being in the Marines is about soldiering at its most demanding.'

Let's do it!

If you are interested in joining the Royal Marines you should visit the Royal Navy website (www.royal-navy.mod.uk) and research into the following sections to gain a better understanding of what is required:

- Recruitment
- Fitness tests
- The training required to be a Royal Marine
- Careers with the Royal Marines.

Royal Air Force

Unlike the army and the Royal Navy you will not have to pass a fitness test before you join the RAF. However you will need to have a detailed medical. After you become a recruit you will be tested for your fitness at *RAF Halton*. On completing your recruit training you will have to pass the following tests:

- Multi-stage fitness test (stamina)
- Press-ups – 1 min (muscular endurance)
- Sit-ups – 1 min (muscular endurance).

You will have to meet the following standards:

RAF Fitness Test				
Gender	Age	Shuttle run	Press-ups	Sit-ups
Male	17–24	8.8 (9.1)	11 (13)	28 (35)
Male	25–29	7.8 (8.1)	10 (12)	26 (31)
Female	17–24	5.2 (6.01)	8 (10)	20 (25)
Female	25–29	4.7 (5.06)	7 (9)	20 (22)

Table 3.5

Note that the scores in the brackets are the test standards for the RAF fitness test, which must be performed by all RAF personnel once a year.

Police

To enter the police force you have to pass three fitness tests:

- Multi-stage fitness test (stamina) – to level 8 shuttle 1 (8/1); this test will be discussed later in this section.

- Grip dynamometer test (strength) – 32 kg, you are allowed two attempts.
- Dynamic strength test – as assessed through a Dyno machine. You must be able to push 34 kg and pull 35 kg.

The dynamic strength test is important because as a police officer you will have to arrest and restrain struggling individuals. The test measures your upper body strength. In the test you have to perform five seated chest pushes and five seated back pulls on the Dyno machine.

Fire service

The fitness tests for the fire service are very specific. You are tested on your ability to perform tasks which will be vital for your job, for example performing a ladder haul. You will have to pass the following tests:

- *Breathing apparatus test* You will have to follow a specific route wearing a breathing apparatus facemask.

  You will have to overcome certain obstacles whilst having limited visibility. You will also be asked to identify a number of objects during the test. This test is designed to test your ability to move in an area which has restricted access and to retain important information.

- *Ladder haul* This test is designed to assess your strength to extend a 13.5 m fire service ladder. You have to haul a weight using a rope attached to equipment specifically designed to simulate operating a ladder.

- *Ladder climb* As the name suggests, you have to climb a ladder to a specific height.

  While you are on the ladder you will also have to identify objects at ground level. After this you have to go further up the ladder and dismount into the building. This will test your calmness, confidence and ability to deal with heights.

- *Lift test* This is another test of strength as you have to lift and lower a weight using a piece of fire service equipment.

Performance

This section discusses in depth the different aspects of fitness tests, ranging from the purpose of them to the need to have tests on a regular basis.

Test protocol

Each fitness test has a specific protocol. A test protocol is a system of rules which sets out the correct way of using the test. If you do not follow the correct protocol the results will not be valid or show a true presentation of your fitness. The protocol for each test should state the following:

- The equipment to be used – e.g. treadmill

- The duration of the test – e.g. three minutes
- The correct technique – important when doing the push-up test
- The type of facilities required – e.g. a gymnasium
- Who to use the test with – e.g. schoolchildren only
- The sequence of activities – e.g. run for three minutes and then take the pulse rate for 15 seconds
- The data required – e.g. pulse rate or distance covered in metres.

Purpose of fitness tests

Fitness testing is used for a variety of reasons:

- For selection purposes – the public services will use a number of fitness tests to make sure you are fit enough to join their service.
- Identifying strengths and weaknesses – e.g. stamina is important for Royal Marines who are tested to make sure they are at the correct fitness level before going into combat.
- Identifying the stage of rehabilitation after injury or illness – the fitness test will be able to inform you of your recovery after any injury.
- To gain a baseline score – they provide information on your current fitness level (baseline score) prior to starting a fitness programme. Re-testing yourself again after a significant number of training weeks makes evaluation possible as to whether the programme has been a success.

Shuttle runs

Shuttle runs will be performed during the multi-stage fitness test, which you will find on page 130.

Sit-ups

The sit-up test measures muscular endurance in your abdominal muscles.

Remember, muscular endurance is the ability of a specific muscle or muscle group (abdominals in this test) to make repeated contractions over a period of time. An example is a firefighter climbing a rope, which involves using their arm muscles. This requires muscular endurance.

However, it is also important for the firefighter to have upper body strength for a rope climb. To test for muscular endurance a helper is needed to hold

Figure 3.12 *Climbing a rope tests muscular endurance*

your feet so they don't move. For the test you lie on a mat with the hips flexed and knees flexed to 90°, with the feet flat on the mat.

A full movement for the test requires the elbows to touch the knees in the upward movement and the shoulders to touch the mat after the downward movement.

Grip tests

Grip tests are used to measure the strength you can generate in your grip. Grip strength is important in a number of situations, such as

- holding a heavy weapon, as you have to in the armed forces
- escorting a troublesome inmate to their cell, as you may have to in the prison service.

A dynamometer is used to measure grip strength. This involves squeezing, pushing or pulling to measure your grip strength, which is measured in kilograms (kg).

The handgrip test must not be used to assess the muscular strength in other muscle groups.

To get a general idea you can compare your score against the table (Table 3.6).

Figure 3.13 *A dynamometer for measuring hand grip strength*

Grip: muscular strength in kilograms	
Rating	Kilograms
	73.0
	69.5
Super	65.5
	64.0
	62.0
Excellent	60.0
	58.5
	56.5
Good	55.0
	53.0
	51.0
Average	48.5
	48.0
	45.5
Fair	44.0
	42.0
	40.0
Poor	38.0
	36.5
	33.0
Very poor	29.0

Table 3.6

Body fat percentage measurement

Measuring the body composition concentrates on measuring the percentage of body fat and the fat-free body tissue. However, there are a variety of methods for measuring your body composition. This section discusses the different methods available to assess body composition.

 Key point

The body is made up of either body fat or fat-free body tissue such as bone.

Bioelectrical impedance

This is one method of assessing body composition. It requires less skill and experience because it is easier to administer. The machine shown in Figure 3.14 passes an electronic current (non-harmful) through your body and records the impedance (opposition) to the electronic current.

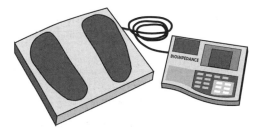

Figure 3.14 *A bioelectric impedance machine*

The currents flow through tissue with a high water content faster than tissue with less water, such as fat. The speed at which the current moves is measured and determines the body composition. A common impedance machine requires you to remove your footwear, including socks, and to stand on the machine, which will then produce a computer printout detailing components of body composition such as fat-free mass.

The protocol for bioelectric impedance is

- no drinking 3–4 hours prior to the test
- no physical activity (moderate/high intensity) 12 hours prior to the testing session
- no intake of alcohol two days prior to testing and no caffeineted drinks – e.g. coffee or coke.

BMI

Another method of evaluating body composition is BMI (body mass index), which evaluates your weight in relation to your height using the following equation:

$$\frac{\text{Body weight (kg)}}{\text{Height in metres squared (m}^2\text{)}}$$

This method assesses the appropriateness of your weight in comparison to your height. For example, if your height is 1.70 m and your weight is 70 kg, then:

1.70 m × 1.70 m = 2.89 m^2
therefore 70 kg/2.89 m^2 = 24.22 BMI

This can be evaluated using the following BMI classification table:

Classification	BMI score
Underweight	Under 20
Normal weight	20 to 25
Overweight	25 to 30
Very overweight	30 to 40
Seriously overweight	Above 40

Table 3.7

Multi-stage fitness test

The multi-stage fitness test, also known as the bleep test, is used to measure your stamina. The test is progressive in terms of intensity (speed) and is used to predict your stamina based on how far you can progress during the test.

The equipment required for the test is minimal and consists of the multi-stage fitness test audiotape, audio cassette player, cones and a facility that is in excess of 20 m in width or length. As the test progresses the beeps on the tapes become faster making you run faster. If you miss three consecutive beeps then you have to stop the test.

Figure 3.15 *Multi-stage fitness test*

Before starting the test you should do a basic but suitable warm up, which should include a stretching programme for the full body. The following should be taken into account to maintain your health and safety:

- non-slippery surface to avoid injuries
- well-ventilated room to aid cooling to avoid overheating
- suitable running footwear with adequate grip to avoid falling or tripping
- no eating 2–3 hours prior to the test to avoid discomfort
- avoid dehydration by ensuring a high fluid intake prior to testing – over the previous day.

1.5 mile (2.4 km) performance timed run

In this test you run the designated 1.5 mile distance as fast as possible.

Fitness category	13–19 years	20–29 years	30–39 years	40–49 years
Men				
Very poor	>15:31	>16:01	>16:31	>17:31
Poor	12:11–15:30	14:01–16:00	14:46–16:30	15:36–17:30
Fair	10:49–12:10	12:01–14:00	12:31–14:45	13:01:15:35
Good	9:41–10:48	10:46–12:00	11:01–12:30	11:31–13:00
Excellent	8:37–9:40	9:45–10:45	10:00–11:00	10:30–11:30
Superior	<8:37	<9:45	<10:00	<10:30
Women				
Very poor	>18:31	>19:01	>19:31	>20:01
Poor	16:55–18:30	18:31–19:00	19:01–19:30	19:31–20:00
Fair	14:31–16:54	15:55–18:30	16:31–19:00	17:31:19:30
Good	12:30–14:30	13:31–15:54	14:31–16:30	15:56–17:30
Excellent	11:50–12:29	12:30–13:30	13:00–14:30	13:45–15:55
Superior	<11:50	<12:30	<13:00	<13:45

Table 3.8   < Less than; > greater than

To get an idea of where you stand in terms of fitness you can compare your time against the above table before you go for your official fitness test.

Annual fitness checks

Most of the public services require you to take an annual fitness test. This is to ensure you have maintained a good standard of fitness. As already discussed in the case of the RAF, you have to take the following fitness tests every year:

- Multi-stage fitness test (stamina)
- Press-ups – 1 min (muscular endurance)
- Sit-ups – 1 min (muscular endurance).

Use of repeat fitness tests to establish gains

A fitness test should be used on a regular basis to make sure you have increased your fitness levels.

 Key point

It is suggested that a fitness test is used every four weeks to make sure your fitness programme is working.

An example of this is shown in the following case study.

Case study

Passing the fitness test for the army

Jenny, aged 18, last year applied for the army but failed the fitness test, for which she had to run 1.5 miles in 12 minutes.

The following is a fitness programme that Jenny followed to take the test again and pass it.

Identification of needs — to run
1.5 miles in 12 minutes

↓

Pre-training fitness tests (baseline
scores) — 14 minutes 34 seconds

↓

Fitness programme (3 months) —
interval training — 3 times a week

↓

Post-training fitness tests (after
training) — 11 minutes 49 seconds

↓

Interview/fitness test —
11 minutes 32 seconds

1 Why was it important for Jenny to get a baseline score?
2 Why was it important for Jenny to have a clear goal of 12 minutes for the run?
3 Why do you think Jenny did better in her second fitness test with the army in comparison to her post-training fitness test time?

 Key point

If the re-test fitness levels are deemed to be *significantly* higher than the baseline scores, this will serve to motivate you into carrying on with your fitness programme.

Adaptations act as a lever to change structure and content

Unlike the case of Jenny, a fitness programme may not produce the results we want – for a variety of reasons.

Let's do it!

In small groups, produce a spider diagram which aims to highlight the reasons why your fitness may not improve as much as you like.

You can start by using the following example:

Missing training sessions ← Reason for lack of significant improvement in fitness

By regularly using fitness tests you can identify areas of weakness in your fitness, which should lead to making changes in your fitness programme, for example by increasing the intensity of the programme.

Case study

On-going fitness testing

Remember, Joe, Sadie and Tariq wanted to apply for the public services when their diploma course finished in the summer. Below are the results of the on-going fitness testing they underwent up until their interview.

	Joe	Sadie	Tariq
Age	17	18	20
Public service	Army	Police	Police
Public service fitness test	1.5 mile run (2.4 km)	Grip strength test	Multi-stage fitness test (bleep test)
Target	Best effort	32 kg	Level 8 shuttle 1
Results (3.02)	18 minutes 32 seconds	20 kg	Level 9 shuttle 5
Results (3.04)	16 minutes 01 seconds	27 kg	Level 10 shuttle 2
Results (3.06)	14 minutes 14 seconds	27 kg	Level 10 shuttle 5
Results (3.07)	13 minutes 15 seconds	33 kg	Level 11 shuttle 2

Table 3.9

1 Why do think the three applicants had on-going fitness testing until their interview?

2 Can you make any suggestions as to why Sadie did not improve her strength between February and April?

3 What do you notice about Joe's fitness test times?

4 Do you think the three applicants will now be able to pass the fitness tests at interview?

CHECK WHAT YOU KNOW

1 Which fitness tests do you need to pass to join the army?
2 Which fitness tests do you need to pass to join the fire service?
3 What is the difference between strength and muscular endurance?
4 What is the basic protocol of the multi-stage fitness test?
5 Why is it important to have repeated fitness tests and how often should they be held?

In summary

- Each public service will ask you to perform a variety of fitness tests at the interview stage, except the RAF.
- To become a royal marine you will need a higher level of fitness.
- The fitness tests for the public services will concentrate on your stamina, muscular endurance, strength and body composition.
- If you use a fitness test on a regular basis (every four weeks) you will be able to check if you have made any improvements in your fitness.

Assessment activity

It is important that when you go for your fitness test at your interview you are at the standard that enables you to pass the test.

For the assessment you will need to do the following tasks to achieve a *pass* (P2):

1 You are to undertake one appropriate fitness test used by the public service of your choice, for example the press-up test.

2 You will also need to highlight the protocol used within your chosen fitness test.

3 As you will need to complete this fitness test on a regular basis, you will need to write down your result in the box labelled 'test 1'.

To help you provide the evidence for your assessment your tutor may want to video you completing the fitness test. You should also use the following information sheet.

Name _____

Fitness test _____

Description of test _____

Test number	Date	Result
1		
2		
3		
4		
5		
6		

To gain a *merit* (M1) you will need to carry out some analysis of your personal fitness results. You may want to write a brief paragraph (200 words) concentrating on the following points:

- Was the result what you expected, if not why not?
- How far away is your result from the target result?
- Are you on schedule to meet your target result?
- How is this going to help you with your fitness training?
- Will you have to adapt your fitness training?

To gain a *distinction* (D1) you will need to carry out the above analysis of your personal fitness results. You will also need to evaluate your results by comparing them to relevant fitness data. Therefore you should compare your data against the specific tables within this unit, for example the grip strength table on page 128. If you cannot locate a suitable table you should contact your public service, as they should able to provide you with some relevant information.

Assessment activity

Regardless of the grade you want for this unit you will need to complete the following activity.

You will need to produce a poster which explains the use of fitness tests for your public service. The poster should be informative and colourful with the use of images and written information, which will be important. You should include

- the name of the public service
- the tests they use
- the fitness standards required
- how often you are tested
- the reasons for repeating the fitness tests.

Body systems

In the public services you need to have a sound understanding of how the body works, as you may need to use this understanding in specific situations, such as when first aid is required. Understanding the human body also increases our awareness of health and fitness issues.

Body systems

There are several important human body systems, for example the cardiovascular system. The body systems work together to ensure we can function when we are sleeping, resting, working or exercising. These body systems are:

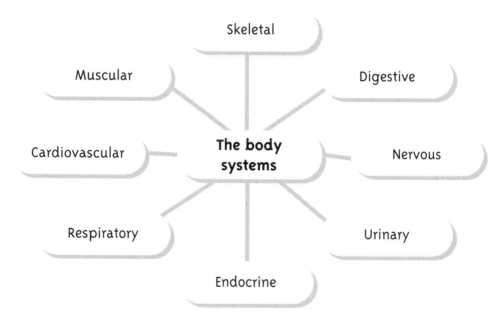

Figure 3.16 *The systems of the human body*

The eight body systems will now be discussed.

Muscular system

Every movement, for example marching on parade, fighting a fire or just blinking your eyes, requires the use of your muscular system. The body contains three types of muscle. These are:

- *Skeletal* This is used during activity – e.g. triceps and biceps (also known as voluntary muscles).

- *Cardiac* This is used during activity – e.g. the heart muscle.
- *Smooth* This is not used during activity – used during digestion and by other body organs. You are not conscious of using your smooth muscle.

Skeletal muscle is the main type of muscle used during exercise. The skeletal muscle is joined to your skeletal system (bones) and allows your bones to move at the joints (knee, shoulder, etc.).

Although there are over 350 muscles in the body they do not all work at once when performing an activity. For example, when someone is running they use only certain muscles.

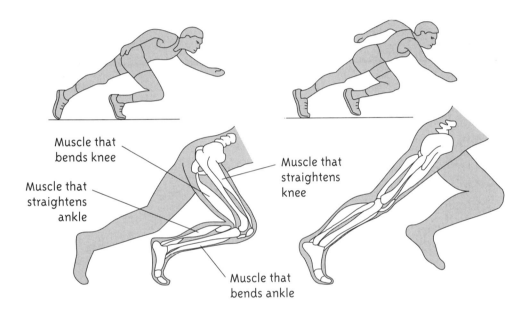

Figure 3.17 *Muscles you use when running*

Within a skeletal muscle there are numerous muscle fibres in tight bundles. These fibres provide the force required to either pull or squeeze things, for example squeezing a fire extinguisher. They work by either shortening or contracting, which allows movement to take place. When the muscle contracts it becomes short and fat to feel.

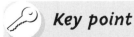 **Key point**

Muscles can only work by pulling, they cannot push.

When we exercise and perform movements the muscles work in pairs known as antagonistic muscles. This can be seen in the diagram of the biceps and triceps, which work together.

Arm bent (flexed)   **Arm straight (extended)**

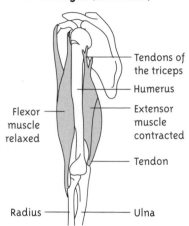

Origin of the
biceps muscle — Scapula

Origins of the
triceps muscle

Tendons of
the triceps

Biceps muscle
contracted

Humerus

Flexor
muscle
relaxed

Extensor
muscle
contracted

Triceps muscle
stretched thin by
the pulling action
of the biceps

Tendon

Insertion of
the biceps

Insertion of
the triceps

Radius — Ulna

Figure 3.18 *Triceps/biceps muscles*

When we examine the muscular system for movement we must also consider the skeletal system because they work together.

Skeletal system

The human skeleton is made up of more than 200 bones and has five key functions. The functions are

- protection – the heart is protected by the rib cage
- supporting the body – it allows us to stand upright
- allows movement with the help of muscles
- makes red and white blood cells
- storage and release of minerals.

 Key point

The skeletal system works in conjunction with the muscular system to allow movement during exercise.

You can see from Figure 3.19 how important the skull and the thoracic cage (rib cage) are. The role of the skull is to hold the brain in place and protect it from impact, for example when you get hit on the head by a ball when playing tennis. The skull consists of two sets of bones:

- Cranial bones – these are at the top of the head and provide protection
- Facial bones – these secure the teeth and provide a framework for the eyes.

The thoracic cage includes the

- ribs (used for protection)
- sternum (piece of bone shaped like a dagger)

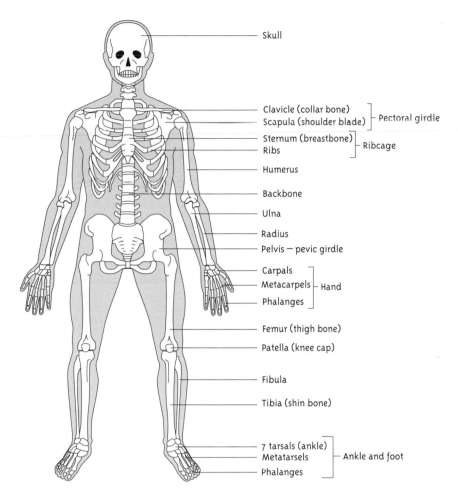

Figure 3.19 *Skeletal system*

- costal cartilages (secures the ribs to the sternum)
- intercostal muscles (used when we breathe)
- vertebrae (required for support).

The thoracic cage is important because it protects the heart and the lungs. Most importantly it is used when we breathe as it allows air to enter and leave our lungs. It also supports the shoulder and upper limbs, which is important for when we exercise.

An important set of bones for exercise is the backbone, which is also known as the vertebrae. This is made up of 33 separate bones and allows us to bend and twist when exercising.

The vertebrae are hollow and within them is the spinal cord. The role of the vertebrae is to protect the spinal cord, which is connected to the brain. All the vertebrae have discs of cartilage between them. The job of the cartilage is to stop the vertebrae rubbing together.

Key point

The human body has limbs which are classed as the legs (lower limbs) and the arms (upper limbs).

Where two bones meet, for example the tibia and femur, you will find a joint. Joints within your body, for example the knee joint, allow you to move. However some joints allow more movements than others. There are also different types of joints within your body.

Let's do it!

Research the joints in the human body and complete the following table. The ball and socket joint has been done as an example.

Joint	Where in the body	Type of movement
Ball and socket	Hip and shoulder	All directions
Hinge		
Pivot		
Gliding		
Fixed		

Table 3.10

Through your research you may have come across joints called synovial. Most movement during exercise occurs at a synovial joint, for example the hinge joints.

The ends of the bones are covered with cartilage, which is a smooth, tough and flexible connective tissue. The synovial membrane contains synovial fluid, which oils the joints and makes movement easy.

Key point

It is the role of *ligaments* to hold the bone and joint together. The muscles are connected to the bones by *tendons*.

When we exercise the muscles pull on tendons and move the bone.

Digestive system

The energy we need to exercise comes from the food we eat. The food we eat travels through one long tube. This starts in the mouth, passes through the oesophagus and is broken down into smaller pieces in the intestine. The process of breaking down food is known as digestion. The food is broken down by enzymes which help in producing the chemical reactions required for digestion. The final destination of the food molecules are the cells of the body where they can be used for exercise. The digestive system includes a number of key body parts:

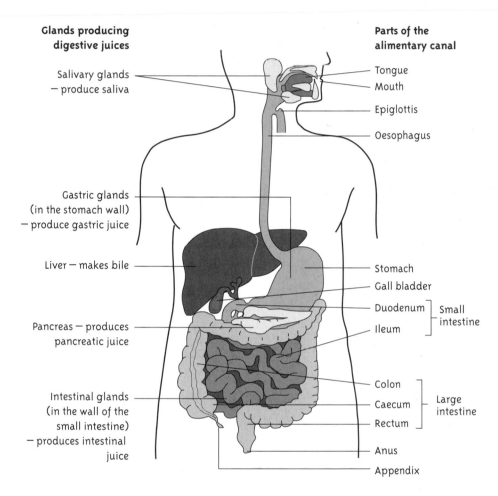

Figure 3.20 *Digestive system*

The digestive system consists of the alimentary canal, which begins at the mouth and ends at the anus, as you can see in the diagram. The oesophagus carries the food we eat to the stomach from the mouth. Food is then passed to the small intestine and then to the large intestine, from where it passes to the rectum. It ends up at the anus, where the waste material is passed out. The food is propelled through the alimentary canal by a motion called *peristalsis* (contractions of the gut wall).

Before the food can get into our blood or the cells it must pass through the wall of the alimentary canal. This is called *absorption*. The walls are made up of living cells, which will only allow small molecules to pass through.

Big molecules such as carbohydrates cannot pass through until they are broken down and finally absorbed by digestion. It is at this stage that the cells provide the energy by which the muscles are powered when you exercise, as in using the biceps.

Nervous system

In some public service work you need to react quickly to certain situations, for example if you are a policeman and someone throws a punch at you, you will need to move fast to avoid being injured.

When you have to react quickly your body responds by using two body systems, the nervous and endocrine systems. The endocrine system will be discussed later.

The nervous system sends *electrical* signals around your body which stimulate your muscles causing them to move, whereas the endocrine system sends *chemical* messages around your body. Your nervous system includes the following:

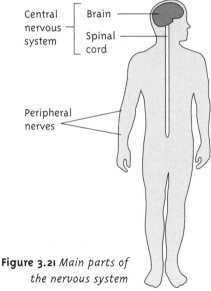

Figure 3.21 *Main parts of the nervous system*

The central nervous system consists of your brain and the spinal cord. The main role of your nervous system is to control movement. It helps you with coordination so that all your body parts work in the correct order. The nervous system is also responsible for actions such as blinking and breathing.

When we move it is because of the reactions involved in a chain of events, starting with a stimulus and ending in a response. The chains are:

Stimulus → Receptor → Coordinator → Effector → Response

Imagine burning yourself on the cooker. The stimulus is the heat from the cooker and the receptors located under your skin tell you it's hot. The effectors, which are the muscles in your arms, allow you to move away from the cooker. Finally, your response is moving your hand away quickly.

Cardiovascular system

The cardiovascular and respiratory system work together to ensure your exercising muscles receive the oxygen needed, and they also help with the removal of waste products. The cardiovascular system has three main parts. These are

- the heart
- blood
- blood vessels.

This system transports the food, oxygen, waste products and carbon dioxide around the body in the blood. At the centre of the system is the heart, which pumps the blood around the body. The blood vessels make up the rest of the cardiovascular system and their role is to transport the blood around your body to and from the heart. There are two main types of blood vessels: the arteries and veins.

Key point

Veins carry the blood to the heart and arteries carry the blood away from the heart.

The arteries have branches called capillaries, which contain the red blood cells. The following diagram is a basic overview of the cardiovascular system:

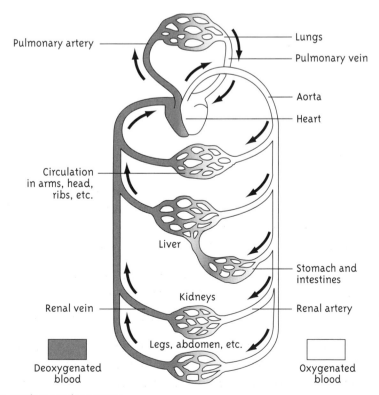

Figure 3.22 *Cardiovascular system*

The heart has two parts: a left side and a right side. Remember that the blood on the left side does not mix with that on the right side.

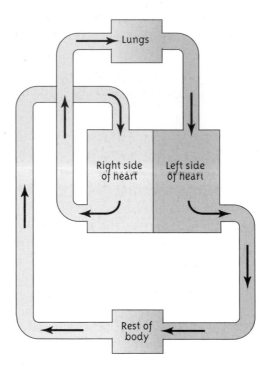

Figure 3.23 *The circulation of blood*

The diagram shows that the right side of your heart pumps the blood into your lungs, where it picks up the oxygen. The oxygenated blood is then returned to the heart. It is the job of the left side of your heart to pump the oxygenated blood to the rest of your body, for example the muscles. When it reaches the muscles it releases the oxygen and becomes deoxygenated and then returns to the heart.

Let's do it!

The cardiovascular system involves other important features, for example blood pressure. You are to do research into blood pressure and then present your findings to the rest of the group through a five-minute presentation. Here is a list of the questions you may want to find answers to:

- What is blood pressure?
- What is systolic pressure?
- What is diastolic pressure?
- How do we measure blood pressure?
- How does exercise affect blood pressure?
- What is the link between stress and blood pressure?

Respiratory system

The respiratory system provides the oxygen we need to release energy and is sometimes referred to as the pulmonary or ventilatory system. Through respiration our body uses oxygen and produces carbon dioxide, as you can see in the table below.

Gas	Breathing in	Breathing out
Oxygen	21%	16%
Carbon dioxide	0.04%	4%
Nitrogen	78%	78%

Table 3.11

Oxygen is needed to release energy so that we can exercise. The oxygen enters our body through the respiratory system, the main part of which is the lungs and air passages.

Oxygen enters the lungs from the atmosphere through *inspiration* (breathing in) and oxygen and carbon dioxide leave the body through *expiration* (breathing out).

Smoking can have a major influence on your health and fitness. It especially affects the respiratory system. Over 100,000 deaths a year in the UK are attributed to smoking. It can cause a range of diseases, from lung cancer to coronary artery disease. One of the many toxic chemicals in tobacco is nicotine, which causes the addiction to smoking. Nicotine raises your blood pressure and the tar in tobacco causes chronic irritation of the respiratory system.

Through smoking carbon monoxide enters the bloodstream by way of the lungs and interferes with the level of oxygen in the cells. This means that when you are training there is less oxygen in your body to produce energy. Also you will find it harder to exercise and will be out of breath sooner.

Endocrine system

The endocrine system sends chemical messages around the body. It is also known as the hormonal system and helps coordinate the body. Our body has a number of glands.

The glands produce hormones which are carried around the body by the blood. The hormones tell the different parts of the body what to do, as you can see in the following table:

Gland	Hormone	Function
Adrenal	Adrenaline	Prepares the body for heightened activity
Pancreas	Insulin	Reduces blood sugar levels
Ovary	Oestrogen	Helps with the menstrual cycle
Ovary	Progesterone	Helps with pregnancy and the menstrual cycle
Testis	Testosterone	Produces male secondary sexual characteristics and helps with sperm production

Table 3.12

During exercise your body releases a large amount of endorphins, which are powerful mood-elevating chemicals (hormones) in the brain. Through exercise you are able to relieve negative emotions such as frustration and anger. The benefits of exercise on the psychological state can be summarised as

- increased self-esteem
- reduced anxiety levels
- increased confidence
- enjoyment.

Urinary system

The urinary system works better during homeostasis. This is also known as the excretory system and involves the removal of waste from the body. The waste is generated from the chemical reactions which take place in the body, for example in digestion. The waste excreted includes carbon dioxide and urea (urine). These waste products need to be removed to avoid the body being poisoned. The liver and kidneys play an important role in excretion, as you can see from Figure 3.24.

The kidneys' main function is to clean your blood by removing the urea from the blood and excreting it as urine. In Figure 3.24 you can see that the skin excretes

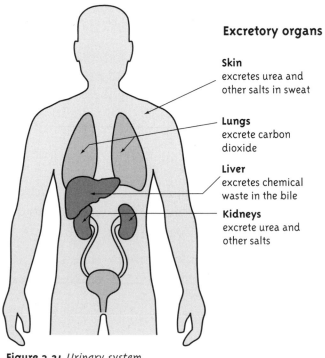

Excretory organs

Skin
excretes urea and other salts in sweat

Lungs
excrete carbon dioxide

Liver
excretes chemical waste in the bile

Kidneys
excrete urea and other salts

Figure 3.24 *Urinary system*

minerals in your sweat. This excretion is increased when you exercise because you sweat more during exercise.

 Key point

If you are exercising a lot it is important that your drinks include sodium, potassium and calcium. These minerals are important because they help the muscles to work and help the absorption of water.

Operation of systems at rest and during exercise

In our everyday lives our body remains in a steady state, for example your hormones remain steady. This steady state is known as *homeostasis*. Imagine the inside of your body as being the water in your bath. Before you get in it is still and calm (homeostasis). However, if you get in and out again you disturb the water causing many ripples and mini-waves (not a steady state). After a time the bath will return to homeostasis (calm).

The loss of homeostasis in the body is caused by certain factors, for example

- illness – your body temperature will rise
- exercise – your heart rate increases
- stress – during a driving test your muscles may become tense.

After a time your body will return to normal (homeostasis).

When we start to exercise there are a number of changes which occur within the body. These changes mean the body is no longer in a state of homeostasis. Figure 3.25 shows these changes:

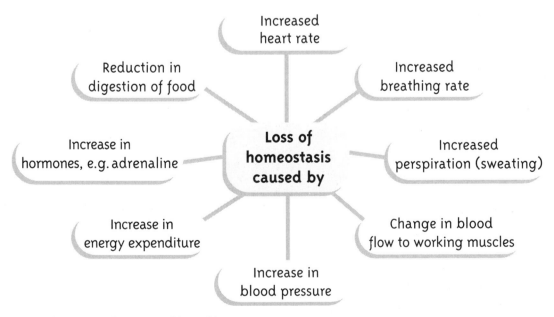

Figure 3.25 *The causes of loss of homeostasis*

Principles

We sometimes talk about health and fitness as if they were the same, however there are important differences. It is possible to be healthy but not fit and it is possible to be fit but not healthy.

Key point

Remember, health and fitness are different concepts.

Definition of health and fitness

There are different definitions of fitness – it is a complex subject. It can be defined into two main areas:

- Health-related fitness – a level of fitness based on fitness test scores, which should lead to a low level risk of developing health problems.
- Skill-related fitness – a level of fitness which allows the individual to perform an activity, task or sport.

The following table summarises the health-related components and introduces you to the skill-related components of fitness.

Health-related fitness	Skill-related fitness
Strength	Agility
Muscular endurance	Balance
Aerobic fitness	Coordination
Flexibility	Power
Body composition	Reaction time
	Speed

Table 3.13

As you can see from the table there is a clear difference between health-related and skill-related components of fitness.

General fitness

If you have a good level of general fitness you will have a blend of all the components of fitness, for example good strength with stamina.

You will be able to cope with the physical demands of your job, as well as play sport and exercise regularly.

Specific fitness

When you enter a specific public service, for example the fire service, you will need to have a specific or certain level of fitness. In the fire service you will need good upper body strength, whereas in the Royal Marines you will need an excellent level of stamina. For the fire service you will need the strength to lift yourself up a ladder, in the Royal Marines you may need to march for 30 miles a day, which obviously requires stamina.

 Key point

It is important that you train to have a specific fitness for your public service because it will make certain physical demands of you.

Components of fitness

The main components of fitness related to health are:

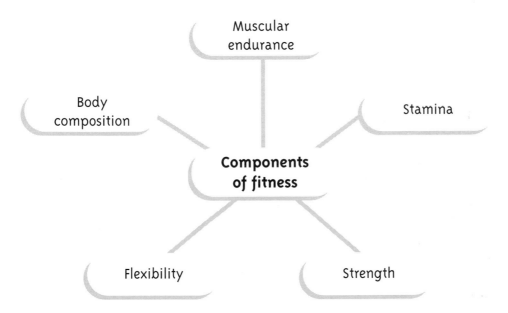

Figure 3.26 *The components of fitness*

The only component of fitness we have not yet discussed is flexibility.

Good flexibility enables you to pick up something heavy from the ground, for example if you are a paramedic you need to be able to pick up a stretcher with someone on it. Flexibility is defined 'as the specific joint's ability to move through a full range of movement', for example the knee. A flexible joint has a greater range of motion, which will aid movement.

CHECK WHAT YOU KNOW

1 Name *five* of the body systems.
2 What are main functions of the skeletal system?
3 What is a role of an enzyme?
4 What is the difference between a ligament and a tendon?
5 What is the difference between the terms 'health' and 'fitness'?
6 What are the main five components of fitness?

In summary

- The body systems, for example the muscular system and the endocrine system, work together during rest and exercise.
- Some systems, like the cardiovascular system, have a more important role when we exercise.
- The terms 'health' and 'fitness' do relate to each other, however there are important differences.
- The main components of fitness are strength, muscular endurance, flexibility and body composition.

Assessment activity

You are to prepare and present a presentation (10–15 minutes) to your group titled 'Body Systems'. You should look to use visual aids and handouts when presenting with diagrams, which will be important.

- To gain a *pass* (P4) you will need to describe the major body systems (remember there are eight) and the principles of health and fitness. You should look to use diagrams, for example of the heart. You also need to identify the main parts and the function of the system. In terms of health and fitness you should try to define them both and explain them. It would also be a good idea to identify factors which affect them, for example health is influenced by a lack of sleep.
- To gain a *merit* (M2) you will first have to meet the pass criteria. In addition you will need to analyse the operation of the major body systems in relation to health and fitness. This is where you need to link the body systems to the concepts of health and fitness. For example, you may make comment that

  'If you do not train the cardiovascular system it will have an effect on your stamina because your heart helps pump the oxygen to the muscles required for exercise, for example running.'

To gain a *distinction* (D1) you have to meet the pass and merit criteria. In addition you will also need to evaluate the main components (e.g. flexibility) of fitness and their importance in the public service activity. An example of this could be

'North Yorkshire Fire Service states on its website that you need good strength to carry the ladders used in fire fighting. Therefore you can strongly argue that upper body strength is vital for the job.'

Assessment activity

You will only need to complete this assessment if you wish to achieve a *distinction* (D3). You are to produce a report on the main components of fitness and their importance in public service activity. You should try to relate the fitness to the public service in which you are interested, for example the fire service. You may want to use the following outline for the report:

- Front cover page, including name, student number etc.
- Contents page
- Introduction
- Components of fitness (strength, stamina, muscular endurance, flexibility and body composition)
- Description of the activities in the public service – for example a police officer may have to chase a suspect through the town centre
- Fitness for the activities – it is important you have good stamina so that you will be able to catch the suspect
- Conclusion
- Bibliography

Nutrition

Being physically fit is important for all the public services and having a good level of fitness will help us stay healthy throughout our lives. However, being physically fit must be matched with a good healthy diet. A healthy diet will reduce the risk of developing certain conditions, for example high blood pressure or becoming overweight. The food we eat plays an important role in our fitness levels and in our ability to perform exercise. A poor diet may

- cause us to run out of energy for exercise
- increase the chance of getting an illness or injury
- lead to dehydration (shortage of water).

This section will introduce you to the basic concept of nutrition, whilst linking it to fitness and health.

Nutrition

Our body whether exercising or not needs oxygen, water and nutrients to work on a daily basis. There are five main nutrients (or food groups) in the body. These are

- carbohydrates
- fats
- proteins
- vitamins
- minerals.

It is important we eat the correct amount of these nutrients to maximise our physical fitness and help us maintain a healthy lifestyle.

Components of nutrition

The following table outlines the main functions of the five main food groups (nutrients).

Food group	Function
Carbohydrate	Provides the body with energy for exercise
Fat	Provides stored energy for exercise
Protein	Required for growth and repair
Vitamins	Important for chemical reactions within the body
Minerals	Helps with fluid balance

Table 3.14

Energy balance within the body

To control weight and reduce body weight, exercise needs to be linked to a reduction in calorie intake, for example a reduction in fatty foods.

(a) calories in food > calories used = WEIGHT GAIN

(b) calories in food < calories used = WEIGHT LOSS

(c) calories in food = calories used = WEIGHT BALANCE

Figure 3.27 *Calorie balance*

You can see that when your calorie intake matches your expenditure through daily activities (including sleeping and exercise) the individual's weight stays the same. However too little or too much calorie intake compared to expenditure will lead to either weight loss or gain. This highlights the importance of regular exercise and health-related fitness for weight control. The following table outlines the recommended daily calorie intake:

Age range in years	Occupational category	Energy (kcal)
Boys		
9 up to 12		2500
12 up to 15		2800
15 up to 18		3000
Girls		
9 up to 12		2300
12 up to 15		2300
15 up to 18		2300
Men		
18 up to 35	Sedentary	2700
	Moderately active	3000
	Very active	3600
35 up to 65	Sedentary	2600
	Moderately active	2900
	Very active	3600
65 up to 75	Assuming a sedentary	2350
75 and over	life	2100
Women		
18 up to 35	Most occupations	2200
35 up to 55	Very active	2500
55 up to 75	Assuming a sedentary	2050
75 and over	life	1900
Pregnancy 2nd and 3rd trimester		2400
Lactation		2700

Table 3.15

Nutritional value of food and planning dietary needs

In deciding your calorie balance and nutritional intake you need to know the nutritional value of the food you eat and the amount of calories you need for exercise.

Let's do it!

One way of finding out our dietary intake of fat is through reading the labels of the foods we eat. For this activity you should all bring in three labels from the foods you eat, preferably tins or packets of food. In your group you should aim to discuss the following points:

1 Are there any similarities and differences between the foods you have brought in, within the group?
2 What percentage of your three foods comprise fat?
3 Do you think that the labelling is adequate on all the samples?
4 Why do think the correct labelling of food is important?

When you are planning your dietary needs there are a number of things you will need to consider in terms of a decrease or increase in your calorie intake.

You need to *decrease* your calories:

If you are injured and are not exercising
If you are not playing sport because it is the off season
If it is summer, as not so many calories are needed to keep you warm
If you are older, because your metabolism slows down
If you have excessive amounts of body fat

You need to *increase* your calories

If you increase the amount of training you are doing
If you are playing sport because it is the competitive season
If you are below the recommended calorie intake for your age/sex
If it is winter, as more calories are needed to keep you warm

Impact of good and bad nutrition on health and fitness

Your diet has a major influence on your health and fitness.

Diet and health

In the UK and the USA it is widely accepted that too many people do not eat a balanced diet. Lack of a balanced diet leads to a number of health problems, for example cardiovascular disease. In the UK 36% of deaths in men aged less than 75 years old are caused by cardiovascular disease.

The biggest problem is that we tend to eat too many saturated fats. Three types of fats are found in food. These are

monounsaturated

- polyunsaturated
- saturated.

Eating a healthy balanced diet will help you reduce the risk of developing certain conditions, for example coronary heart disease.

 Key point

Remember, you do not need to cut out your favourite foods totally in order to have a healthy diet, you simply need to adjust the amounts of foods you eat, for example you can increase your dietary fibre through eating more fruit.

The kind of diet you have can also help to improve certain health conditions. It has been found that making certain adjustments to diet can improve the following conditions:

- *Asthma* – cutting down on salt can reduce the effects of asthma.
- *Cancer* – the risk of certain cancers is lower in people who eat a diet full of vegetables, fruit and starchy foods, for example cereals.
- *Anxiety* – if you suffer from stress you can reduce the effects by cutting out caffeine and alcohol. At the same time you should take vitamin supplements and stay well hydrated.
- *Heart conditions* – fruit and vegetables include vitamins C and E, which have been shown to protect the heart.

Diet and fitness

There are certain dietary rules that can help you with your fitness training. When you exercise you should follow these general guidelines:

- Don't drink alcohol before or after exercise.
- Don't eat a large meal for three hours prior to exercise.
- Avoid fatty foods for your energy source.
- Avoid excessive amounts of caffeine – e.g. coffee.
- Don't eat during exercise.
- Avoid excessive amounts of salt prior to exercise.
- Make sure you drink plenty of water before and after exercise.
- If you eat before exercise make it a small snack like a banana.
- Use carbohydrates as your energy source.
- After exercise make sure you re-fuel by having carbohydrates.
- If you have a sports drink have one that has some sugars, calcium, potassium and sodium.

Water

Water is the most important fluid for the human body and is vital for a healthy lifestyle. Water maintains our cells and transports the nutrients and oxygen around the body along with the removal of waste matter. It is widely accepted that you should have between 2 to 3 litres per day, more if you are exercising. It is important to have more when you are exercising because you lose water through sweating and cooling down.

Alcohol

It is accepted that without any significant risk to health

- women can drink 2 to 3 units of alcohol a day
- men can drink 3 to 4 units a day.

One unit is classed as half a pint of lager or a pub measure of spirit, a glass of wine is 2 units and alcopops is 1.5 units. Alcohol will affect your sporting performance and exercise, as it can significantly affect your balance and coordination. Here are a few practical points:

- After you exercise make sure your first drink is not an alcoholic one.
- If you get injured, for example develop a large bruise, avoid alcohol after 24 hours of exercise.
- Avoid alcohol 24 hours before a match or competition.

Assessment activity

You are to produce a poster (600 mm × 900 mm) which highlights the importance of good nutrition and its impact on health and fitness. Your tutor will provide you with the poster paper. You should look to use both colourful images, for example a plate of chips, and text. The poster must contain a title and your name.

- To gain a *pass* (P5), you will simply need to explain the importance of good nutrition and its impact on health and fitness. For example, you could report that 'You should eat 60% carbohydrates, 25% fat and 15% protein on a daily basis because this will help you remain healthy and fit' and 'If you eat too much fat this can lead to heart problems.' You could include a pie chart to show this.

- To gain a *merit* (M3), you will need to meet the pass criteria (see above). You will also need to analyse the impact of good nutrition and diet on health and fitness. You will need to bring in some evidence to support the points which you make. For example, 'Hypertension (raised blood pressure) is a big health problem, which effects 20% of the adult population in the world (World Health Organisation, 1994). It has been shown that excessive amounts of salt in your diet can raise your blood pressure. Therefore you should avoid adding extra amounts of salt to your diet, for example table salt.' It will also be important for your poster to be presented well, for example colourful with important images.

- To gain a *distinction* (D2), you will need to meet the pass and merit criteria (see above). Your poster should also evaluate the impact of good nutrition on the human body. Therefore, unlike for the pass and merit criteria, you will need to show a good understanding of the body systems. For example, you could report, 'If you eat too much fat this can lead to an increase in cholesterol, which is a waxy substance. The cholesterol over a period of time builds up in your arteries, which are important for the circulation of blood. This build up is called arteriosclerosis, which can lead to a heart attack.' It will also be important for your poster to be presented well, for example colourful with important images. You will need to show a thorough understanding and knowledge of the relationship between diet and the human body.

Diet

People in everyday life often misuse and misunderstand the word 'diet'. They use it in conjunction with some plan to lose weight, for example the Zone Diet or the Atkins Diet. However a diet is simply the food we eat. To go on the Atkins Diet is not to start a diet but to change your diet.

Dietary requirements to maintain health and for exercise

To maintain a healthy body you can use the following food pyramid as a guideline.

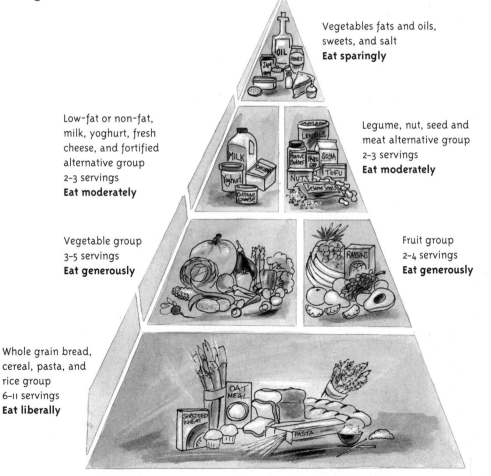

Vegetables fats and oils, sweets, and salt
Eat sparingly

Low-fat or non-fat, milk, yoghurt, fresh cheese, and fortified alternative group
2–3 servings
Eat moderately

Legume, nut, seed and meat alternative group
2–3 servings
Eat moderately

Vegetable group
3–5 servings
Eat generously

Fruit group
2–4 servings
Eat generously

Whole grain bread, cereal, pasta, and rice group
6–11 servings
Eat liberally

Figure 3.28 *Food pyramid*

The food pyramid outlines what you should eat on a daily basis for good health. The idea is that you eat more servings from the bottom layer and a reduced amount from the middle and top layers because they are not as healthy for you. Each level of the pyramid provides a wide range of servings from each food group. From this you can see that it is important you eat a variety of foods. If you follow this pyramid it will help you with your weight and health. Generally speaking, you should aim to eat the proportions shown in Figure 3.29.

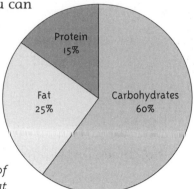

Figure 3.29 *The proportions of food you should aim to eat*

Recommended Nutrient Intake (RNI)

To maintain our health we should we eat a certain amount from all the food groups each day. The amount we require is known as the RNI (Reference Nutrient Intake), which is the amount of a nutrient sufficient for most individuals. For example, the RNI for a male aged 19–50 is 55.5 grams per day for protein.

Nutrient	RNI (19–50 year olds)	RNI (50+ year olds)
Energy (kcal)**	1940 (females) 2550 (males)	1900 (females) 2550 (males)
Protein (g)*	45 (females) 55.5 (males)	46.5 (females) 53.3 (males)
Fat (g)	33% of energy	33% of energy
Carbohydrate (g)	47% of energy	47% of energy
Minerals		
Calcium (mg)	700	700
Zinc (mg)	7 (females) 9.5 (males)	7 (females) 9.5 (males)
Potassium (mg)	3500	3500
Manganese (mg)	NA	NA

Vitamins		
Vitamin B2 (mg)	1.1 (females) 1.3 (males)	1.1 (females) 1.3 (males)
Vitamin B1 (mg)	0.8 (females) 1.0 (males)	0.8 (females) 0.9 (males)
Vitamin B6 (mg)	1.2 (females) 1.4 (males)	1.2 (females) 1.4 (males)
Folate (mcg)	200	200
Carotene	NA	NA
Niacin (mg)	13 (females) 17 (males)	12 (females) 16 (males)
Pantothenate (mg)	NA	NA
Vitamin B12 (mcg)	1.5	1.5

Table 3.16

* RNI = Reference Nutrient Intake

Food group system

The food group system consists of five main groups:

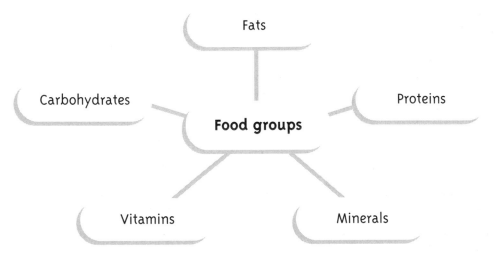

Figure 3.30 *The five main groups of food*

Here we will discuss in more depth these food groups, highlighting such issues as the function and food sources.

Carbohydrates

Carbohydrates, also known as starches and sugars, are our main source of energy and should make up 60% of our daily intake. Carbohydrates are

made up of sugars and are found in all foods, except meat. Examples are
- apples
- potatoes
- oatmeal
- chocolate
- rice
- pasta.

They are also found in breads, cereals and grains. The main role of carbohydrates is to provide us with the energy required to live and to exercise.

When they enter the body carbohydrates are broken down and turned into glucose. Glucose can be used straight away for exercise and is carried in every cell within the body. However not all the glucose is required immediately and what isn't needed combines to make glycogen. This is stored in the liver as energy, which can be used at a later time. Some glycogen is stored in the muscles and is the main fuel source for muscles during exercise.

Carbohydrates can either be classed as being 'simple' or 'complex'. Simple carbohydrates include
- fructose, i.e. sugar found in fruits
- galactose
- glucose.

In comparison complex carbohydrates are
- dried peas and beans
- grains, including oats, rice and wheat
- bread, cereals and pasta
- vegetables, including potatoes and peas.

Carbohydrates are simple or complex because of the way they are formed. Too many carbohydrates in your diet can increase your blood cholesterol levels (a waxy fatty substance found in the blood). It can also raise your blood sugar level, which could be fatal if you suffer from diabetes.

Fats

Our daily diet should include 25% of fat. As with carbohydrates, proteins and alcohol, fat provides the body with calories. The calories are used by the body to provide energy so that we can do everyday things like sleep or run for the bus.

Key point

A diet including fat should not be viewed as being a bad diet as it depends on the amount and type of fat eaten.

Fat is found in foods such as meat, dairy products and oils. If we eat too much fat the body stores it in fat cells for use at a later date. Fat plays a vital role in the transportation and absorption of fat-soluble vitamins, which will be discussed later.

Let's do it!

Did you know that a change in diet which reduces the intake of fat could reduce your chance of developing

- obesity
- heart disease
- cancer.

In groups, produce an A3 poster showing the side-effects on your health of eating too many fatty foods. You should try to keep the language simple and image colourful. Your target group is police officers over the age of 45, who have not had a fitness test for many years and eat a number of takeaways a night.

To lower your daily fat intake you could

- cut down on red meats and eat fish
- choose low fat products
- remove the skin from poultry
- trim off visible fat.

Proteins

Proteins are made up of amino acids of which there are 20 different types. It is not important to know them all, however it is important to know that the body can only make 13 of them. The other 9 must come from the food that we eat, and are therefore known as 'essential' amino acids. Proteins are required to help us grow and develop properly and should form 15% of our daily diet.

Key point

When we exercise for over three hours constantly, the body uses proteins as an energy source instead of carbohydrates and fats. An example would be a long run.

Protein is found in a number of food sources, such as

- beef
- lamb
- fish
- poultry
- eggs
- shellfish.

Protein is important for fitness because it helps to repair the body's cells when they are damaged or worn out, for example a torn hamstring. It is specifically important for our organs (e.g. heart), muscles, nervous system, blood vessels and skeleton.

Let's do it!

In pairs, research the terms 'complete' and 'incomplete' proteins. Try to discover the difference between them and find examples of food sources for both types of proteins.

Unlike carbohydrates and fats, the amount of protein required on a daily basis is small, with our daily diet providing a sufficient amount.

If we eat too much protein it can be very harmful to the kidneys, which break down the protein in our diet. Excess amounts makes the kidneys work a lot harder. So you need to work out how much protein you need to eat every day – which is quite easy to do.

Key point

As a rough estimate, we need to eat 1.0 grams of fat per kilogram of our body weight. For example, if you weigh 60 kg then you will need 60 grams of protein a day.

From Table 3.17 you can see how much protein is in some foods.

Vitamins

They may only be in very small amounts, however vitamins are vital for maintaining life. One of their main roles is to act as an enzyme, which causes reactions within the body, such as that required to heal a wound. Unfortunately our body cannot make vitamins, so we need to get them from our food or vitamin supplements. They come in two forms: fat-soluble and water-soluble.

Key point

A vitamin that is fat-soluble is one that you do not need daily because your body stores them for the future.

Key point

A water-soluble vitamin is one the body cannot store, so you need it every day.

The protein content of various foods	
Food	**Protein (g per portion)**
Meat/fish/poultry	
Red meat (4 oz portion)	32
Chicken (6 oz portion)	45
White fish (6 oz portion)	30
Oily fish (6 oz portion)	30
Sausages (1)	10
Mince (4 oz)	25
Tinned tuna (4 oz)	25
Dairy products and eggs	
Milk ($\frac{1}{4}$ pint)	6
Cottage cheese (4 oz)	15
Fromage frais (4 oz)	8
Cheddar cheese (2 oz)	14
Yoghurt (1 carton)	8
Eggs (4)	8
Pulses and nuts	
Kidney beans (8 oz boiled)	15
Baked beans ($\frac{1}{2}$ large tin)	10
Nuts (2oz)	13
Cereals	
Bread (2 slices)	6
Pasta (6 oz boiled)	5
Rice (6 oz boiled)	6

Table 3.17

The following are the vitamins we need.

- *Vitamin A* is a fat-soluble vitamin that is found in foods like liver, cheese and eggs. It has a number of key functions. It
  - helps strengthen immunity from infections
  - helps maintain good skin
  - aids your vision in dim light.

However it is important to know that too much of it makes your bones more likely to fracture.

- *Vitamin B_6* is found in a number of foods, such as
  - whole cereals
  - eggs
  - milk
  - potatoes.

Let's do it!

Carry out research to answer the following questions regarding Vitamin B_6

1 What other foods contain B_6?
2 What happens if you have too much of B_6?
3 What function does B_6 have?

- *Vitamin B_{12}* is found in all forms of meat, for example beef and seaweed, and is a water-soluble vitamin. It has a role in
  - releasing energy from food
  - making red blood cells and maintaining the nervous system.

- *Vitamin C* is also known as ascorbic acid and is found in a number of fruit and vegetables such as oranges and sweet potatoes. In most cases you will get all the vitamin C you need through your normal food intake. It
  - helps the body absorb iron
  - keeps cells healthy.

  However too much of it will lead to diarrhoea and flatulence.

Figure 3.31 *Fruit and vegetables are sources of vitamin C*

- *Vitamin D* is only found in a small number of foods, such as oily fish, liver and eggs, and is fat-soluble. Fortunately most of our vitamin D comes from sunlight. As in the case of vitamin A, too much of it will weaken your bones, but it does help keep bones and teeth healthy.

- *Vitamin E* is another fat-soluble vitamin and is found in nuts and seeds amongst other things. It is required for protecting cell membranes and there is little evidence to what the effects are of having too much.

- *Vitamin K* is fat-soluble and is found in green leafy vegetables, such as broccoli and spinach. It can also be found in meats such as pork. The body stores this vitamin in the liver and it helps with the healing process.

Minerals

Minerals are important to most parts of the body, such as the bones, and to our fluid balance. There are a number of key minerals which you have probably heard of, such as iron and calcium. Our mineral intake comes from food or mineral supplements, usually in tablet form.

The following table outlines some important minerals.

Name	Sources	RNI (per day)	Functions	Effects of having too much
Calcium	Milk Cheese Cabbage	700 mg	Helps build strong bones and teeth Aids muscle contraction Aids blood clotting	Stomach pain and diarrhoea
Copper	Nuts Shellfish Liver	1.2 mg	Helps produce white and red blood cells Vital for child growth	Stomach pain and diarrhoea Long-term effects are damage to liver and kidneys
Iron	Beans Nuts Whole grains	8.7 mg (men) 14.8 mg (women)	Carries oxygen around the body Makes red blood cells	Nausea and vomiting
Potassium	Bananas Beef Pulses	3500 mg	Controls fluid balance Lowers blood pressure	Stomach pain and diarrhoea
Sodium				
Zinc				

Table 3.18

Let's do it!

Aim to complete the above table for both sodium and zinc. You should also try to research the link between sodium and blood pressure because sodium can have a big influence on health.

Health Development Agency guidelines

In England the Health Development Agency, formerly known as the Health Education Authority, is the leading organisation involved in

- promoting health
- helping people make improvements in health
- working with others to reduce health inequalities.

It also advises the government on health promotion strategies, an example being the stop smoking campaign. Most importantly, its job is to communicate to us on public health issues, such as the need to cut down on salt within our diet. It also recommends that we use the following plate of food as a guideline:

Figure 3.32 *A balanced diet is important for our health and fitness*

This plate represents the desirable balance of foods for the promotion of good health. In general the suggestion is that we

- eat at least five portions a day of fruit and vegetables (excluding potatoes)
- eat enough bread, other cereals and potatoes to make up one-third of our diet
- include some wholegrain products to increase the amount of dietary fibre we eat
- eat moderate amounts of meat, preferably a lean cut
- eat oily fish at least twice a week
- eat a moderate amount of milk and dairy products
- make foods containing fat and sugar the smallest part of our diet, for example biscuits and cakes.

CHECK WHAT YOU KNOW

1 Which mineral is important for strong bones and teeth?
2 Name the *three* types of fat and explain the difference.
3 What does RNI stand for and mean?
4 Briefly describe and explain the importance of the food pyramid.
5 Provide a list of *five* key carbohydrate, fat and protein sources.

In summary

- Generally, we should eat more fruit and vegetables whilst reducing our fat, salt and sugar intake to maintain a healthy diet.
- We should not think of the word diet as being only to with initiatives such as Atkins, as whatever we eat is our diet, so we are always on a diet.
- We should aim to have 60% carbohydrate, 25% fat and 15% protein in our daily diet.
- The five main food groups are carbohydrates, fats, proteins, vitamins and minerals.
- By changing our diet to include healthier foods we can reduce the chance of getting certain diseases, such as forms of cancer.

Assessment activity

Regardless of the grade you want to work towards you will need to complete the following assessment activity.

You are to produce a report on the following tasks:

1 Plan a dietary programme (P6), which can be fairly simple in nature. There are many approaches you might take, for example you may produce a bullet point list (an example is shown below):
   - Reduce the amount of salt intake
   - Eat five portions of fruit and vegetables
2 Explain the Recommended Nutrient Intake (RNI). You may want to provide a number of food examples in relation to the RNI.
3 Explain the food group system. You will need to mention carbohydrates, fats and proteins.

If you are working towards a *distinction* (D2) grade you should complete the following task in addition to the above tasks (1–3):

4 From Task 1 you will need to make clear recommendations explaining briefly the nutritional value of food. For example, you could report:
   - Reduce the amount of salt intake through not adding table salt to meals and reducing the foods which include a high level of salt, for example pork pies. Use low sodium salt substitute for cooking purposes if salt cannot be avoided. Switch from tinned vegetables to fresh vegetables, as these have no added salt, unlike the tinned foods.

Resources

Books

Bean A (1994) *The Complete Guide to Sports Nutrition*, London, A & C Black

Bean A (2002) *Kids' Food for Fitness*, London, A & C Black

Dick F W (1992) *Sports Training Principles*, London, A & C Black

Griffin J (2001) *Food for Sport – Eat Well, Perform Better*, London, The Crowood Press

Jones M (1994) *Biology for IGCSE*, Oxford, Heinemann

Maud P J and Foster C (1995) *Physiological Assessment of Human Fitness*, Leeds, Human Kinetics

Powers S K and Howley E T (1997*) Exercise Physiology Theory and Application to Fitness and Performance*, Brown and Benchmark

The British Medical Association (2001) *Illustrated Medical Dictionary*, London, Dorling Kindersley

Williams G (1996) *Biology for You*, Cheltenham, Stanley Thornes

Fact sheets

Health Education Authority, 'The Balance of Good Health'
Health Education Authority, 'Enjoy Healthy Eating'
Health Education Authority, 'Cancer: How to Reduce Your Risks'

Journals

Navy News
RAF News
Soldier

Websites

Army – www.army.mod.uk
BBC – www.bbc.co.uk/news.
Government Statistics – www.statistics.gov.uk
Police – www.policecouldyou.co.uk
RAF – www.raf-careers.com
Royal Marines – www.royal-marines.mod.uk
Royal Navy – www.royal-navy.mod.uk
World Health Organisation – www.who.int

Workplace welfare

Introduction

Within any place of work, whether the local police station or the local supermarket, the health and safety of yourself and others is so important and cannot be overstated. Having poor health and safety awareness or poor workplace welfare could lead to injury or even death. Work-related accidents kill over 300 people per year and over 2 million people in the UK suffer illnesses caused by their work. Preventing accidents and ill-health should be a key priority for everyone within the workplace.

The aim of this unit is to assist you in your knowledge and awareness of workplace welfare. Many factors are important in workplace welfare, such as safe working practices, emergency procedures, first aid and risk assessment. Here is a list of some of the other topics you will be studying:

- Roles and responsibilities for all
- Evacuation procedures
- Emergency equipment
- Hazards and risks
- Codes of practice
- Manual handling

You will also explore the legal implications of workplace welfare to the public services and the individuals. Some public services and individuals fail to comply with the legislation covering workplace welfare, so it is important for you to know the consequences of this.

You will have the chance to produce evidence for your key skills work in communication, information technology, improving your own learning and performance, problem solving and working with others.

You will have to do practical work throughout the unit, for example doing personal research and contacting health and safety officers. Therefore it is important that you get access to a variety of people, such as the local fire prevention officer or the health and safety officer from your local authority.

How you will be assessed

For your assessment of this unit you will need to complete a number of activities (known as assessment activities) to meet the assessment criteria. You will achieve a pass, merit or a distinction grade. The assessment activities are designed so that you can meet all the criteria required to pass the unit. If you wish to do the extra work you will also be able to meet the merit and distinction criteria through the assessment activities. However your tutor may set you other activities other than the assessment activities, which will also allow you to meet the assessment criteria.

As the assessment criteria can be met through a variety of methods you will have to complete a number of activities ranging from a presentation to a case study. Generally, in your assessments you will have to look at the

- various Acts and regulations
- roles and responsibilities set out in the legislation
- steps to be taken when discovering an incident
- requirements in the production of a risk assessment
- regulations concerning the provision of first aid
- the term 'manual handling'.

After completing this unit, you should be able to achieve the following outcomes:

1 Explore the provisions set out in health and safety at work legislation and explain the terminology, summarising the possible outcomes of failing to comply.
2 Explain emergency procedures, outlining differing practices in specified situations.
3 Explore the purpose of risk assessments and describe the methodology used.
4 Explore the requirements for additional safe working practices and describe their integration into the work environment.

Health and safety at work

Before starting the unit it is important you understand three key terms which are used throughout: health, safety and welfare.

Put simply, being healthy means being fit and well, for example we do not have an injury such as a sprained ankle. It also involves our state of mind and the way we think about things. For example, someone who has been in a car crash and then develops a fear of going in a car again would not be regarded as being healthy. Health also involves our ability to interact socially with the people we live with in our community. The World Health Organisation defines health as being 'a state of complete physical, mental and social well-being, not merely the absence of disease'.

Safety is also a complex term to explain and understand. Generally, safety means freedom from danger. However if you think about everyday life you can see that we are never totally free from danger. Even in our homes we face dangers, for example the electrical wiring in the kitchen is a potential source of danger. In thinking about safety you should consider the level of danger you are in. The level of danger normally relates to your environment and what you are doing at that time.

Welfare is a general term directly related to your health and safety. It is important for your employer to look after your welfare. For example, if your employer makes you work a 100-hour week or makes you work in a very noisy environment, then they are not looking after your welfare.

All companies and organisations must take health and safety very seriously at all times to avoid injury, illness or even death.

The public services are responsible for staff, visitors, and anyone else who enters their facilities, even at sea or in the air. The public services must meet the legal requirements imposed by law. This section concentrates on the major Acts of legislation which are designed to improve and maintain workplace welfare.

Terminology

There are a number of key terms you will need to know and be expected to learn for this unit. These key terms will form the basis of your assessment activities.

Basic terminology used in health and safety legislation

You need to be able to understand and explain the following terms:

- Health and Safety at Work Act 1974
- Health and Safety Commission
- Health and Safety Executive
- Local authorities
- Approved code of practice
- Duty of care
- Hazard
- Risk
- Control measures
- Competent personnel
- Accident management.

Health and Safety at Work Act 1974

The Health and Safety at Work Act (HASAWA) 1974 is the main piece of legislation covering workplace welfare. A number of other key Acts of legislation fall under the Health and Safety at Work Act 1974, for example the Health and Safety (Display Screen Equipment) Regulations 1992. The Health and Safety at Work Act 1974 is an umbrella Act which covers other important Acts which we will discuss later.

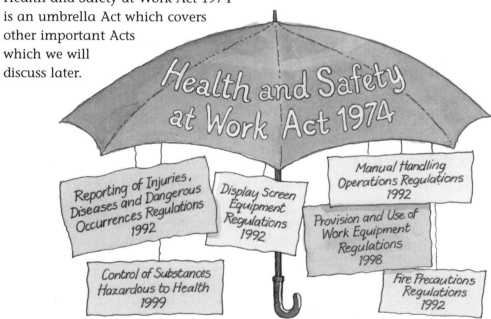

Figure 5.1 *Some of the legislation that comes under HASAWA*

Health and Safety Commission

The Health and Safety Commission (HSC) is responsible for health, safety and welfare in the workplace in this country. It advises the government on standards and regulations relating to workplace welfare.

Key point

The HSC aims to protect the health, safety and welfare of people at work.

The HSC is also responsible for proposing new laws and updating old laws with the aim of improving workplace welfare, which is enforced by the Health and Safety Executive.

Health and Safety Executive

The Health and Safety Executive (HSE) works for and advises the HSC on health and safety policy. It is also responsible for enforcing health and safety law in the workplace in the UK, along with the local authorities. It is the enforcing authority for the following workplaces:

- Factories
- Construction
- Mines and quarries
- Hospitals
- Schools
- Airports
- Police authorities, forces and fire authorities.

All workplace accidents in which those who are injured are off work for at least three days must be reported to the HSE. The following must be reported to the HSE:

- Death
- Loss of vision
- Amputation
- Fractures – not hands or feet
- Unconsciousness through shortage of oxygen
- Accident causing hospitalisation for more than one day
- Illness as a direct result of inhaling or absorbing a hazardous substance.

The HSE also
- inspects workplaces
- investigates some accidents and causes of ill-health
- publishes advice and guidance
- provides information on health and safety.

Local authorities

Local authorities also enforce HASAWA in workplaces such as
- shops
- market stalls

- most offices
- hotels
- restaurants
- night clubs
- zoos.

Your local authority will have departments and trained specialists to deal with health and safety issues. They will enforce the standards within specific organisations, such as the local army training college. If there is a specific issue, for example the level of hygiene in a kitchen, then an environmental officer may be called on to evaluate the standards of hygiene.

Approved code of practice (ACOP)

Approved codes of practice are documents that have a specific legal standing and are used by the public services. They offer practical examples of good practice, give advice on how to achieve compliance with the law, and can be issued by the HSC. Employers who have not followed an ACOP and who are prosecuted for a breach of health and safety law are likely to be found at fault by the courts.

Key point

The ACOPs provide practical advice and examples of good practice, which the employer and employee should follow to maintain the safety of the workplace.

Duty of care

Current health and safety legislation stipulates that employers have a duty of care towards their employees. The duty of care is a general legal duty that all organisations have to avoid carelessly causing injury to employees. This is regardless of the size of the organisation.

Case study

Failure to care

A volunteer is left unsupervised in a local fitness suite looking after a group of school children. Whilst doing some cleaning, the volunteer gets some bleach in one of his eyes, which requires first-aid treatment. Under the law the owner of the local fitness suite has a duty of care to the volunteer. The owner could be liable for failing to supervise and train the volunteer and for failing to provide protective gloves and goggles.

So, duty of care also extends to those who do not get paid for their work, such as students on work experience. Therefore statutory responsibility not to harm or damage the health of people working for organisations applies to both employees and volunteers.

Hazard

A hazard is something that has the potential to cause harm.

Figure 5.2 *A hazard such as ice on the road can cause harm*

In the cartoon the ice is the hazard because it causes the car to skid, which may cause the driver harm, if the car crashes and the driver suffers a broken arm. Think about the various hazards in your college, school or workplace.

Let's do it!

In pairs, draw up a list of 10 hazards which you find in one of the following locations in your college or school:
- fitness suite
- gym
- refectory
- computer suite
- sports field.

The type of hazard in the workplace will depend on the public service you enter. As a paramedic in the ambulance service you will face hazards such as
- muscle injuries caused by lifting
- tiredness caused by unsocial hours
- infections
- stress
- assaults
- infected needles.

Let's do it!

In pairs, draw up a list of 10 hazards which you would find in one of the public services you are interested in joining. For example, if you were interested in the coastguard service one hazard would be the weather.

It is important to reduce the number of hazards we face in the workplace to ensure our health and safety. However the dangerous nature of public services, such as the fire and rescue service, makes it impossible to reduce all the hazards. A firefighter will always face the hazard of fire. However, the risk of being harmed by the hazard can be reduced by wearing the correct clothing and having in-depth training.

Risk

A hazard is strongly linked with risk. A risk is the likelihood of a hazard causing harm to someone facing the hazard. It is important that we assess the risk as being low, medium or high.

In the case of traffic lights the green light is in the low risk category. Given that it isn't always possible to work without risk, we need to behave in ways that reduces the risk – to a low risk. In the case of traffic lights we should not drive off on an amber light (medium risk) because there is a significant amount of risk involved. Activities with a high risk (the red light) should also always be avoided because of the degree of danger.

Let's do it!

In pairs you drew up a list of 10 hazards within your college or school. You should now label these hazards as being low, medium or high risk based on your assessment. To give you an idea here are some examples:

- Red (High) – sustaining an injury because you failed to wear shin pads in hockey.
- Amber (Medium) – falling over and landing on glass on the football pitch.
- Green (Low) – being electrocuted while on the treadmill.

Risks can be reduced if we use control measures, which will now be discussed.

Control measures

We can reduce the risk of a hazard causing us harm if we used control measures. These help identify how you can reduce or even eliminate risks altogether. For example, if you are in the army on an overnight exercise and have identified the cold weather as a hazard during the night, you need to put in place control measures to reduce the risk. These could be to

Figure 5.3 *Having the right equipment for the conditions reduces the risk to health and safety*

- ensure all the tents are suitable and have no damage
- pack an extra layer of clothing
- pick a location which reduces the effects of the weather.

Let's do it!

In pairs you drew up a list of 10 hazards and the risk they posed in your college or school. You should now identify one control measure for each hazard.

Competent personnel

Employers must appoint competent people to ensure that they meet the provisions of health and safety legislation. Those appointed must be capable of carrying out tasks such as monitoring the sell by dates on food. For this they need to be given

- adequate information
- the correct instruction
- training
- support.

Competent personnel must have a good understanding of the current best practice, and so it is important they have ongoing training. However it is paramount to know the limitations of your own experience and knowledge, for example if you are not confident in first aid you should not perform it.

Case study

The need for support

Brian, aged 23, has just been taken on by the prison service to work at his local prison. After only two weeks' training within the prison he has been given some roles and responsibilities to do with workplace welfare. One of those roles is to offer the inmates basic advice on drug abuse. However, Brian has not been given support in doing this work and after a while it is clear he has limited experience in dealing with drug issues.

1 In your opinion, how do you feel the prison service is letting down the inmates, in terms of their welfare?
2 Who is responsible for this situation and why?
3 If you were in Brian's position what would you have done when you were asked to perform the roles and responsibilities?
4 Why do think it is important for an employee to receive the correct training and support?

The case study shows that the prison service (employer) has a major responsibility for their employees' health and safety training and support. If a person fails to provide a necessary standard of work, the employer still has a degree of responsibility to have ensured at the outset that the person was given the necessary training and support to do the job competently.

Accident management

Even though control measures have been put in place to maintain workplace welfare, there is always the chance of an accident.

A public service needs to have a plan to deal with an accident – this is known as an Emergency Action Plan (EMA). An EMA comes into force when there is an accident and is designed to maintain the health and safety of all those involved. Later in the unit we will discuss the EMA required for dealing with fire and bomb threats.

Legislation

In the UK our law comes from three different sources. These are
- European law
- case law or common law
- legislation or statute law.

The UK as part of the European Union is subject to regulations made by the European Commission. Health and safety regulations come to us in the form of European directives. These direct us to introduce specific pieces of legislation, for example the Health and Safety (Display Screen Equipment) Regulations 1992, which will be discussed later.

The UK parliament also passes laws, known as case or common law, which are administered by the law courts. Judges decide how the law should be applied in a specific case or how a dispute between two parties should be settled.

UK legislation or statute law is brought into being by Acts of parliament. Before an Act becomes law it starts out as a bill, which is discussed and voted on by the House of Commons and House of Lords. Once this has been passed it becomes an Act of law, which is a piece of legislation. The Health and Safety at Work Act 1974, which you have already been introduced to, is an example of legislation.

 Key point

The term 'legislation' relates to the body of laws made by the UK parliament, for example the Health and Safety at Work Act 1974.

We will now highlight the main pieces of legislation which are related to workplace welfare.

Acts and regulations

Within each piece of legislation there are parts called regulations.

 Key point

A regulation is a prescribed rule which must be followed to maintain workplace welfare.

An employer or employee who breaks a regulation can be prosecuted by the HSE. Every piece of legislation, for example the Health and Safety Information for Employees Regulations 1989, has a large number of regulations. You don't need to understand all the regulations, as they can be quite complex. You should concentrate on the most important ones. This section will highlight the main pieces of legislation which are related to workplace welfare and identify the key regulations.

In general, the law in the UK states that

- employers have to look after the health, safety and welfare of their employees
- employees and the self-employed have to look after their own health and safety
- everyone has to take care of the health and safety of other people – such as members of the public who may be affected by their work activity.

Health and Safety at Work Act (HASAWA) 1974

This is the main law in the UK that relates to workplace welfare. It has now been updated by the Workplace (Health, Safety and Welfare) Regulations 1992. All public services must comply with this law, including all the uniformed services.

The main focus of the Act is to protect the following people:

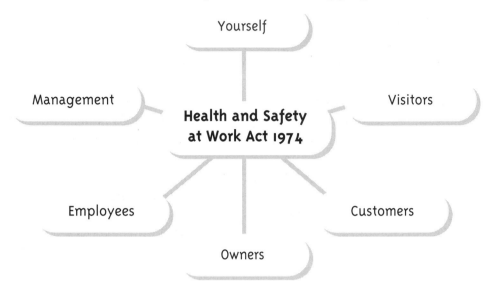

Figure 5.4 *The sort of people HASAWA is meant to protect*

The law states that employers must

- have a general duty to provide for the health, safety and welfare of those they employ
- consult employees about health and safety arrangements on a regular basis
- have a written health and safety policy
- ensure that non-employees (visitors or customers) are not at risk
- provide information on work-related hazards and the precautions required to contain them.

The law also states that the employee (you) must

- take reasonable care of their own health and safety at all times whilst working
- take reasonable care of the health and safety of others who may be affected by their actions, for example a fellow employee
- cooperate with the employer and other relevant organisations to ensure that the requirements of the Act are met
- not misuse equipment provided to maintain health and safety, for example the fire hose.

Key point

All employers and employees must adhere to the Health and Safety at Work Act 1974.

Case study

Failure to follow health and safety guidelines

Navid, aged 23, has just joined the local fire service as an auxiliary firefighter, whilst also working as a painter and decorator. After only two weeks training Navid was asked to drive one of the fire engines. Whilst driving Navid crashed the engine into a wall on the way to an incident. It emerged that Navid had received no training to drive the engine.

1 Who was to blame for this incident and why?
2 How does this incident relate to the Health and Safety at Work Act 1974?
3 What would you have done in Navid's position, when asked to drive the engine?
4 Which organisation would have investigated this incident?

Any employee or employer found to be negligent under this Act can be prosecuted through a criminal action and face a number of punishments. This will be discussed later.

Health and Safety (First Aid) Regulations 1981

Under these regulations employers have a duty to ensure adequate first aid provision for employees when they are injured or become ill at work. Employers should provide

- first-aid equipment – first-aid boxes
- a dedicated room for first aid
- trained first-aiders who have a first-aid certificate.

There are no clear guidelines on the contents of a first-aid box.

A qualified first-aider has four clear aims. These are to

- preserve life
- ensure the condition does not get any worse
- aid recovery
- ensure information is passed on to the emergency services – name of casualty, symptoms and any treatment you have given.

Figure 5.5 *A basic first-aid box*

Working Time Directive and Working Time Regulations 1998

These regulate the maximum working hours for employees (including night-shift employees) and are therefore important for health and safety in the workplace.

Let's do it!

Carry out research into the Working Time Directive and Working Time Regulations 1998. In small groups, do research into one of the following areas (choose one per group):

- Working time limits
- Working at night
- Health assessments for night employees
- Time off
- Rest breaks at work
- Paid annual leave.

Present your findings to the rest of the group, so that they get an overall understanding of the regulations.

Noise at Work Regulations 1989

Under the Noise at Work Regulations 1989, employers and employees have obligations which they must meet to reduce the risk of damage to hearing within the workplace.

In 1999 the Health and Safety Executive estimated that 1.3 million people in the UK were exposed to noise levels which could damage their hearing. Furthermore, statistics show that 56% of employers neglect noise problems.

Under the regulations the employer must

- reduce the risk of hearing damage to the lowest practical level
- appoint a competent person to carry out regular noise assessments (who must also keep a record of these assessments)
- reduce the risk of exposure to noise as far as is reasonably practical by means other than ear protectors
- mark ear zone protection zones with signs as far as is reasonably practical
- provide information and training about the risks to hearing
- provide ear protectors and ensure they are maintained and repaired.

The employees must

- use ear protectors
- use other protective equipment
- report any defects in the protective equipment.

Case study

Noise regulatons

Whilst studying health and safety at her local college, Sarah, who is interested in joining either the fire service or Royal Navy, has being doing some research on the Noise at Work Regulations 1989. She has a number of questions which she needs answering.

1 What activities in the fire service and Royal Navy may affect her hearing and need noise protection?
2 What health and safety signs should the employer put in place when an employee is working in a noisy environment?
3 What are the possible fines for breaking the Noise at Work Regulations 1989?

Failure to comply with the Noise at Work Regulations 1989 contravenes the Health and Safety Work Act 1974 and may lead to fines and prosecutions for the employer.

Health and Safety (Display Screen Equipment) Regulations 1992

This covers employees who operate display screen equipment (e.g. a computer screen) on a regular basis.

They apply wherever an employee uses a display screen, such as in
- offices
- computer suites
- educational environment
- hospital ward
- the home.

Under this law the employer's duty is to
- assess the risks to health from display screens
- reduce the risks identified through risk assessment
- ensure employees have regular breaks or changes in activity to reduce contact with display screens
- ensure display screen users have eye and eyesight tests on request
- provide further tests at regular intervals
- provide tests for those requesting them – for example someone who had been suffering from headaches
- provide spectacles for those whose tests show they require them for working with display screens
- give staff training for display screen users.

Key point

Employers must provide and pay for a professional eyesight test when requested by an employee.

Work Place (Health, Safety and Welfare) Regulations 1992

These regulations do not apply to transport, construction, mines and quarries. They set general requirements in

- ventilation
- lighting
- room space
- temperature
- work stations.

These factors, which can have a big influence on your workplace welfare, will be discussed in depth later.

Reporting of Injuries, Diseases and Dangerous Occurrences Regulations (RIDDOR) 1995

These require organisations to notify the HSE when accidents occur which cause serious or fatal injuries or lead to a lengthy period off work. In addition, the organisation must keep records of all notable injuries, dangerous occurrences and diseases. These records must be kept for three years and should show the following information:

- Date/time and place of the event
- Personal records of those involved – witness, first-aider etc.
- A description of the event
- Injuries occurred
- First-aid treatment
- Name of the reporting person.

Control of Substances Hazardous to Health (COSHH) 1994

There are a number of substances in the workplace which may be hazardous to your health. They include

- toxic materials
- corrosive or irritant material
- biological products – e.g. bacteria.

Employers have the duty to

- minimise any health risks to employees using appropriate equipment and procedures
- assess the risks to health from any substances used or stored in the workplace

- inform employees about any health hazards arising from any substances used or stored in the workplace
- monitor situations with regard to effectiveness of protective measures and health of employees.

Manual Handling Operations Regulations 1992

Poor handling of items such as equipment, machinery and supplies causes more than 1 in 4 accidents in the workplace. These accidents lead to injuries such as

- pulled muscles
- broken bones
- cuts and bruises
- trapped nerves.

Any of these could lead to pain and time off work. In some cases there may be permanent disablement. The employee may be at risk if they

- are physically unsuited for the task
- are wearing unsuitable clothing and footwear
- have not received adequate and suitable training.

These regulations were brought in to reduce the injuries caused by poor manual handling in the workplace.

Figure 5.6 *Carrying anything that is too heavy for you is a risk to your health*

Key point

The Manual Handling Operations Regulations 1992 do not set limits for weights that can be lifted by the employee.

Although there are no limits to the weights that employees are allowed to lift, the employer does have the duty to

- avoid hazardous manual handling where possible
- use machinery to help where possible – e.g. a fork-lift truck
- consider the load to be moved through risk assessment – by considering the shape and size of the load
- reduce the risk of injury as far as possible
- provide information on the weight of each load.

The employee must use the correct system of work provided by the employer.

Health and Safety (Safety Signs and Signals) Regulations 1996

Organisations must ensure they have standardised signs relating to health and safety. Such signs use different colours to stress the message they convey.

- A sign with a green square or rectangle with white lettering or symbols usually indicates an exit or first-aid post.
- A sign with a blue circle containing lettering or a symbol indicates something that you must do, for example wear ear protection when working in a noisy environment.
- A white circle with a red border and red lettering informs you that you should not do something; an example is a no-smoking sign.
- A yellow triangle with a black border and black lettering and symbols warns you of a hazardous situation.

Management of Health and Safety at Work Regulations 1999

Such regulations cover every work activity and explicitly state what employers are required to do about health and safety in the workplace. The main requirement of employers is that they carry out a risk assessment. This is a paper-based procedure which aims to reduce the risk of injury and illness in the workplace. It will be discussed in depth later in the unit. The regulations also set arrangements for appointing competent personnel in the workplace.

Let's do it!

There are a number of laws which apply to workplace welfare. In small groups, conduct research into the following regulations:

- Chemicals (Hazard Information and Packaging for Supply) Regulations (Chip 2) 1994
- The Health and Safety Information for Employees Regulations 1989
- Electricity at Work Regulations 1989.

After researching these regulations, prepare and present a five-minute presentation to the rest of the group on the main points of the regulations. You should also try to relate the main points to working in the public services.

Assessment activity

You should complete this assessment activity regardless of the grade you are working towards.

For a *pass* (P1) you are to prepare a 10-minute presentation which you will present to your peer group. The title of your presentation should be called 'Acts and Regulations'. Within the presentation you will need to give an overview of the various Acts which apply to workplace welfare, for example the Manual Handling Operations Regulations 1992. It is suggested that you concentrate on four for your presentation. It will be important to identify and explain any terminology used, for example duty of care. You will not need to go into too much depth regarding the regulations, just outline the main points. To make the presentation look more professional and interesting you should look to use

- handouts
- pictures
- OHPs
- PowerPoint presentations.

Health and safety

As you have seen, there are a number of regulations which the public services must follow to maintain workplace welfare. Due to the nature of the work, for example the equipment used or the tasks performed, a public service will have its own particular roles and if violated, then the individuals or public services will have to face the consequences, which might be a fine. In this section we will consider the specific responsibilities and consequences of failing to act.

Roles and responsibilities placed upon a chosen public service

So far we have looked at the following regulations to improve workplace welfare:

- Health and Safety at Work Act 1974
- The Health and Safety (First Aid) Regulations 1981
- Working Time Directive and Working Time Regulations 1998
- The Noise at Work Regulations 1989
- The Health and Safety (Display Screen Equipment) Regulations 1992
- The Work Place (Health, Safety and Welfare) Regulations 1992
- Reporting of Injuries, Diseases and Dangerous Occurrences Regulations (RIDDOR) 1995
- Control of Substances Hazardous to Health (COSHH) 1994
- The Manual Handling Operations Regulations 1992

The Health and Safety (Safety Signs and Signals Regulations) 1996

The Management of Health and Safety at Work Regulations 1999.

Each public service will have to comply with the above regulations as well as others we have not discussed. However, each public service, because of the nature of the jobs in each one, will have to comply to regulations for a variety of reasons.

Let us consider the ambulance service and which regulations it has to comply with. For example, it will have to comply with:

Reporting of Injuries, Diseases and Dangerous Occurrences Regulations (RIDDOR) 1995 (e.g. if a paramedic suffers from a slipped disk whilst carrying a casualty).

Control of Substances Hazardous to Health (COSHH) 1994 (e.g. a paramedic will be carrying and using a number of medications, therefore these must be stored in an appropriate manner).

Working Time Directive and Working Time Regulations 1998 (e.g. a paramedic cannot be forced to work over the specified work time regulations).

From these examples you can see that the ambulance service has a duty and responsibility to

record the accident in the accident book and include any changes required to reduce the risk of this happening again

provide the appropriate facilities required to store the medications, for example a lockable cupboard

produce a suitable shift timetable which does not force a paramedic to work more than what is prescribed in the regulations (although they may be asked on a occasional basis but only if the paramedic agrees).

Let's do it!

Using the above as an example and guideline, you are to investigate the public service of your choice in relation to the regulations. You should consider three sets of regulations that are linked. It is important that you discuss the implications for the public service.

Managers and the individual – current legislation, e.g. duty of care, safety of self and others

The managers of an organisation, including the public services, have a responsibility under legislation to maintain workplace welfare. They have a duty of care (level of responsibility) for all who enter their organisation, including, for example, contractors or visitors. The work carried out in an organisation should not affect the welfare of all those in the organisation. In summary, the management should have a clear health and safety policy, which should contain

- a general statement of commitment
- a summary of responsibilities for all levels of employee, particularly those with safety duties
- a collection of the organisation's own rules and regulations to ensure workplace welfare
- details of the significant findings of risk assessments
- the date the policy was last revised.

Assessment activity

You should only complete the following assessment activity if you are interested in gaining a *distinction* (D1) grade. You are to produce an investigation report into two case studies. The case studies should be based on a public service of your choice and they need to be from the last four years to make them relevant. Within the case studies there will need to be some form of negligence relating to health and safety measures. Your analysis and report should centre on the following key areas:

- Description of the case studies
- Acts of health and safety which are involved in the case studies
- Identification of the hazards responsible for the incident/accident
- Identification of responsibility with explanation
- Description of the outcomes, for example a fine of £1000
- Recommendations for the future – this may come from a case study, for example increased staff training, or based on your understanding and knowledge of control measures.

You may find it a challenge to locate specific case studies relating to the public service of your choice. Therefore you should seek advice from

- your tutor
- a health and safety advisor
- a solicitor who specialises in health and safety legislation
- a health and safety officer from your local authority.

Failure to act

To ensure health, safety and welfare of their employees at work employers must work within the legislation at all times, ensuring they follow the regulations.

In some cases the organisations do fail to abide by the regulations, which may lead to an accident, illness or death. This failure could result in a criminal prosecution. It could lead to an employee suing for personal injury or in some cases the employer being prosecuted for corporate manslaughter. This section will identify the possible consequences of failing to act.

Consequences of failing to comply with current legislation

Under the Health and Safety at Work Act 1974 failure to comply with regulations by employees, employers, manufacturers etc. can lead to prosecution. The magistrates court will initially deal with the offences. However, more serious offences, such as a fatal accident, will be prosecuted in the crown court, where the defendants will be tried by a jury. The two types of courts can impose the following punishments:

- Lower court maximum – £20,000 fine and/or six months imprisonment
- Higher court maximum – unlimited fine and/or two years imprisonment.

Some of the reasons for prosecuting someone are

- breaking of health and safety regulations
- obstructing an inspector
- making a false statement on a report
- changing safety equipment.

However the HSE may not prosecute an offence straight away as they may want to

- give the organisation improvement notices with a specified time limit
- temporarily or permanently close the building (or part of building).

The outcome of negligence

Negligence can lead to certain outcomes, for example a broken leg or loss of sight. However, negligence doesn't always lead to an injury or illness, perhaps only to a near miss. No matter what the outcome, the organisation should review its workplace welfare after such an incident. The outcomes of negligence can range from no injury or illness to that of death.

Tribunals

Tribunals are judicial bodies established to resolve disputes over employment issues. Examples of the issues they cover are

- failure to allow time off for trade union duties
- failure to allow time off for ante-natal care
- unfair dismissal because of disability
- failure to allow time off to seek work during a redundancy situation.

They also deal with workplace welfare issues, for example failure to allow a safety representative time off to carry out duties or undertake training. A tribunal is similar to a court but is less formal, for example nobody wears a wig. The hearings are open to the public and they work independently with the aim of being fair and just. Therefore, it is possible for an employee or group of employees to take an employer to a tribunal over certain workplace welfare issues, for example a breach of the Working Time Directive and Working Time Regulations 1998.

Compensation and civil claims

When an employee suffers an injury or illness because of malpractice in the workplace, they can make a civil claim in the courts. Such a claim can be made because there has been a breach of duty or breach of contract.

CHECK WHAT YOU KNOW

1 What does HSC stand for?
2 Name two main points of the Health and Safety (First Aid) Regulations 1981.
3 What does the term 'duty of care' mean?
4 What does RIDDOR stand for?
5 Which Act covers the usage of computer screens?

In summary

- The Health and Safety at Work Act 1974 is the major piece of legislation responsible for health and safety in the UK.
- The Health and Safety Executive is the main agency responsible for enforcing health and safety in the UK.
- The responsibility for health and safety in the workplace falls on everyone, for example the employer, employee and any visitor.
- Failure to comply with health and safety legislation can lead to criminal convictions.

Assessment activity

You should only complete the following assessment activity if you are aiming to gain a *merit* (M1) or *distinction* (D1) grade.

You are to produce a 10-minute presentation which will be presented to your peers with the title 'Health and Safety Issues Within the Public Services'. The presentation will be based on the public service of your choice. Within the presentation you will need to concentrate on the following areas:

- Health and safety issues – for example in the fire and rescue service it is important that the firefighters wear the correct protective equipment, e.g. heat-resistant gloves.
- Consequences of failing to act – e.g. fines, civil claims etc.

Assessment activity

You are to complete this assessment activity for a *pass* (P2) and regardless of the grade you are aiming for. Through your research for the assessment activity on page 191, you are to produce research notes which are clear and concise. The following is an example of how you can set out your notes. You should concentrate on three key pieces of legislation.

Roles and responsibilities set out in the legislation

Control of Substances Hazardous to Health (COSHH) 1994

Employers have the duty to minimise any health risks to employees using appropriate equipment and procedures.

Practical applications

Therefore, if you have to work with hazardous substances your employer should provide you with protective equipment, for example rubber gloves.

Outcomes of failing to comply

Employee – they will receive burning to the hands
Employer – they will receive a fine of £20,000 and/or six months imprisonment

---

Emergency procedures

You may face many different emergencies while working in the public services. So it is important for you and your colleagues to behave in a professional manner to maintain health and safety and reduce the risk of injury, or even death.

Emergency procedures

You need to know the correct emergency and evacuation procedures in your workplace for emergencies such as fire and bomb threats. This will save time and more importantly save lives. We will now discuss the correct emergency and evacuation procedures for dealing with a fire and a bomb threat in a public service building.

Action to be taken when discovering an emergency situation

Fire

In the UK every year over 700 people are killed by fires and 14,000 are injured. Preventing fires happening is obviously the best policy, however if a fire does break out you need to know what to do.

If you discover a fire in its early stages, for example a fire in a waste paper bin, it's possible for you to deal with it yourself by using fire extinguishers – this will be discussed later. However, remember that fires can spread very quickly and produce smoke and fumes which can kill in seconds. If you have any doubt about what you should do about putting out a fire, you should not tackle it yourself.

 Key point

If a fire breaks out, get out of the building and call 999. Do not go back into the building. Always put your own and other people's safety first.

When you discover a fire you should

- ensure everyone knows – sound the alarm
- not delay – do not waste time
- not investigate the fire or search for valuables or pets
- shut doors
- get everyone out, using escape routes, and stay together
- after you are out, call 999 using a mobile, a neighbour's phone or a phone box.
- not assume someone else has called – take control and phone the emergency services yourself.

When you call the emergency service you should give the following information:

- Address
- Name
- Phone number
- Location of fire – room number and floor
- How the fire started
- Any trapped person, including location
- Basic description of building – e.g. multi-storey prison.

If you have phoned the emergency services do not hang up until the operator has finished talking to you as they need to get all the important information they need from you.

 Key point

Do not re-enter a building on fire for any reason. When the fire brigade arrives you will need to be there to tell them about anyone who is trapped.

You should also wait in a safe area, which will probably already be designated – an example may be the car park or sports field.

Bomb threats

There is very little chance of you finding a suspect package that contains an explosive device, however it is vital that you always remain vigilant, especially in these times when we are being warned of possible terrorist attacks.

If you discover a suspect package you should

- call the police using the 999 system
- do not move or handle the package
- clearly mark the location of the device (use a bright coloured object or coloured paper)
- Report the *exact* location of the package to the police.

The police will have direct contact with a bomb disposal team and will make all the necessary arrangements for the safe disposal of the device.

The types and packages you may suspect as being dangerous are

- any envelope or package with suspicious or threatening messages written on it
- letters with oily stains
- no postage stamp, no franking or no cancelling of the stamp
- envelopes which have a strange odour or feel like they contain powder.

Evacuation procedures

A safe and efficient evacuation procedure is needed to deal with any emergency situation. However, because of the differences in public service buildings each organisation will have a site-specific evacuation procedure. This is because each building will have different

- number of floors
- exits points
- exit routes
- assembly points.

Evacuation of employees and visitors from public services buildings

The following general evacuation procedure has been designed to cover all the things you need to do in an evacuation procedure.

> If you discover a fire you should sound the alarm by breaking the glass

↓

> Do not stop to collect valuables or personal possessions

↓

> You must leave the building via the correct exit routes

↓

> Do not use the lifts, as they may be a fire hazard

↓

> Leave the building in an orderly fashion without putting others at risk

↓

> You must assemble at the designated assembly points

Within the building there should be designated areas, for example at the end of a corridor, where a responsible person must take disabled employees and visitors. Once outside remain at the assembly points until you are given permission to re-enter the building. This will either come from the fire brigade or a designated fire marshal.

The same evacuation procedure will be followed for a bomb threat.

Let's do it!

In your college or school you will have a specific evacuation procedure for either a fire or bomb. This evacuation procedure should be stored centrally, possibly at the reception area. You are to locate the fire evacuation procedure. Once you have done this you should read it and make sure you know the main points. In pairs you should have a question and answer session where you test each other's knowledge and understanding.

Exits

In the event of danger, it must be possible for employees to evacuate the workplace as quickly and safely as possible. In the case of exits it is important that

- they lead as directly as possible to a place of safety, for example the car park
- emergency doors should normally open in the direction of escape
- emergency routes and exits must be indicated by signs
- sliding or revolving doors must not be used for exits specially intended as emergency exits
- emergency doors must not be locked or fastened so that they cannot be easily and immediately opened
- emergency doors must be wide enough to allow the safe passage of wheelchair users
- emergency routes and exits requiring illumination must be provided with emergency lighting of adequate intensity in the case of failure of the normal lighting.

Access

Exits should have clear access so that they can be used effectively in case of emergency.

Figure 5.7 *Fire exit sign*

Let's do it!

In your workplace (if you have a part-time job) or college/school there will be a number of exits which must remain free from obstruction. Within your group, draw up list of the possible objects, for example chairs, which may reduce the access. Walk around your workplace or college/school and note down any issues of safety which you feel need addressing.

Ensuring signs are illuminated or clearly visible

Any workplace in which fire safety legislation applies must be provided with fire safety signs which comply with the Health and Safety (Safety Signs and Signals) Regulations 1996. All safety signs should be of sufficient size and positioned so that they are legible and easy to see. It is also important that specific safety signs are adequately illuminated, as they will need to be read in certain situations, for example through smoke if there is a fire. Table 5.1 provides a guideline as to the distance at which signs can be viewed:

Symbol height (mm)	Viewing distance (metres)
100	17
110	19
120	20
130	22

Table 5.1

From any point within a building a person should have sight of the nearest exit. If this is not the case, then a sign or series of directional signs should guide people to the exit.

Figure 5.8 *Fire exit signs will direct you to the assembly point*

Marton LRC
Middlesbrough College
Marton Road
Middlesbrough
TS4 3RZ

Signs and general maintenance

The purpose of safety signs used for evacuation are to
- warn people of hazards
- identify safe routes for escape
- provide instructions
- indicate the location of fire equipment.

There are six categories of sign. These are
- safe condition
- mandatory
- fire equipment
- warning
- prohibition
- supplementary.

Let's do it!

Conduct research into the various signs and complete the following table.

Category	Shape	Colours	Examples
	Square or rectangular	White symbol or text on a green background	Fire exit sign
Mandatory			Keep shut sign on fire door
Fire equipment	Square or rectangular		Fire extinguisher sign
Prohibition	Circular with cross band		No smoking sign
	Triangular	Black symbol or text on a yellow background surrounded by a black triangle	Caution – risk of danger
Supplementary			Directional arrow used with fire exit signs

Table 5.2

Emergency and exit lighting is an essential feature of building safety, allowing staff and members of the public to be effectively and safely evacuated from the building by the fastest and safest route in case of an emergency.

Special lighting can be used to illuminate certain areas so that people evacuating the building in the case of an emergency can find their way more easily to safety. This kind of lighting works independently of the building's power supply and will normally last up to three hours.

Equipment

A fire may break out no matter what safety precautions are in place. For such an emergency the building should be equipped with certain pieces of equipment, such as a fire hose, which can be used to fight the fire or reduce the damage by stopping the fire spreading. You also need to use the correct piece of equipment at the right time and in the right way; for example a powder-based fire extinguisher should only be used in certain situations.

 Key point

Using the fire equipment in the incorrect way can cause the fire to become worse and can endanger lives.

The following discusses the different types of equipment and highlights the methods for use.

Types of equipment available

The equipment used to prevent or treat a fire includes

- extinguishers
- blankets
- hoses
- sprinklers
- lighting
- ladders.

Fire extinguishers

A fire extinguisher is the main piece of equipment used for fighting fire in the workplace. They are cylinders which contain a pressurised substance, usually powder, water, foam or carbon dioxide.

The procedure for using a fire extinguisher is to point the nozzle hose at the fire and shoot a jet of the substance at it. Usually, fire extinguishers are highly effective in fighting small fires and can be used from some distance from the fire. However if

Figure 5.9 *The right fire extinguisher needs to be used to fight the appropriate fire*

the fire extinguisher is having no effect and the fire is now out of control, then you should leave it for the fire brigade to deal with. The disadvantages of fire extinguishers are they

- require servicing and checking (normally once a year)
- are relatively expensive (upwards of £20)
- can make the fire worse and could endanger lives if you use the wrong ones.

Key point

If your extinguisher has been used, even if for a couple of seconds, it must be refilled according to the manufacturer's instructions.

Fire extinguishers should be fixed where you can reach them quickly. They should be positioned on an escape route, near an outside door or on route from the living areas. They should be properly fixed to the wall at an appropriate height but out of the reach of children. They should not be positioned above cookers or heaters or in other places of high temperatures.

Let's do it!

You probably don't know where all the fire extinguishers are in your school/college, however it is important to know for safety reasons. In pairs within your group, walk around and locate the fire extinguishers, making a note of the colour of each.

You will probably have noted that the fire extinguishers have different colours. These colours indicate the type of fires the extinguishers are used for fighting. They are listed below with warnings about how you must *not* use them.

- White markings (water filled) – used for wood, paper and plastic fires. DO NOT use these on electrical fires.
- Blue markings (powder filled) – used for fires fuelled by flammable liquids and can be used on electrical equipment. DO NOT inhale the powder.
- Black markings (carbon dioxide filled) – used for electrical fires. DO NOT use in an unventilated area because you will not be able to breathe.
- Cream markings (foam filled) – used for burning liquids, e.g. oil. DO NOT use on electrical fires.

Fire blankets

Fire blankets, which are made of fire-resistant materials, are effective for fat pan fires, which are a major cause of fires in kitchens. For this reason the best place to store them is in the kitchen. However the blankets are not so effective for general use. Some fire blankets can be used again, however some need to be thrown away after use because of the damage caused when putting a fire out.

Case study

The danger of a chip pan fire

In October 2000 Sharon Evans heated her chip pan and put in the chips as she'd done on many occasions. However this time the pan caught fire. She said that 'I turned off the gas but the flames did not stop' and 'I nearly turned and ran but I caught sight of the fire blanket on the wall. I'd never used it before but I put it right on top of the pan and the flames disappeared, I can't describe my relief!'

1 What was the hazard in this case study?
2 Why should Sharon not have thrown water over the flames?
3 If the fire blanket had not worked what action should she have taken?
4 Are there any control measures she could put in place the next time she uses the pan?

Source: www.firekills.gov.uk

Fire hose

Fire hoses are normally located in large buildings, storage warehouses or large garages. They should be located where they are prominent and always accessible, such as in corridors.

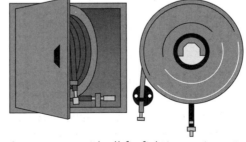

The hoses are attached to the mains water supply and can unroll to a length of up to 50 metres. As with fire extinguishers, it is important that you only use them on certain fires and they should not be used for electrical fires.

Figure 5.10 *As with all firefighting equipment fire hoses should be free from obstruction*

Sprinklers

Most public service buildings are fitted with sprinklers to reduce the risk of fire damage and loss of life.

As many rooms as possible in a building should be fitted with sprinklers, which are directly linked to the water mains. They are activated by heat at high temperatures, so they don't go off accidentally.

A sprinkler system should be installed along with smoke alarms.

The smoke alarm alerts you to slow-burning, smoke-generating fires, which may not generate enough heat to activate the sprinklers.

Key point

A quarter of all people killed in home fires are asleep at the time. A smoke alarm would save most of them.

Activated sprinklers also set off the fire alarm in a building so that people throughout the building are alerted that a fire has broken out and that they should immediately follow the emergency and evacuation procedures.

Ladders

When the normal evacuation routes in a building are blocked by fire or smoke, an emergency fire ladder can be used to evacuate people.

When not in use the fire escape ladder is usually stored in a small, neat white box, permanently secured to the wall underneath a windowsill. In a building which has more than one level it should be stored upstairs. In an emergency, simply remove the cover, attach one end of the ladder to the windowsill, throw the rest of it out of the window from where it will hang, and then descend to the ground and safety. The ladder rope is fire retardant and has a fluorescent colour, ensuring good visibility in low light situations. The plastic rungs are also flame retardant and have anti-slip features so that you can easily grab hold of the ladder on the way down.

Figure 5.11 *You can save yourself in a fire emergency if you have an emergency ladder*

Provision of emergency equipment in public service buildings

Public service buildings should have the following equipment in place to maintain workplace welfare:

- extinguishers
- blankets
- hoses
- sprinklers
- alarms
- lighting
- ladders.

Key point

Due to the design and layout of public service buildings, each one will be different in terms of the provision and location of its safety equipment.

Let's do it!

Visit a local public service building, which will be arranged by your tutor. Observe and note down the provision and location of the building's safety equipment. You should also consider

- the signs used for workplace welfare, for example fire exit signs
- other equipment which may cause harm, for example speaker systems.

CHECK WHAT YOU KNOW

1 What is the correct procedure for dealing with a bomb threat?
2 Why will every public building have a slightly different evacuation procedure?
3 Why is it important to have evacuation drills?
4 What is the colour and the main function of exit signs?
5 What are the different types of fire extinguishers and what fires they are used for?

In summary

- There are specific procedures to follow when dealing with a specific situation, for example a bomb threat.
- It is vital that you follow the correct procedure to reduce the risk of injury to yourself and others.
- Exit routes from buildings should remain clear with signs clearly visible to allow for a quick and safe evacuation.
- There are numerous pieces of equipment available for fighting fire, ranging from fire hoses to fire blankets.

Assessment activity

You should complete this assessment activity (P3) regardless of the grade you are working towards. On the visit of your local fire prevention officer to speak to you at your college/school you should aim to discover information from them which will enable you to complete the following worksheet, which is based on the response to an incident and the evacuation procedure. Stage 1 is given as an example of what you need to do in the case of a fire.

BTEC First Diploma in Public Services (Level 2)

Student's name _____   Date _____

Fire officer's name _____

Type of incident: <u>fire</u>_____

_____

Action on discovering an incident:

Stage 1: Sound the alarm – to make sure everybody in the building is alerted to the situation

Stage 2:

Stage 3:

Stage 4:

Stage 5:

Stage 6:

Stage 7:

Stage 8:

Stage 9:

Stage 10:

Evacuation procedure:
Write a 200-word description of an evacuation procedure:

Assessment activity

You should complete this assessment activity if you are working towards a *merit* (M2).

You are to produce a research project titled 'Emergency Equipment'. You are to investigate the different types of emergency equipment and their usage. The project should have the following sections:

- Front cover, including your name etc.
- Contents
- Introduction
- Regulations of emergency equipment, for example fire exits and that they should not be locked
- Emergency equipment (this could be in the form of a list showing when they should be used)
- Sources – state where you got your information from, for example an Internet website address.

The use of pictures would be beneficial, for example a picture of a fire blanket.

Risk assessments

Under the Management of Health and Safety at Work Regulations 1999 employers have to carry out a risk assessment of health and safety in the workplace. Generally, a risk assessment is the main tool a public service uses to improve its workplace welfare. The risk assessment is:

'Nothing more than a careful examination of what, in your work, could cause harm to people, so that you can weigh up whether you have taken enough precautions or should do more to prevent harm.' [HSE (2001)]

This section will concentrate on the process of risk assessments, which will form an important aspect of your assessment.

Risk assessment

It is important to understand that each public service will have a different style of risk assessment. However all risks assessments are designed to improve the health and safety of all those in the workplace. It is your role to understand the basic concepts of risk assessments so that you can apply your knowledge and understanding in any public service.

Definition

A risk assessment is defined as a systematic general examination of a work activity to identify any hazards involved and the likelihood of these hazards causing harm.

Let's do it!

In small groups within in your group, complete the following table, which highlights work activities which require a risk assessment. An example has been done for the fire service.

Name of service	Work activity requiring a risk assessment
RAF	
Royal Navy	
Army	
Police	
Fire	Being lowered into an old well to save a child
Ambulance	
Customs and excise	
Coastguard	
Prison service	

Table 5.3

As you can see, it is important to identify any hazards which are present in a public service. Most risk assessments will contain a number of hazards.

Purpose

The purpose of a risk assessment is to prevent accidents by identifying hazards and reducing the risk of injury from those hazards to as low is reasonably practical. They are also used to ensure that an organisation complies with any legal requirements relating to workplace welfare.

It also important that employers

- provide clear information and training for employers – so they know how to perform a risk assessment
- set up emergency procedures – required in case of an accident or emergency
- appoint competent personnel to help them make arrangements identified in the risk assessment – to put in place the control measures.

Use

A risk assessment should be carried out if

- a new piece of equipment is to be used
- an existing piece of equipment is to be used for a new task
- a member of staff is training on the equipment
- the environmental conditions change – e.g. weather, floor surface, etc.
- an accident has taken place
- legislation changes
- it is within an annual review.

Format

There are usually five stages in a risk assessment. They are

- Stage 1 – Identification of hazards
- Stage 2 – Identification of who will be harmed
- Stage 3 – Evaluation of the risks and whether the precautions already in place are sufficient or more are required
- Stage 4 – Record your findings
- Stage 5 – Review the assessment and make changes if required.

Stage 1 Identification of hazards You can only do this if you are in the place you are assessing so that you can see the possible hazards. You must identify the significant hazards, such as a naked flame, and ignore trivial ones, such as the temporary lack of toilet rolls.

 Key point

Ask your work colleagues if they know of any hazards within the workplace as they may have more knowledge about this than you do.

Stage 2 Identification of who will be harmed Here you need to identify who may be harmed by hazards. The spider diagram may help you:

Figure 5.12 *The sort of people who can be harmed by hazards in the workplace*

As you can see there are quite a lot of potential victims of hazards in the workplace.

Stage 3 Evaluation of the risks and whether the precautions already in place are sufficient or more are required You will need to consider the level of probability (likelihood) of the hazard occurring and therefore causing harm to someone. The probability can be expressed through the following scale:

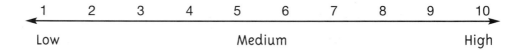

You also need to consider the severity (seriousness) of the injuries that might be incurred because of the hazard, for example 2 = bruise and hand, 10 = death.

You will also need to list the existing measures which are already in place and evaluate whether they are adequate. If they not adequate then you will need to add more control measures.

Stage 4 Record your findings If your organisation has more than five employees, which will be the case in the public services, you will need to record your findings of the risk assessment. So you will need to write down the significant hazards, for example faulty wiring. Your employer should tell you what the findings of the risk assessment are.

A risk assessment doesn't have to be perfect, it just needs to be suitable and sufficient for the particular workplace environment. The HSE recommends that

- a proper check is made
- you have asked everyone who may be affected
- you have dealt with the significant hazards
- the control measures are reasonable and the risk should be low.

Stage 5 Review the assessment and make changes if required When a hazard analysis and risk assessment is complete and all the control measures are in place, the assessment will need to be reviewed periodically to ensure it is still valid. This could be because

- work methods have changed
- an accident has occurred
- additional control measures have been introduced
- the technology has changed
- regulations have changed.

Documentation

The format of a risk assessment form is likely to vary according to the organisation. However they will do the job they are designed for if they are done correctly. Here is an example of a risk assessment form:

Management of Health and Safety at Work Regulations Risk Assessment Record					
Directorate:	Work activity to be assessed:		Name of assessor:		
Section:	Date of assessment:		Position:		
Activity/Process occupation	What hazards to health and/or safety exist?	What risks do they pose to employees and other persons?	Precautions already taken?	Risk level achieved? (H/M/L)	Are additional measures necessary? (Note: This section must be completed if risk level is HIGH)

Are any special groups at risk?   YES/NO

If YES, who are these, and how many? _____

_____

Figure 5.13 *The risk assessment form suggested by the HSE*

Let's do it!

In small groups, discuss the similarities and differences between the two forms.

Contributory factors

There are many factors which may have or could contribute to an incident or accident within the workplace. A contributory factor is something which has the potential to cause an accident, for example poor lighting would be classed as a contributory factor. Other contributory factors may include

- space constraints
- uneven or slippery floors
- extremes in temperature
- stairs/steps/ramps to negotiate
- ventilation problems.

There are also many more.

The HSE estimates that human error is involved in approximately 80% of all accidents in the workplace. It also suggests that 'organisations must recognise that they need to consider human factors as a distinct element, which must be recognised, assessed and managed effectively to control risks'.

Key point

When performing a risk assessment you need to consider the contributory factors. If you can reduce the number of contributory factors you will reduce the risk of an accident taking place.

Identification and evaluation of hazards (high, medium or low risk)

When you perform a risk assessment you are looking for hazards. Remember, a hazard is something with the potential to cause harm, for example an overloaded socket. When you identify a hazard it may be classed as either being physical, chemical, biological or a natural phenomena.

- Physical hazards – manual handling, noise vehicles, computers, etc.
- Chemical hazards – toxic substances, acids, cleaning products, etc.
- Biological hazards – animals, plants, vegetation, etc.
- Natural phenomena – heat, cold, water, snow, etc.

Key point

It is important you identify hazards which are realistic. A vehicle with a faulty break is a hazard, whereas a meteorite is not, as this is not a realistic hazard.

You should remember also to evaluate the risk of the hazard using the traffic light system:

- Red (High)
- Amber (Medium)
- Green (Low).

Precautionary measures

A precautionary measure is one which is already in place to prevent an accident occurring, for example a paramedic who wears rubber gloves when dealing with a casualty to avoid cross-infection. Within the workplace there will be a number of precautionary measures which will reduce the risk of a hazard causing harm.

Let's do it!

On your own, list the precautionary measures already in place either in your workplace (if you have a part-time job) or in your college/school, for example having a crash mat in place when performing sit-ups is a precautionary measure.

Control measures

Control measures are also used to reduce risk. These are often based on not doing certain things. For example, deciding not go for a run in the local park after it has rained eliminates the risk of slipping on excess water along the route you usually take. However, in the workplace you cannot avoid working in order to reduce risk, an example being fuelling a fighter plane in mid-air. Therefore, the control measures that are put in place must be reasonable in relation to the situation.

Case study

Introducing control measures

The local college has sent 14 students for a four-day look at life with the army at the local barracks. On the second day the students are to do the assault course.

An army captain, who is responsible for health and safety at the barracks, has put in place a number of precautionary measures in relation to the assault course, for example training for all army personnel who are in charge of the assault course.

However on the morning of the second day it is raining. The captain has assessed that it is still viable to do the assault course, however she is going to introduce a number of control measures.

1 What extra hazards can you identify due to the change in weather?
2 What other precautionary measures do think will be in place?
3 Can you suggest any control measures which could be included?

Let's do it!

In small groups, use a risk assessment form (use an example from this unit) to complete a risk assessment for an activity in your college or school, for example a football match or a training session in the fitness suite. Remember, you will become competent and efficient in performing risk assessments through practice, as it will help you identify the key hazards.

CHECK WHAT YOU KNOW

1 What is the purpose of a risk assessment?
2 Briefly sketch out a blank risk assessment form?
3 What is the role of a control measure?
4 Why is it important to categorise a hazard as being low, medium and high risk?
5 When planning an activity, for example a riot training day in the police force, at what point should the risk assessment be done and why?

In summary

- A risk assessment is used to reduce the risks in the workplace with the aim of maintaining health and safety.
- A risk assessment may come in a variety of forms, depending on the organisation.
- The main components of a risk assessment are hazard, risk and control measures.
- It is paramount that a risk assessment is updated on a regular basis to maintain health and safety.

Assessment activity

You are to complete this assessment activity regardless of the grade you are working towards. Using a risk assessment of your choice (you may use one from this student handbook) you are to perform a risk assessment on an activity or facility of your choice. Within your college or school, you may want to use the following facilities:

- Fitness suite
- Gym
- Swimming pool.

Furthermore, within your course you may select an activity, for example a training session within the public service fitness unit.

Once you have performed the risk assessment, you are to produce a 500-word report on the requirements of the production of a risk assessment, for example it is important for the risk assessment to identify all the significant hazards. Hopefully, you will find that performing the risk assessment will help you in understanding the requirements for the production of a risk assessment.

Assessment activity

You should only complete this assessment if you are working towards a *distinction* (D2). Through the contacts you have made in your course, you are to make contact with the public service of your choice. Through discussion, you are to locate a current risk assessment used by the public service which relates to safe working practices. Based on the risk assessment you are to produce a 500-word report centred on the link between the risk assessment and safe working practices in the emergency procedures of the public service. For example, the fire and rescue service will have a risk assessment for travelling at high speeds when attending a fire. Therefore, part of the risk assessment may centre on the need to have a trained driver to reduce the risk of injury to others on the road.

Safe working practices

Any organisation must have safe working practices which are used daily to maintain workplace welfare. For example, a safe working practice for the ambulance service would be to check regularly that the ambulances have a full complement of rubber gloves to reduce the risk of cross-infection. This section will highlight specific areas which should be included in safe working practices, for example the need for good ventilation and light within the workplace.

Codes of practice

Under the Workplace (Health, Safety and Welfare) Regulations 1992 employers have to consider the following aspects of health and safety in the workplace:

- Ventilation
- Temperature
- Lighting
- Workspace
- Workstations
- Washing and sanitary conveniences
- Accommodation for eating and changing facilities.

The above aspects are also part of a number of ACOPs which are approved by the HSE as previously discussed. Furthermore, it is important they are included within an organisation's internal code of practice. A code of practice is devised by an organisation to maintain health and safety. Although this isn't compulsory, it should be used as an example of good practice.

Health

Ventilation

All work areas should be well-ventilated with fresh air. In some workplaces this isn't possible, so the regulation provides that employees should have an adequate break in a well-ventilated area. To ensure this all air-conditioning systems must be kept in good working order through regular maintenance checks. Some systems will purify the air to eliminate dust or fumes, however they must have an effective device to give visible or audible warning of failure. The level of dust and fumes in the workplace must be controlled under the COSHH regulations.

Temperature

During working hours, the temperature in workplaces inside buildings should be reasonable. A reasonable temperature is suggested as one that provides reasonable comfort without special clothing: a temperature of 16° C for normal workrooms and at least 13° C if the work involves severe physical effort. A thermometer must be provided to enable employees to determine the temperature of the workplace.

Excessive heat in the workplace can

- lead to accidents because it lowers concentration levels
- cause dehydration through loss of fluids due to sweating and this can leads to cramps, headaches and tiredness
- lead to heat stroke if the temperature of the blood rises above 39° C, and can cause confusion, incoherent speech and even death.

Figure 5.14 *The temperature in a workplace must be reasonable to work in*

The sort of control measures that could be put in place in the working environment to avoid hazards are:

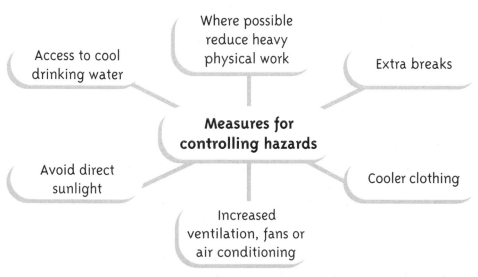

Access to cool drinking water

Where possible reduce heavy physical work

Extra breaks

Measures for controlling hazards

Avoid direct sunlight

Increased ventilation, fans or air conditioning

Cooler clothing

Figure 5.15 *The sort of control measures that need to be in place to avoid heat hazards in the workplace*

The effects of excessive cold in the workplace can cause

- frostbite
- tiredness and fatigue due to the body over-working to keep warm
- broken bones due to slipping hazards.

Let's do it!

Within your group, draw up a list of 10 control measures which you could put in place for working in a cold environment (inside and outside).

Lighting

Every workplace should have suitable and sufficient lighting and this should come from natural light as far is practical. Different work may require different light levels. You should be able to work safely and without straining your eyes. For office work better lighting is required. Light should be provided on stairs to avoid the risk of injuries. Windows and skylights that allow in natural light must be kept clean so that employees get as much light as possible. Emergency lighting must be available where failure of artificial lighting would create a hazard.

Room space

Every room in which people work should have sufficient floor area, height and unoccupied space for the sake of health, safety and welfare. In an office the requirement is a minimum of 11 m^3 per person. However many offices have a lot of large pieces of equipment, such as a photocopiers. So, the room should have extra space to accommodate the extra equipment. When assessing a room's height any distance over 3 m should be classed as 3 m.

Workstations

As most workplaces now use computers and need space for computer workstations it is important they follow these principles:

- Employees should be able to move freely and move quickly in an emergency.
- Footrests must be provided for work that is carried out in a seated position.
- The workstation must be arranged in a way that is suitable for the employee and for doing the task, such as typing a letter.
- A suitable seat must be provided for work that can or must be done seated.

Figure 5.16 *The organisation of workspace needs to take into account a range of factors to ensure health and safety*

Safety – maintenance of the working environment

The regular use of safety checks will ensure that all equipment within the workplace is suitable to use. The health and safety officer can perform some safety checks, for example checking the computer chairs. However, some pieces of equipment need to be checked by a professional who has technical expertise.

Welfare

Washing and sanitary conveniences

It is important that the workplace has suitable and sufficient washing facilities in the toilets, as you can pass on infections through poor washing of your hands after you have been to the toilet. The washing facilities must be readily accessible and in the immediate area of sanitary conveniences. The facilities provided must include

- a supply of clean hot and cold (or warm) water
- soap or other means of cleaning
- towels or other means of drying.

The rooms used must be adequately ventilated, adequately lit and kept clean. An ACOP states that 1 wash station should be provided for the first 5 employees and an additional 1 for every 25.

As well as washing facilities, suitable sanitary conveniences must be provided. They must also be accessible, ventilated, well lit and clean. Separate rooms are needed for both sexes, except where each convenience is in a separate room capable of being secured from the inside. The ACOP also states that 1 toilet should be provided for the first 5 employees and an additional 1 for every 25.

In work areas where there is no running water or sewer, chemical toilets should be provided.

Accommodation for eating and changing facilities

Where facilities for changing clothing are required, as in the police force, there needs to be separate facilities for men and women.

Under Regulation 23, suitable storage must be provided for employees' clothing that is not worn at work and for special clothing which cannot be taken home, such as a uniform.

As most people need to eat and rest in the workplace employers need to provide suitable and sufficient facilities for doing this. Rest rooms and rest areas must include suitable arrangements to protect non-smokers from discomfort caused by smokers and the possible effects of passive smoking.

Drinking water

An adequate supply of drinking water needs to be provided for people in the workplace and needs to be readily accessible. Disposable drinking cups should also be provided unless there is a water jet.

First aid

No matter how effective risk assessments are there is always the risk that someone in the workplace will be injured or become ill. Under the Health and Safety (First Aid) Regulations 1981 it is the responsibility of the organisation to provide adequate and appropriate personnel (a first-aider) who can provide first-aid treatment. A first-aider must be trained in first aid and hold a current first-aid certificate – which will be discussed later. Employers should also provide the personnel with the appropriate first-aid facilities and equipment. Under the regulations the minimum required at work is

- a suitably stocked first-aid box
- an appointed person (this will be discussed later) to take charge of first-aid arrangements.

The following highlights the main duties of the employers.

Duties imposed on employers

Facilities

One of the main duties of employers is to provide a first-aid room, where first-aid needs justify it, as in a large building. The first-aid room must be clearly signposted and identified by white lettering or symbols on a green background.

The first-aid room should have
- soap and paper towels
- sink with hot water and cold running water
- drinking water and disposable cups
- first-aid box
- container suitable for the safe disposal of clinical waste
- a couch (or folding bed) with waterproof protection and clean pillows and blankets
- a chair
- a telephone
- an accident book.

Trained staff

Not all the employees will be fully trained first-aiders, however for health and safety reasons it is advisable that as many as possible should be qualified. The more employees that are qualified in first aid the better equipped the public service will be to deal with an incident/accident. First-aiders must be trained and have a qualification by the HSE. Currently, first-aid certificates are valid for three years and refresher courses must be started before the certificate expires, otherwise a full course will need to be taken again. In your study programme it is probable that you will take a first-aid qualification, which will be invaluable when you are applying to join the public service of your choice.

Appointed person

An appointed person is someone authorised to take charge of a situation, for example someone who can call an ambulance in a case of injury or illness. They act in the absence of the trained first-aider or when a first-aider is not required. Appointed persons are recommended to undergo emergency first-aid training in order to comply with the training of employees' duties in legislation.

If you have to give first aid you will need to log the following information in the accident book, which is usually located in the reception area of a building:

- Name of the casualty
- Date
- Time
- Location
- Injuries
- Treatment
- Circumstances of the accident
- Witness personal details – in case of a follow up investigation.

Let's do it!

On your own, devise a report form which deals with an accident which has just taken place. You should fill in the report form as the first-aider, making sure you fill in all the information required, such as the time and the location.

Key point

Whenever you deal with an accident and use first-aid material, such as a triangular bandage from the first-aid box, you must replenish the material immediately.

Information regarding first-aider and location of equipment

Notices giving information about first-aiders or appointed persons and the location of the first-aid box must be placed in every main room of a building, for example the fitness suite in a police station. These should inform employees who the first-aiders or appointed persons are, where they are and where the first-aid box is located. First-aiders are responsible for ensuring the notices are kept up to date and that they are readily visible at all times. The first-aider must make sure to make the information available for people with reading or language difficulties. Also, any visitors will need to be informed of basic information, such as the extension number of a first-aider.

A first-aider must always be available when people are working. However, there are no clear rules on how many are required. This depends on the circumstances of the organisation, such as the size or location.

Assessment activity

You should complete this assessment activity regardless of the grade you are working towards. You are to take part in a 10-minute mini-group (4–5 members) discussion on the topic of first aid (P5). Before the discussion you should research the topic and make rough notes, which you can use in your discussion to prompt you. You need to contribute to the discussion to show that you have met the criteria, which will be assessed by your tutor who should produce a witness statement. You can fill in the following sheet with your research. An example has been done for the implications for the public services.

BTEC First Diploma in Public Services (Level 2)

Student name _____ Date _____

The Health and Safety (First Aid) Regulations 1981 – Key points:

Implications for the public services:
In a public service building they should have a number of first-aid boxes, which are maintained after use.

Equipment and electrical safety

The types of equipment needed for workplace welfare in the public services includes

- furniture
- computers
- vehicles
- radio
- telephone
- cell phones
- protective clothing.

Some of this equipment is electrical and needs to be handled carefully.

All electrical portable appliances powered between 40 and 240 volts and connected to the mains by a cable and plug, for example a kettle, must be tested. This testing is done yearly and is called PAT testing (Portable Appliance Testing). PAT testing is performed under the Electricity at Work Regulations (1989).

When dealing with electrical equipment it is important that you

- do not attempt to repair equipment unless you are authorised to do so
- report faulty equipment and prevent others using it until it is repaired
- do not place drinks where they may spill onto electrical equipment
- do provide sufficient socket outlets and avoid the use of adapters. Overloaded sockets can become a fire hazard.

Furniture

Most people tend to see offices as low risk environments. This is true compared to a firing range or an aircraft carrier. However, remember that accidents do occur in offices. It is important that everyone is aware of the potential hazards and that they cooperate as required, to ensure hazards are minimised and the risks of accidents reduced. You need to consider the furniture and workspace when trying to maintain workplace welfare. You need to think about office furniture such as

- computer desks
- filing cabinets
- chairs
- bookcases
- shelving systems.

It is important you

- do not lean back on your chair/make sure it has a back rest
- do not have a workstation or chair behind a door
- do not leave drawers open whilst unattended
- do not stand on a chair with wheels to reach a box
- do not position a shelving system directly above a workstation
- place heavy goods on low shelving
- do not leave paper, files etc. on the floor
- use, if possible, cupboard doors that are sliding (open doors can become a trip hazard)
- empty the bins on a regular basis
- do not have cables (from computer) trailing across walking routes
- do not store heavy files/boxes in high or awkward positions.

Computers

If working on a computer you need to:

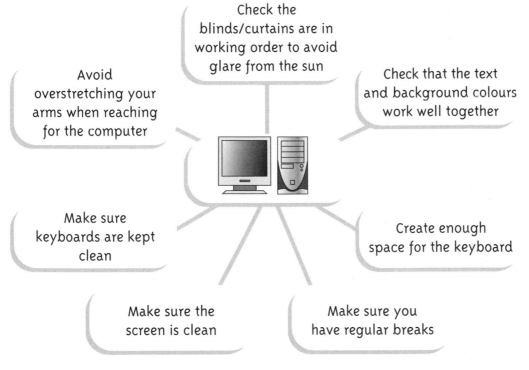

Figure 5.17 *Basic health safety tips for working at a computer workstation*

In the case of a computer chair you should consider not using armrests, as they prevent you getting close enough to use the equipment comfortably. You should sit with your back straight and your shoulders relaxed. Your eyes should be at about the same height as the top of the screen. All this means that the chair should be adjustable so that anyone sitting on it can adjust it to suit their size and physique.

Computers are often connected to printers, scanners, etc. by way of electrical cables. The following are guidelines on how to follow safe practice in using cables:

- Never use a coiled extension cable without fully unreeling the cable – it can overheat and cause a fire.
- Rubber and plastic covered cables should be kept away from hot surfaces.
- Ensure that no bare wires are showing.
- Trailing cables should be located within an appropriate cable duct.
- Cables should not stretch across gangways where they can be walked on or run over by trolleys.

Let's do it!

In pairs, design an A4 poster which could be displayed on an office noticeboard. You should stress the key health and safety points when working with a computer.

Vehicles

In working in the public services you are likely to use a range of vehicles in your job.

Let's do it!

As a group and with the aid of your tutor, draw up a list on the whiteboard of the possible vehicles you may have to drive in the public services – an example would be a jeep if you were in the army.

Here are some tips for driving a vehicle over a long distance:

- Look at maps and plan your route thoroughly.
- Research the roads you are using to avoid road works.
- Estimate travel times, so you can plan rest breaks, which will be important.
- Check the vehicles parts – e.g. filters, belts, fluid levels – and that the oil has been changed recently.

 Key point

Each year about 3500 people are killed on our roads and 40,000 are seriously injured.

Before each journey check
- the condition of your wiper blades
- that your signals work, including your brake lights
- the tread on your tyres
- the vehicle is prepared for the weather conditions.

When driving
- wear your seat belt
- do not use your mobile phone
- avoid road rage
- be careful and slow down in wet conditions.

Figure 5.18 *Road rage has become an increasing problem and hazard in recent years*

Let's do it!

On your own, research the top 10 road safety tips on www.thinkroadsafety.gov.uk/advice/toptentips.htm. Also on this website, look into the advice for driving in wintry conditions.

Telephone

The telephone is the main method for communicating within the workplace, and there are safety points in using the phone that you need to keep in mind. These include:

- Use a cordless phone if possible to avoid trailing cords that could be tripped over.
- Do not use a phone if your hands are wet.
- When speaking on the phone do not perform another task as this may lead to a distraction which could involve unsafe practice.
- To avoid congestion, attach the telephone to the wall if possible and not behind a workstation.
- Do not have a phone cord stretching across walkways where someone could trip over it.

Cell phones

Cell phones, commonly known as mobile phones, are part of our everyday lives. We use them for work and for private communication.

Case study

Are mobile phones safe?

A major study into the safety of mobile phones has reported that they may affect the health of people who use them. Researchers in Finland have suggested that the radiation associated with mobile phones causes changes in the brain. The two-year study concluded that even low-level emissions from handsets are damaging.

1 Why is it important for researchers to investigate this possible problem?

2 What role do mobile phones play in the work within the public services?

3 Why is further research required into the safety of mobile phones?

Source: http://news.bbc.co.uk

The precautions you can take to reduce any health risk from mobile phones includes

- keeping your conversations to a minimum
- using hand-free kits where possible
- buying phones with external aerials so that the phone is held as far away from the head as possible
- not using phones which have a high SAR value (i.e. it emits more radiation).

Key point

From 1 December 2003 a change to the Road Vehicles (Construction and Use) Regulations 1986 meant that anyone caught driving a motor vehicle and using a hand-held mobile will face a £30 on-the-spot fine, which rises to £1000 if the case goes to court (the fine is £2500 for drivers of vans, lorries, buses and coaches).

Radio

As with mobile phones, two-way radios (used for communication) should not be used while driving. As also in the case of mobile phones, you should turn them off at petrol stations to avoid the possibility of triggering an explosion in the petrol pumps. You should also switch off radios (used for recreation) wherever there are large quantities of flammable liquids. The risk is that the radio may produce a spark which could cause the flammable liquids to explode.

Protective clothing

Personal protective equipment (PPE) must be worn by employees exposed to hazards in the workplace, such as flying fragments of metal. PPE includes items such as

- lifejackets
- safety harnesses
- eye protectors
- gloves
- safety helmets.

If you work outside, PPE must be provided to protect you from the cold and wet weather.

Figure 5.19 *It is vital to have the correct equipment to protect yourself from the hazards of your workplace*

In the photo the firefighters are wearing protective gloves, trousers, jacket and helmet face shield.

 Key point

Employers cannot charge employees for the use of PPE if the law requires it.

Kettles and food preparation

Here are a few tips for using a kettle in an office environment:

- Preferably use kettles/water boilers in designated kitchens.
- Do not have a kettle on your desk.
- Where kettles are used in offices they must be located in a safe position, for example on a suitable surface.
- They should be positioned at a high suitable height and clear of doors where there is a risk of a door being opened and knocking over a kettle which could result in someone being scalded.
- Do not place hot drinks where they could be easily spilled
- Other items such as microwaves, toasters, refrigerators, vending machines, etc. should be placed in a designated area outside the office.

When considering workplace welfare in the office you need to assess things such as

- the systems for those with hearing difficulties
- photocopiers
- printers
- other items specifically related to your public service building.

Training requirements to enable correct usage

To ensure workplace welfare for all it is important that you are trained to use the items discussed previously, for example a new tank in the army. You also need to be trained when circumstances change in the workplace, such as having to use new equipment or having to follow new legislation.

Figure 5.20 *You need to have the correct training to carry out certain tasks*

Manual handling

In the public services there will be occasions when you have to lift and carry a heavy or large object. So, it is important that you follow the correct procedure when performing such a task to avoid injury to yourself or others.

Let's do it!

In small groups, complete the following table, which helps you begin to identify specific heavy or large objects you may have to deal with. Try to think of at least two objects in each public service. An example has been done for the ambulance service.

Name of service	Heavy or large object
RAF	1 2
Royal Navy	1 2
Army	1 2
Police	1 2
Fire	1 2
Ambulance	1 Casualty on the stretcher 2
Customs and excise	1 2
Coastguard	1 2
Prison service	1 2

Table 5.4

Requirements to provide training for correct lifting techniques

Although no limits are set as to the amount that can be lifted, the employer has the following duties to:

- avoid hazardous manual handling where possible
- use machinery to help where possible – e.g. a fork-lift truck

- consider the load to be moved through risk assessment – by considering the shape and size of the load
- reduce the risk of injury as far as possible
- provide information of the weight of each load.

The employee must use the correct system of work provided by the employer. The following diagrams should help you when handling heavy weights. When you are lifting and carrying a heavy object you should consider the following steps:

1 *Think about the object you are going to lift* Decide whether you need help or a lifting device like a pulley system.

2 *Position of your feet* Make sure your feet are apart in a balanced position so that you do not stumble or lose your balance.

3 *Body position* Bend your knees and make sure your back is straight. Make sure you get a good grip and make sure you do not kneel.

4 *Movement* Make sure the movement is smooth and controlled, not rushed and jerky.

5 *Feet movement* Make sure you move your feet and avoid twisting to ensure you do not get a back injury.

6 *Position of the object* Keep the object close to yourself at all times to avoid extra stress on your arms.

7 *Putting the object down* Make sure you do not drop the object by rushing. You should check your feet position again before putting it down.

Figure 5.21 *Make sure you use the correct technique when handling a heavy weight*

When you perform a manual handling risk assessment you should consider

- the task being performed
- the individual carrying out the manual handling operation
- the load(s) being moved
- the equipment being used
- the environment.

CHECK WHAT YOU KNOW

1 What is a code of practice?
2 Name *four* pieces of first aid equipment you would expect to find in a first-aid box?
3 Why is it important to wear protective clothing? Giving *two* examples you would use if you were a paramedic.
4 Name *three* methods of communication in relation to safe working practices within the public services.
5 Name *three* hazards within a kitchen and outline *three* methods for reducing the risk of the hazards you have identified.

In summary

- The main responsibility for first aid in the workplace is imposed on the employer, as they need to provide the training and resources.
- When considering health and safety within the workplace you must consider the ventilation, lighting and room space.
- Protective clothing must be suitable for the task and should be worn at all times.
- It is important you follow the correct manual handling procedures at all times to avoid injuries to yourself and others.

Assessment activity

If you are aiming for a *merit* (M3) grade you should complete this assessment activity. You are to fill in the following table, which aims to link the different forms of protective equipment and clothing and their purpose for enhancing safety. Firstly, you need to identify the piece of protective equipment and clothing, for example rubber gloves. Secondly, you will then need to explain the purpose of the equipment or clothing, as you can see from the example.

Equipment/clothing	Purpose
1 Rubber gloves	To reduce the chance of cross-infection when treating a casualty as a paramedic
2	
3	
4	
5	
6	
7	
8	
9	
10	

Table 5.5

You may want to identify protective equipment and clothing from the public service you are interested in, or you may do a more general list.

Assessment activity

You should complete this assessment activity (P6) regardless of the grade you are working towards. You are to produce a poster no larger than 600 mm × 900 mm which has the title of 'Manual Handling'. For the poster to be interesting and informative you should look to use colour, images, such as someone lifting a heavy object, and text. You will probably find the internet a good resource for the images.

- You should outline what the term 'manual handling' means. You may want to identify manual handling tasks in the public service of your choice. It may also be useful to identify the types of injuries that can be incurred from poor manual handling. This would be a good opportunity to also mention the Manual Handling Operations Regulations 1992.

- It is also important for you to look at the training requirements for manual handling, for example a paramedic will need some training in carrying a casualty. You should provide images of the correct procedure for lifting a heavy object, such as keeping your back straight.

Resources

Books

Barker, R, Saipe, R, Sutton, L, and Tucker, L (2003) *BTEC National Sport*, Oxford, Heinemann

Outhart, T, Taylor, L, Barker, R, and Procter, N (2000) *Advanced Vocational Leisure and Recreation*, London, Harper Collins

Saipe, R (1999) *Working in Sport and Recreation*, Cheltenham, Stanley Thornes

Journals

Navy News
RAF News
Soldier

Leaflets

HSE (1992) 'Personal Protective Equipment at Work Regulations 1992'

HSE (1994) 'Manual Handling: Solutions you can Handle 1981'

HSE (1997) 'First Aid at Work: the Health and Safety (First-Aid) Regulations 1981'

HSE (1997) 'The Health and Safety Executive – Successful Health and Safety Management'

HSE (1998) 'Five Steps to Risk Assessment'

HSE (1998) 'Reducing Noise at Work, The Noise at Work Regulations 1989'

HSE (2000) 'The Health and Safety Executive and You'

Websites

Army – www.army.mod.uk
Government Statistics – www.statistics.gov.uk
Police – www.policecouldyou.co.uk
RAF – www.raf-careers.com
Royal Marines – www.royal-marines.mod.uk
Royal Navy – www.royal-navy.mod.uk
World Health Organisation – www.who.int

Outdoor activities and the public services

Introduction

This unit guides and supports you through the requirements for the unit on outdoor activities in the public services.

Today, outdoor activities are not just leisure pursuits, but are also used for educational and personal development purposes, and these are the themes which will be explored in this unit.

Some of the themes that courses and projects develop are teamwork, problem solving and confidence building. These will also be explored. Perhaps you already know that outdoor activities contribute a lot to young people's development through your own experiences, and they are valued aspects for many public services organisations.

Responsibilities for running these courses/projects/residentials rest with a mixture of highly qualified instructors and many enthusiastic volunteers. The instructors tend to supervise the activities, which can be a range of things such as climbing, canoeing, caving and camping, while the group leaders (volunteers) provide all the logistical support to make it happen. The unit will help you weigh up roles, responsibilities and aims of many of the schemes in operation today, which are run by a selection of organisations which specialise in community-related projects using the outdoors.

How you will be assessed

The assessment requires you to take part in at least two activities so that you can have first-hand experience and maybe improve your skills as well. You will also do some research into schemes that organisations run to help benefit young people and show how these are used by the public services.

After completing this unit, you should be able to achieve the following outcomes:

1 Participate in outdoor activities and identify how an individual can benefit from them.

2 Examine youth and community projects in our society and their use of outdoor activities and residentials.

3 Examine how public services may be involved with outdoor activities and youth and community projects.

4 Describe the benefits of outdoor activity residentials and the responsibilities of organisers.

Outdoor activities

Outdoor activities

Types of providers, locations and activities

These vary greatly but can be found throughout the UK, close to towns, further into the countryside, on the coast and in more remote locations. Some examples are given below:

- In the public sector – local authority centres usually in hilly areas with rivers and lakes nearby, which can be used for activities such as walking, canoeing and caving, for example the Peak District.
- In the private sector – small companies offering specialist courses such a hang-gliding, pony trekking or diving around the coast of Wales.
- In the voluntary sector – clubs and community groups going off into the countryside or larger charitable organisations such as Outward Bound or the Scout movement, who run courses in the Lake District and parts of Scotland.

Increasingly leisure providers also offer their venues as locations, for example hotels with lakes for watersports, sports centres with indoor climbing walls, or parks with bike trails, so clearly outdoor activities can take place in urban locations too.

A safe outdoor environment

Outdoor activities providers tend to promote their facilities as a 'safe environment' for learning and development to take place. This means safe in terms of the equipment used, the staff supervising the activities and the level of activities undertaken. When you make your trip as part of this unit you should be able to assess whether these were safe for your group.

To get the most benefit out of these types of activities, locations and courses there needs to be opportunities and the right environment for public services groups to achieve a range of things. Some examples are

- overcoming fears – this requires achievable tasks, supportive leaders, and help from other members of the group
- developing confidence – this needs patience, gradually increasing targets being set, repetition of skills and a sympathetic group and leader
- organised learning – structured programmes that bring out the best in people and allow time to reflect on strengths and weaknesses
- development activities – the chance to lead, or go first, or help get someone else through a difficult task.

Think about it

Have you ever been in a similar challenging situation and been grateful to someone else or proud of your input? If so how much did it mean to you?

The range of outdoor activities

Although personal development is a key theme it cannot happen in the outdoors without activities to foster it. Most centres will develop their own activities and locations or use the natural environment to stage them. Typical examples might be:

- Rock climbing – this can be done on sea cliffs, quarries, or natural crags.
- Abseiling – this often uses the same locations as rock climbing but many organisations use man-made structures too, such as old viaducts, towers or bridges.
- Mountain craft – this is obviously done in hilly areas, such as the Pennines or the Lake District.
- Campcraft – this can take place anywhere in the countryside, either in a designated campsite or in the wild (with permission).
- Water-based activities – examples are canoeing, rafting, sailing, which need rivers, lakes and estuaries.
- Caving – this is more likely to be in limestone areas such as the Peak District.

Let's do it!

As a group discuss what skills or abilities each of the above activities help bring out. Create a chart to capture your opinions.

Let's do it!

Can you identify three areas of the UK that would be suitable for hiking, climbing and water activities, *other than* those mentioned above?

Each activity has to be tailored to suit the weather and the ability of the group, therefore centres running courses or activities need to have a range of locations and levels of activity available, so that they can assess which format will suit a certain type of group, for example beginner, primary school children, intermediates such as scouts, or experienced teachers and leaders.

Figure 7.1 *Outdoor activities help personal development and teamworking skills*

Outdoor activities based on site

Many centres will also have a repertoire of activities which can be used on their own site to help develop personal skills. These will depend on the natural or man-made features which are available, such as

- tall trees to build a high level ropes course, for example most of the Outward Bound centres (very much a confidence builder)
- a small coppice of trees where a blind trail can be set out using ropes or string for people to follow who are blindfolded (a good communications exercise)
- problem-solving equipment, for example logs, planks, ropes and barrels which are used to build structures (a team-building task)
- two trees close together to create a spider's web of ropes to pass people through (great for trust building)
- walls of logs or sleepers for groups to climb over (which tests commitment and planning).

 Think about it

During your residential part of this unit, assess which problem-solving tasks produced
- good team work
- good communications skills
- confidence boosts.

Personal benefits from different activities

A number of these have been signposted in the previous section, and, as with the activities themselves, centres can choose from their repertoire others which will test other skills or bring out other group dynamics. This is usually agreed between the staff accompanying the group and the instructors before the residential takes place. Staff will give an idea of what they want the group or individuals to experience and instructors compose a problem-solving or activity session to meet those needs. Some examples are:

- *Developing confidence* This might be based on some perceived element of risk such as zip rope slide or short abseil, where individuals have to face certain fears and overcome them, which boosts their confidence.

- *Testing skills* This can be done on the water or land by setting out a course to be navigated, such as a slalom course for canoeists or an orienteering course for runners. Skills of navigation, technique, speed and the least number of errors come under the spotlight here.

- *Challenging views* This can be achieved by group interaction, perhaps through a construction task which has a number of solutions. The best solution has to be agreed by everyone before the build can begin, for example before building a raft, as this often leads to heated debate about what is the best style.

- *Trust* This is a key teamworking skill and is often tested by people completing a short backward fall 'off a log' into the arms of team mates. You just have to believe they will catch you!

Let's do it!

Think of another activity based on water which might test or develop coordination and cooperation skills.

Use of the outdoors by the public services

The previous sections will have given you a good idea how many organisations can use the outdoors, and the public services are no exception. Probably the three most common uses are

- for team-building purposes, for example to help people who are new to fit in, to help groups bond to improve a team's performance

- to provide a different experience than normal, for example to challenge individuals or groups, to get them out of their normal habits and areas, to see who is the most adaptable or can lead

- developing fitness, for example prior to an event or challenge, to improve stamina and strength, to blow away cobwebs of inactivity and lethargic lifestyles.

The following section will explore some of these ideas and other benefits in more depth.

Skills and abilities – benefits for the public services

The key issue in all the work that goes into creating activities that will help people develop their personal skills and abilities is how transferable that type of learning or benefit is to their work situation – this is usually called 'transferability of skills'. This will often depend on the skills of the instructors or leaders in relating what has been learned or experienced into everyday work contexts such as clearer communications or spending more time planning. These 'transferable skills' are valuable to public service organisations for they are usually the things that 'make it tick', that is run effectively. So, organisations hope that time and money invested doing the outdoor activities will produce a more effective workforce.

This is particularly true for the public services in a number of ways, which we will consider now.

1 *Teamwork* A better understanding can be given by setting a series of teamwork task or scenarios in the outdoors, then reviewing how well groups and individuals performed. The review after each task is a most important part for it gives a chance for feedback on good and bad points and a chance to revise tactics for the next task, that is carry forward what the team did well and be aware of what they did not do well. It is also a chance to note these types of learning points to take back to the workplace for action there too – that is transferability.

2 *Roles and responsibilities* These can be clearly carried out in the outdoors context, usually through simple tasks. Plans are made and jobs allocated, so if someone does not do a good job it is clear to the others and may determine the success (or not) of the task set. These roles and responsibilities are not always made clear at work or effectively carried out, whereas the outdoor tasks usually show up strengths and weaknesses in individuals. Ideally, the team will rally round or help someone out because they can clearly see the problem – another useful learning point which all public service organisations can benefit from. It is also a chance for individuals to shine and show their personal skills more openly, for example in leadership or planning.

3 *Confidence building* In earlier sections we have described some activities to help people in this respect. A boost to confidence may well be carried back to the work context as someone becomes more assertive or more communicative as a result.

4 *Problem-solving skills* These can be built up through experience of a range of tasks, which gives people a generic model they can also use at work. A suggestion is given in the following figure.

Gather as much information about
the problem as possible

↓

Discuss what options might be
used to solve it (brainstorm)

↓

Evaluate a shortlist of those
solutions most likely to succeed

↓

Make a plan of how this could be
done and set some criteria by which you
will know you have been successful

↓

Carry out that plan and evaluate
the outcomes

5 *Planning and organising* These are two of the most important abilities for a work context. Outdoor activities can set a range of tasks such as planning a route, organising what supplies to take, packing a rucksack, and so on. Groups and individuals must agree what goes into the plan, how they will check if it is going to plan and how they will organise themselves into roles and responsibilities to see the plan through.

6 *Leadership* Perhaps the most important ability of all. Much debate exists about whether leaders are born or made. Setting challenges and tests in the outdoors gives people a chance to try out their skills as leaders and others a chance to assess whether they are good leaders without all the electronic support or resources which are found in the workplace – it's just basic ability or not!

One model which is easy to understand and covers many of these aspects is shown in Figure 7.2, John Adair's model.

 Think about it

How crucial do you think leadership skills are in the public services?

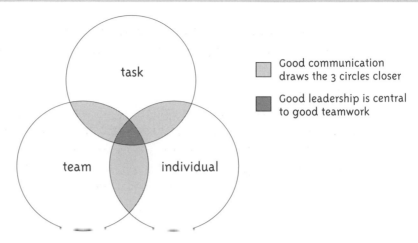

Figure 7.2 *John Adair's three circles model. This suggests that (**a**) individual needs have to be met, (**b**) the task has to be clear and achievable, (**c**) team behaviours need to be positive. When these conditions are met success is a likely outcome*

Let's do it!

Make a list of the top five attributes you think a leader should have, then compare your list to others to see if you agree. Discuss where you do not agree and why.

7 *Communication* Sometimes this is described as the 'glue' that holds organisations together. Good communications have to exist to get work completed, to meet deadlines and keep information flowing to the right people. There are some basic guidelines which outdoor activities can help people instil into their modes of communication:

- Make sure you compose the message so that the receivers of it will understand it clearly.
- Think about the way you should send it, e.g. phone, fax, email, verbal, and when is best.
- Make the message clear with no jargon, vagueness or misleading information.
- Check it has been received and understood.
- Check that someone has taken action and it is the action you wanted.
- Ask for some feedback on what happened as a result of your communication and their actions.

Many communication exercises can be set up in the outdoors – blind sheep, blind rope, caving with communication chains in the dark, collaborative teamworking during an abseil session. You will notice that many of the situations take away the facility to see people, in that way you cannot read their body language to help you get the message across. This highlights the need for clear instructions to be passed, while the element of danger focuses everybody's minds to listen carefully!

Think about it

Transferring good communication practices back to the workplace is perhaps the most valuable contribution that outdoor activities can make for any set of staff and organisation, not just in the public services but in any organisation. What do you think?

8 *Motivation* This is what you might call our 'driving force'. We can be motivated in two ways:

- Intrinsically – from within ourselves, spurred on to achieve a target, or to better our performance (this can be used positively or negatively to do good or to do bad). We usually work harder if there is a high reward.

- Extrinsically – from outside sources, for example friends, role models, bosses. In these contexts we can be motivated because we have to, because we want to, or to avoid punishment.

Outdoor activity courses often give people a chance to try and push their motivation limits higher, by tackling new (sometimes scary) things, by getting them to concentrate under pressure and help to motivate others when they are under pressure. Just getting to the top of a mountain or completing a trek can challenge some people's motivation, that is their ability to stick to the task and see it through to the end. All of these situations help people to explore what motivates them (and what does not) and at what stage others in the team have a cut-off point.

Taking this sort of knowledge back to the workplace is really valuable for teamworking, appraisals, meeting expectations and even promotion purposes. It also gives people an understanding of human nature, which can be valuable in the public services for dealing with members of the public, as well as colleagues.

9 *Identifying and developing flexible skills* This is sometimes called multi-skilling. With more and more organisations functioning with fewer staff, those who remain are being asked to be more flexible in what they do, that is do more varied tasks as part of their job description. This is certainly part of the ethos in the public service. Outdoor development tasks can be structured to put people in demanding situations which are unfamiliar, for example sailing a dinghy, completing an ascent of a mountain, all of which show up a range of skills which some people are capable of picking up quickly. The dynamics of situations will also show who are the best decision makers, ideas people, who are good at seeing a task through or completing

things in detail, all valuable abilities and skills for teams working in the services. Where an obvious gap appears in someone's skills or abilities training can be prescribed or extra sessions scheduled to help them catch up.

Think about it

These types of courses, tasks and experiences are supposed to help identify strengths and weaknesses and to inform staff development needs. What do you think? Was this the case on your residential?

Let's do it!

Carry out a small personal audit by asking the following questions about your strengths and weaknesses:

- Am I good at taking decisions?
- Do I mix well with others?
- What can I do well when in a team?
- What are my best skills and abilities?
- Where do my weaknesses lie?

Public service involvement

The public services have vital roles to play in the safety and welfare of the population, but they also make considerable contributions to the type of training and development we have discussed in the previous section by, for example

- improving people's skills and abilities
- helping raise awareness of the services and what they offer and do
- opening their doors to allow the public to see them at work or in training
- training young people for the services.

In the next section we will consider some of these types of involvement.

Involvement with the voluntary sector

The public services get involved by hosting or helping to run young people's groups such as the sea cadets or scout movement. The activities they run can take various forms, but is likely to be adapted to suit local group needs such as boat-handling skills – power, rowing and sailing – or campcraft and navigation skills.

Figure 7.3 *Volunteers in the public services need to develop certain skills to do what is required, as in the case of being a member of a lifeboat team*

Mountain rescue groups give talks and demonstrations, perhaps on reading the weather or rope/stretcher rescue techniques. The lifeboat service shows training techniques for launching, rescuing and maintaining the boats and equipment, for example. Coastguard stations and harbour masters may also be brought in for their specialities, while police divers can contribute to young people's development and training through dive training sessions.

Let's do it!

Carry out some research in your area to assess what two public service agencies do for young people's groups.

The professional role

In most real-life incidents it is unlikely that just one wing of the professional services would be called into action. These are usually joint operations involving several services, for example a problem in an estuary might involve helicopter, lifeboat, coastguard, police and ambulance teams. So there is a need for a lot of collaborative work. A problem in the mountains might need police, ambulance, dog teams and mountain rescue teams on call as well. So there is a great deal of need for inter-team communications. For a city-based incident, fire, police, ambulance and even specialist army team members might be called in. So there is a clear need for an incident's plan that can be brought into action.

Many of these situations require similar skills to be developed, which outdoor activities can teach or help people to develop, such as

- decisiveness
- working with radios
- reading the weather
- handling craft on water
- navigating
- first aid in the field
- working with people who are scared.

During the residential outdoor activity course you partake in for this unit you may well be introduced to some of these skills. The more adept you become the more value you offer the team, the more versatile your skills are, and the more likely you are to be employed.

The following are scenarios of when young people with outdoor activity skills might be useful:

- If a search was required of difficult terrain or forest, perhaps if children went missing, teams of searchers are always welcome, such as scouts.
- The St John's ambulance corps provide first-aid cover at many outdoor events such as orienteering, fell running and mountain biking competitions.
- Sea cadets might well provide useful skills for organisers of dinghy sailing regattas.
- General stewarding at countryside fairs and outdoor events might be offered by Duke of Edinburgh Award holders.

Think about it

Can you think of other examples you have seen particular to your area?

In summary

Clearly all public service teams need to be able to work together and have skills needed in emergencies. This must be brought into their training routines – to avoid confusion, help smooth operations and give staff the right kind of skills to deal with incidents effectively.

Assessment activity

For whatever grade you are aiming for you need to take part in at least two outdoor activities and prepare a report which has the following sections in it:

1 The value of outdoor activities to the public services as a training method.
2 The types of skills and abilities that public service teams require which can be brought out through outdoor activities.
3 How public services get involved with youth groups to help with personal abilities and technical skills.

Your report should be clearly structured and use case studies or examples to illustrate points.

Youth projects

Much of the emphasis in the last section was on helping to train young people for work in the public services using outdoor activities as a medium. This section will consider how this is done by a number of organisations in the form of youth projects. The focus is still on personal development and life skills.

Youth projects

The Prince's Trust

The Prince's Trust (with Prince Charles as the patron) focuses on helping young people achieve a number of things in their lives, such as

- lifting barriers to progress or success
- improving their personal skills
- giving them openings to a fresh start.

Since its inception in 1976 the organisation boasts to have helped over 500,000 young people all over the UK. They have a particularly good record with people who have been in care, unemployed, struggled at school or in trouble with the law. This would appear to reflect the work that public services undertake too. Further study of their aims reveals the following:

Aims of The Prince's Trust

The Prince's Trust aims to combat
- social exclusion and unemployment
- youth crime and anti-social behaviour
- underachievement or low qualifications
- disengagement and truancy.

The Prince's Trust aims to promote
- citizenship and respect
- financial independence and practical skills
- self-esteem and motivation
- community engagement and regeneration.

Think about it

Which of the previous aims for The Prince's Trust correspond to aims held by public service organisations or their youth wings?

On The Prince's Trust website you can assess how many types of young people it has helped and how it has done this. Examples include ex-offenders who have been helped into education or steady employment; young people helped into self-employment or business schemes; and the unemployed helped into training schemes. Over 600 teams work on personal development every year, as do hundreds of community schemes, for example to create children's play areas. It has involvement in the government's 'New Deal' scheme. It works closely with other partners such as business or public service, for example the Royal Bank of Scotland, the FA Premier League, BT and the civil service and Inland Revenue, plus social services and voluntary organisations.

Such are the problems for young people in the 14–30 age group in our post-modern age (as many as 600,000 are not in education, training or employment and the same number again claim unemployment benefit) that as many as 20% need help with life skills and career choices, clearly a big role which needs to be shared.

The Duke of Edinburgh Award scheme

This scheme is a voluntary, non-competitive programme of practical, cultural and adventurous activities, designed to support the personal and social development of young people aged 14–25 years. It offers an individual challenge and encourages young people to undertake constructive, enjoyable but challenging activities and projects in their free time.

The programme has three progressions based on age and difficulty, which are designated as:

- Bronze award for those aged 14 and over
- Silver award for those aged 15 and over
- Gold for those aged 16 and over.

Each level has four sections, which participants must cover to attain the award:

- Service – helping other people in the local community.
- Expedition – planning, training for and completing successfully a journey (expedition) which can be done on foot; on a bicycle; by canoe; in a boat.
- Skills – covering almost any hobby, skill or interest.
- Physical recreation – undertaking a sport, dance, or fitness activity.

● Residential project – (gold award only) a purposeful enterprise with people not previously known.

Benefits which might accrue doing the 'D of E', as it is often known, could be:

- a sense of achievement
- new skills and interests
- self-confidence and self-reliance
- leadership skills and abilities
- exciting opportunities
- friendship
- experience of teamwork
- national and international connections
- enjoyment.

Each county in the UK which is licensed to run the award will have an organising person, probably supported by a team of volunteers or field workers who assist in its running.

The Duke of Edinburgh Award has in recent years taken on some new areas of focus with which you might get involved with, such as
- providing active citizenship projects for schools
- helping youth offending teams with rehabilitation
- creating volunteers, over 2500 so far.

Let's do it!

Carry out some online research to identify your nearest organiser of the D of E and assess how widespread and popular the scheme is in your area.

Outward Bound scheme

Courses or programmes which can be undertaken with Outward Bound and fall into the category we are learning about come under the umbrella of 'Learning Gateway and Life Skills Option'. The objectives, which bear a certain resemblance to other organisations, are to increase
- self-awareness and self-esteem through success
- understanding of the work ethic, values and citizenship
- self-reliance and responsibility
- teamworking and leadership skills.

Many of these would be facilitated by taking on outdoor activities and tasks, as you can see from the attached programme sample.

Figure 7.4 *The Outward Bound scheme provides young people with opportunities to learn new life skills by engaging in activities such as this*

The following is a sample of the Outward Bound 'Learning Gateway and Life Skills' programme.

	Activity	Learning outcome
Day 1	Icebreakers Log book time	Relationship building Setting out aims and objectives Problem solving and reflection on performance
Day 2	Water activities Ropes course Overnight 'camp'	Teamwork, new skills learning, personal challenge, fun, pairs work Self-organisation, group skills, reflection period
Day 3	Campcraft Navigation 'home' Walking skills	Target setting, roles and responsibilities, motivation, challenge of environment
Day 4	Land-based activities Rock climbing and abseiling Zip wire and trapeze	Confidence, support, achievement, 'getting a 'buzz', reviewing achievements (and failures)
Day 5	Clean-up kit Final challenge Presentations	Action plans Highs and lows Evaluation of skills

Table 7.1

Raleigh International

Raleigh International has a youth development scheme which aims to develop the skills and prospects of disadvantaged and socially excluded young people in the UK. The main means of achieving this aim is through local projects and partnership schemes with other agencies to support joint initiatives. These projects give young people the chance to undertake activities on a weekly basis or go on a UK or international course or expedition. One such programme is called 'Motiv8', which is a well-known project of drop-in schemes run across the country. Raleigh International also works in partnership with other complementary organisations such as the Amber Foundation.

Case study

Raleigh International

Raleigh International's local projects help maintain participants' interests in personal development opportunities. The projects emphasise the concepts of community involvement and social responsibility. (Here you can see parallels with other youth organisations.) They use a range of activities to engage young people such as

- sport – swimming, health and fitness activities
- discussion of 'rules boundaries and consequences'
- anger and stress management
- cultural awareness
- fundraising
- follow-up action plans for individuals.

A typical programme would be:

Day 1 – enrolment and awareness sessions

Day 2 – a taster residential involving teamwork, individual skills and relationships, group skills (communication and conflict)

Day 3 – a workshop to help integration and discussion of issues

Day 4 – preparation for the project or expedition.

Think about it

Why do you think courses like anger and stress management and cultural awareness are included in the above scheme?

Fairbridge

The Fairbridge organisation offers young people long-term personal support and challenging activities in many of the most disadvantaged areas in the country. Their goal is

'to give young people the motivation, confidence and skills they need to change their lives'.

Their programmes are tailored to meet individual needs and can last as long as young people need the support (which can be quite a commitment). Fairbridge focuses on helping young people who have 'switched off' from conventional learning and tries to give them opportunities to do challenging activities in the outdoors such as rock climbing, but also indoor challenges such as running a small business.

Fairbridge tries to provide 'a route back to mainstream society' in deprived areas where marginalised young people live. It aims to help young people gain a belief in themselves, their potential and personal skills in the light of problems they are trying to overcome in their lives. Problems can be anything from drug addiction to crime and unemployment or homelessness. It also works in conjunction with other charities and social and public service organisations to create an integrated approach.

Fairbridge focuses on 13–25 year olds in urban areas, who have, for example, not had much education, training or work experience. Many of the young people do not have the conventional support that we are likely to enjoy such as family, friends and the local community. Fairbridge works with over a 1000 other organisations (many of which will be public services) to provide hope for disadvantaged young people by trying to show them that they have ability and can take opportunities with both hands to prove themselves to themselves and others.

Let's do it!

Compare the above three organisations to identify common themes and approaches using outdoor activities.

Youth groups

A range of these will be touched on in this section, but research should be carried out by you to create a better knowledge of these organisations. Your research should focus on whether the organisations have a national or local focus and how they use outdoor activities to encourage young people to develop skills and abilities relative to this unit.

● *Scouts* The aim of the Scout Association is to

'... promote the development of young people in achieving their full physical, intellectual, social and spiritual potential, as individuals, as responsible citizens and as members of their local, national and international communities.'

The method of achieving the aim of the Scout Association is by providing an enjoyable and attractive scheme of progressive training, based on the Scout Promise and Law, and guided by adult leadership.

Scouting's great strength lies in its grassroots. It is locally that scouts are best able to identify and work directly with those young people most in need. Scouting offers bridges to a world of social involvement and inclusion through education and activity

● *Guide movement* Guides are usually aged between 10 and 14, although some guides like to stay until they are older. Any girl over the age of ten can become a guide as long as she is able to understand, and wants to make, the Guide Promise.

Being a guide is all about belonging to a group, learning new skills, making new friends and helping others. Each guide is encouraged to achieve her own personal goals through a progressive programme with the opportunity to work for a wide variety of badges. This allows the girl to mature and develop at her own pace.

Guides work together in patrols (teams), of four to eight girls, providing a ready-made group of friends and helping the girls to feel that they belong to something special. They elect their own leader. A patrol plans its own activities with the support of the guide leader so that each girl learns to share in decisions that affect herself and others in the patrol.

● *Air training core* The air training corps (ATC) was formed during World War II to provide part-trained personnel for the Royal Air Force. The modern ATC is no longer a recruiting organisation, but rather an organisation offering a wide range of exciting opportunities to young people aged between 13 and 20. However, the organisation is very proud of its continuing strong links with the RAF and can offer an interesting insight into RAF life.

The following are examples of activities and projects:

● Power flight – cadets get the opportunity to fly in the RAF's primary training aircraft, the *Bulldog*. These flights are called air experience flights (AEFs), and cadets get the chance to control the aircraft.

● Gliding – the air cadet gliding organisation is the largest glider training organisation in the world.

● Shooting – cadets get the opportunity to shoot two types of rifle, but there is no pressure put on you to do so in the ATC.

- Camping – the ATC holds regular camps that are usually based in the UK. Many cadets are also selected for camps in Cyprus, Germany or Gibraltar. Annual camp is a week-long trip to an RAF base in the UK, usually taking place once a year for each squadron. Other activities, such as sports events, are arranged and cadets can also do work experience in the base.

- Citizenship training – the aims of the ATC, whilst including the emphasis on developing the individual cadet through instruction and rugged training, also places value on service to the local community.

- Other activities – hill and mountain walking, camping, abseiling, and many other sports, the list is endless. If you are the outdoor type, or even if you are not, the ATC has a lot to offer you. During the winter, night exercises are held. They are often one of the cadets' favourite activities. A 'nitex' generally involves putting on camouflage combats or dark clothes and running about a forest ambushing other cadets in order to complete a set objective.

Army cadet force The army cadet force (ACF) is a voluntary uniformed youth organisation, partly sponsored by the Ministry of Defence. It has been successfully helping young people in their development for over 100 years. There are at present some 50,000 boys and girls aged between 12 and 18 years in the army cadet force nationwide.

The aim of the army cadet force, as described in its charter, is to inspire young people to achieve success in life with a spirit of service to the Queen, their country and their local community, and to develop in them the qualities of a good citizen.

It is one of the country's leading youth organisations and is run on military style guidelines, so a certain amount of discipline is to be expected. The ACF offers a full training syllabus designed to help young people to become good citizens and responsible members of the community. They offer various activities: climbing, canoeing, first-aid training, target shooting, sports, weekend camping, annual camps, courses (cooking, leadership, physical training, communications), musical skills, service to the community, overseas expeditions, participation in the Duke of Edinburgh Award scheme, St John Ambulance, friendship, discipline, leadership, development – and lots of fun!

Girls and boys brigades The Girls' Brigade (GB) is a Christian, international charity working alongside girls and young women of every background, ability and culture. There is a Boy's Brigade as well.

Since its foundation in 1893, GB has become known worldwide as a fun and interesting organisation which offers challenging and relevant activities, the chance to develop skills, as well as care and Christian values for hundreds of thousands of young people.

It is led by Christian women from local churches. These leaders are trained volunteers who are committed to providing a regular meeting time of activities and skills for girls and young women. GB groups (companies) usually meet on a weekly evening in churches, schools and community centres.

Worldwide (GB operates in over 60 countries) the charity seeks to enable girls and young women to develop in confidence, ability, friendship and citizenship, and is committed to nurturing the unique value of every girl in its care.

The Boys' Brigade has been around for more than 110 years and is part of the boyhood experience of many adults. The function is to serve today's young men through:

'The promotion of habits of obedience, reverence, discipline, self-respect and all that tends towards a true Christian manliness.'

Its approach is to capture the energy and enthusiasm of youth and to channel it purposefully. It recognises that the influences surrounding young people are not always helpful and that too many lose control at great cost to themselves, their families and the community. So the Boys' Brigade sets out to

- develop a boy's awareness of his own community and create opportunities for service

Figure 7.5 *Through outdoor activities the Girls' Brigade offers opportunities for enjoyment and friendship*

- develop latent leadership qualities so that boys become contributors to the life of their community – not just takers
- encourage boys to get involved in their company, their church and the community, and this involvement means taking responsibility for what happens.

The Boys' Brigade does not confine itself to well-motivated and prosperous young people. It offers support and interest to the less fortunate and recognises the value of adult interest as young people develop.

Youth clubs

A mention will be made of the type of work these kinds of organisations undertake.

Your research should focus on whether the organisations have a national or local focus and how they use outdoor activities to encourage young people to develop skills and abilities relative to this unit. You should also carry out some personal research to identify some local examples and projects.

- *UK Youth* This is the largest nationally registered youth work charity in the UK. It supports and develops high quality work and educational opportunities for all young people.

  The network of members represents more than 750,000 young people and is supported by some 45,000 volunteer and part-time youth workers representing more than 7000 youth groups, clubs and projects throughout the UK.

UK Youth

UK Youth's special advantage is that young people choose to get involved. It approaches this by enabling young people to develop personal and social skills so they can take responsibility for their actions and control of their lives.

Young people are at the heart of everything it does. The management committee has 22 national members from around the UK who play a role in shaping policies and practice.

The charity depends on public support to continue to develop its role as an innovator in developing services for young people.

Its activities include the following:

- UK Youth has guaranteed places in the Flora London Marathon, the world's greatest inner-city marathon.
- Nigel Mansell UK Youth Golf Tournament is held each spring at the prestigious Woodbury Park Hotel, Golf and Country Club. Spaces for teams sell out early as the weekend includes golf with Nigel Mansell and other celebrity guests.

Other areas worth researching or visiting for further information on youth clubs are

- local community centres
- after-school clubs
- church groups.

In summary

Many of the organisations have similar aims, but slightly different approaches to tackling and supporting these. You can gather the impression that they might all be competing for the attention of young people and scarce resources to deliver their aims.

Assessment activity

For whatever grade you are working towards you have to do this activity. Compare some youth organisations or groups and identify their use of outdoor activities for the benefit of young people. Present your material using real case studies and diverse examples.

To achieve a *pass* (P1) you need to explain the importance and benefits of the activities to the individuals; for a *merit* (M1) you need to analyse the benefits of developing certain skills through these activities; and for a *distinction* (D2) you need to evaluate these benefits.

Community projects

Public service groups and youth groups of the types mentioned in the previous section very often get involved in community projects in their local areas. It involves them 'volunteering' to carry out some work or an activity which has real value to a certain section of the community such as the elderly or disadvantaged. Volunteering is an important way of not only making a contribution to society, but also of gaining experience through project work with new people and resources or finances, which are often in short supply.

In this section you will learn about the nature of projects, volunteering and the benefits to the community. Not all are outdoor activity based but the examples included show good practice in a range of projects.

Community projects

All projects have aims and objectives by which they are guided and evaluated. The content of these aims and objectives gives the project its purpose, sometimes called a 'mission statement'. In the public service context purposes tend to be aimed (or targeted) at certain groups (target groups) in the local community who can clearly benefit from help. Some examples follow.

- *Disabled* Projects might involve youth groups in helping to create disabled access to parks for some simple outdoor recreation. They might be involved in supporting other professionals to provide 'real adventure experiences', such as an abseil or boat trip.

  Volunteers may be used as 'buddies' for the disabled person to motivate and encourage them with sporting skills and competition. Tameside local authority's sport and youth service have a project called 'Disability Active' which runs along these lines.

  Over the past year they have done archery, rock climbing, bush craft and lots more. They also have youth clubs where karaoke, concerts, sports, and awards work are done.

- *Disadvantaged* Projects for this type of group usually involve working with disaffected youngsters who need more structure, facilities and people to lead them. Another Tameside case study gives a typical example on the next page.

Case study

Tameside project

A pilot scheme for the Tameside project began with two 'pods' (porta cabins) – a facility which had heating/lighting/ventilation; tea/coffee making facilities; somewhere to sit/chat/hang out with youth workers. The workers would give advice and direct youths on topics such as harmonising in their communities, alcohol misuse, how to avoid engaging in anti-social behaviour and to signpost them onto facilities that the council and others were offering for young people.

Pods across Tameside showed success in each of their locations. The police experienced a reduction in calls, indicating that young people were adjusting their behaviour. Tameside Council's youth service was meeting and working with more young people at the front line who did not access mainstream facilities. Parents, residents and young people saw a facility being introduced into their specific area for their young people, to help tackle nuisance, annoyance and the anti-social behaviour of young people.

Since April 1998 Tameside Council has expanded the scheme which now runs with eight pods and 24 youth workers plus volunteers. The figures are showing very good results with 700 young people addressed by youth workers in the first three-month phase and over the same period up to 64% reduction in calls to the police where pods were located.

 Think about it

How would you evaluate if the Tameside project was a success, that is had achieved its purpose?

    Elderly Projects for this target group are probably best appreciated at Christmas time when loneliness and lack of mobility can be highlighted. In Scarborough many of the local scout, guide and beaver groups give a few evenings to go carol signing in the many retirement homes around the town. Does this happen in your area?

 Think about it

What benefits might this bring for both the carol singers and the elderly residents?

    Young unemployed This can often stem from lack of education, opportunities or motivation so the purpose of many of these types of projects is to engage young people in meaningful work, which will give them a pathway to employment or education. In the Knowsley area of Liverpool there is a good example of this type of project. Six partner organisations have come together in the Huyton Youth Leadership project to support young people. This project was developed to tackle youth unemployment and a culture of de-motivation. Schools, colleges, the Youth Service, a drugs team, and Weston Spirit have come together to encourage young people to take part in an apprenticeship scheme. These public service organisations cooperate and collaborate in the hope that the recruits will make it through to the end of the four-year-long project and onto jobs or higher education.

- *Truants and young offenders* Anti-truancy schemes already in place showed that education spending targeted at this group could produce a substantial reduction in youth crime rates. In the city of York youth crime figures had fallen by 67% after truancy watch schemes were introduced in 2000, claimed the Schools minister.

  In Hampshire the Education Department's Welfare Service is aiming to reduce truanting within the area through a new anti-truancy pilot scheme operating in certain areas of the county. This is a joint initiative between Hampshire County Council and Hampshire Constabulary. Through this initiative the police will have the power to take truants back to school. The Welfare Service can also offer support and help to pupils, parents and schools who may be having problems with attendance.

Some individuals who show promise, through participating in these schemes, are selected to go on Outdoor Development/Activity residential courses with organisations such as those described on pages 248–253.

Let's do it!

Social inclusion projects are manifold in nature, focusing on black and minority groups, ethnic communities, the disabled and offenders/ex-offenders. The aims of most of these projects are to examine

- the barriers that exist for some people – e.g. organisational, attitudinal
- the steps that need to be taken to give inclusion opportunities – e.g. access
- the benefits which can accrue from inclusion – e.g. citizenship, cohesion.

Carry out some research of your own to identify a social inclusion scheme which uses outdoor activities and evaluate which of the above purposes or aims are being used. Compare your findings with those of others in your class.

The role of the volunteer in projects

The mainstay of many projects is the people who volunteer to work alongside public service professionals and the target group individuals.

Research and practice has clearly shown that not only do volunteers benefit from involvement with projects, but so do the recipients and the wider community. The benefits include

- new networks being created
- new skills and personal development
- improved physical and mental well-being
- being satisfied with making a contribution
- notions of trust and reciprocity are fostered
- cohesion and advancement climates are created.

Roles that volunteers take and responsibilities that they carry out can be very diverse, just as the nature of the projects. Some examples are discussed in the next section to give you a flavour of what volunteers take on.

- *Chairperson* This person helps to steer the project along, taking an overview of all the tasks, roles and responsibilities and trying to ensure that all of these happen as planned.

  Quite often this person will be selected because they meet a range of needs that community projects require, such as
  - good local contacts
  - good communicator
  - leaderships skills.

  On a day-to-day basis the chairperson will call and run meetings, prepare documents and effectively 'head up' the project in a range of ways, such as being a spokesperson with the press and making sure all goes smoothly with all the other agencies involved. In many projects there will be a deputy (chair) leader who can stand in if the chairperson is unavailable, which helps keep continuity and communications flowing.

- *Treasurer* A project which cannot keep within its funding basis is destined to have problems, if not fail altogether, so the role of treasurer is a key one for keeping track of
  - costs, that is every item of resources, people and time that needs accounting for before budgets are set
  - budgets, that is the limits that have been set for each area of spending
  - balances at the end of a project, that is income versus expenditure.

  The treasurer must work closely with the chairperson to keep him or her informed at each stage and also to keep any other team leaders, with budgets, in the picture over their spending. It is fair to say that this person must have a head for figures and on larger projects may have to have an accountant.

Helper or volunteer Usually these people don't need to have experience or obvious skills, just a willingness to get involved with any tasks that come their way. Support (or training if required) is usually given but many just learn as the project progresses.

Volunteering for many of the public service organisations' projects is more than just a job however, it is an opportunity to
- meet new friends
- learn new skills
- put skills to good use
- take part in a team
- make a difference to other people's lives.

Although there may be no pay at the end of the day, the satisfaction of helping young people and achieving some of the above is often reward enough.

Project workers These are more likely to be professional people who work on a project or a range of them as part of a public service team. They will have a good range of skills which have been learned over a number of years of practice and training, such as being
- able to keep calm under pressure
- good listeners with an ear for detail
- practical 'hands on' people
- well organised.

Think about it

What other skills do you think professional project workers would need to have to run an outdoor project which involved restoring a coastal cliff top pathway?

Public services roles in projects

Each public service organisation will have different contributions they can make to community projects depending on their resources, funding and remit or purpose.

In this section we will consider a few, but it is likely that each local area will have its own types, which you can uncover when you carry out your research for this section of the assessment.

1 Advisory roles – at Lickers Lane Community centre in Whiston workers use a combination of outreach and drop-in advisory services to support young women to
- access college courses
- take up new sports
- discover health and beauty activities
- discuss issues that affect their lives.

2 Reduction of crime – by involving young people in projects.

3 Speakers – leaders of groups and public service officers often give talks to interested groups in the community to help them understand local projects which are tackling problems.

4 Charity collections – all voluntary and charitable organisations need donations and funding. Youth groups are often very active in this role; some examples might include: sponsored walks; abseils; collections for car washes or car boot sales.

5 Developmental or educational – in Liverpool's Halewood district there is a project based at the Hilton Grace Community Centre to which young people have been referred because of their behaviour. Workshops, activities and awards are used to help in this scheme. The young people are encouraged to examine their own behaviour and its impact on others.

Benefits to public services

There are three main benefits which can easily be discerned from all the project work which goes on in the community by the public services.

Firstly, involvement in varying roles for various projects produces *a real understanding of community* needs and perceptions. Projects are often in the form of 'outreach work' going out to where disadvantaged people actually live and helping them on their own territory, rather than waiting for them to come in to some centre, which they may not have the confidence to do.

Secondly, projects show *real concern for people*, meeting them face to face, trying to understand their problems and trying to help with solutions. All of this needs to be with belief, commitment and sincerity.

Thirdly, the projects provide *real contact with others* which might be challenging as they will have different attitudes, values and cultural backgrounds. Striving to understand and get along is an achievement in itself.

Organisers' responsibilities

A good deal has been written about these in previous sections under the roles described, for example treasurer, chairperson, volunteer. In this section we shall view some that have not been mentioned, that are sometimes in the background, but do what has to be done to ensure a smooth and safe project completion.

Funding In some projects a whole team will be allocated the role of fundraisers and targets will be set for them to try and achieve. A fund-raising team usually has a brainstorming session to come up with ideas that they might use. The suggestions then have to be reduced to those that are workable. Funding can come from recognised sources such as a government department, local authority or the EU, where a bid is made for funds allocated to help the target group in the community that the project is aimed at. This process is usually lengthy and complex. Fund-raising schemes can be much more fun with all sorts of sponsored events, for example parades, races and stunts. One of the key principles of using funding is to try and ensure that as much as possible goes towards helping the people in need and not on project team expenses such as administration or wages. Organisers need to keep a careful record of all income and expenditure and keep within budget (see page 262).

Trips and visits The complexity of organising a trip or visit for a group is often overlooked, for it is the actual trip that usually gains more publicity. Here is a checklist that might have to be completed before a day trip could take place, for example for a group of young adults to go on a one-day visit to the coast.

To do	Done
• Parental permission	✓
• Booking of transport, entrance fees, lunch	✓
• Route and pick-up and drop-off/stopping points	☐
• Kit list of things to take	☐
• Do's and don'ts list	☐
• Emergency contacts numbers	☐
• Medical and dietary needs	☐
• Wet weather alternative	☐
• Staffing	☐
• Payment system	☐
• Insurances	☐

Let's do it!

Can you add any other items to the checklist from your experience?

Insurances There are many types of insurance which you should research into to make sure you have a good idea what they all cover. Among them you will probably find the following types of insurance:

- Accident – to cover injuries
- Travel – to cover delays
- Public liability – to cover injuring someone else
- Cancellation – to cover costs of rebooking or returning home
- Medical – to cover hospitalisation costs
- Contents – to cover articles in a building
- Buildings – to cover the fabric of the building itself.

It is worth shopping around for the best quotes, especially if it is only for a short period or a trip.

Staffing Probably one of the most difficult things to do is to ensure that sufficient cover is available at all times for all circumstances, such as holidays, sickness, absence, emergencies, personal commitments (family), codes of practice. The organiser compiling any rota has to take many of these into account, but also has to ensure that arrangements are fair and equitable in terms of workload, and that peaks and troughs can be covered with the right numbers and appropriately qualified staff. Keeping a record of hours worked if pay is involved may be an issue too.

External liaison This is a very important responsibility if the project needs to publicise itself or work in partnership with other organisations. Clearly, this person has to be up to date with all progress and complications. They may well be involved with

- the media
- the public
- sponsors
- VIPs
- royalty
- politicians
- other organisations.

Think about it

What sort of skills and support systems do you think the person responsible for external liaison would need?

Record keeping We have mentioned how important this is for the funding aspects, but there are other needs such as writing the report on the project, keeping a note of queries or problems, staff records and participant details, evaluating how it all went for the team, the project and participants, stock control or equipment lists, and, hopefully not, accidents. Can you add others?

○ *Health, safety and security* For every aspect of the project (under the law) a risk assessment needs to take place (see Unit 7 and the next section). However security of premises often falls outside this practice. It is an important issue as often temporary or old premises are used to keep costs down or the organisation works from premises in disadvantaged areas where there is not a lot of respect for property. So organisers must ensure that all reasonable precautions are taken, such as padlocking doors and ensuring windows are locked. Where more valuable equipment might be at risk, greater security measures may be needed, such as lights, alarms or even guards.

Participants on a camping expedition or in dormitories on a 'camp' may also need their security covering, with adults being on hand to ensure this.

In summary

Community projects are very diverse and are aimed at meeting the needs of many different types of community groups. Public service organisations get involved in many different ways in response to expressed needs, for example funding and volunteers. Organisational skills are at a premium amongst leaders, workers and the volunteers, and the work can be very challenging at times, however the benefits to all are often very visible as confidence and success are achieved. Outdoor activity projects are particularly effective in meeting those latter two aspects.

Assessment activity

For whatever grade you are working towards you will need to do the following:
1 Compare a range of youth and community projects which are active in your area and involve the use of outdoor activities.
2 Examine one project in more detail to show its links to a public service and explain the purpose of those links.

To achieve higher grades than a *pass* (P4, P5) you need to analyse these projects to gain a *merit* (M3) and evaluate them for a *distinction* (D3).

Residentials

These are short experiences away from home, usually with a group of peers, where a group is resident in a centre and stays there to carry out a preset programme of activities, which may have a range of themes. For many children this is their first experience away from home on their own, in what is likely to be a strange environment. There are many centres around the country which will offer residentials, some are privately owned, others run by local authorities, and some are run by voluntary bodies or charities. Public service groups are just one of the many types of users.

In this section types of courses and providers will be discussed along with the aims and objectives that residentials can offer and achieve.

Types of residentials

The types of residentials can range from the more leisurely, through service and conservation projects up to the outright sporty and adventurous.

- *Sports* – these are usually adventure-based, such as canoeing and walking, or can be skills-based too, that is improvement or tasters' courses.

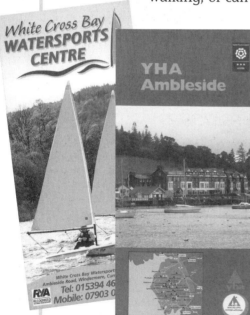

- *Leisure* – these focus on hobbies or interests more, such as photography, bird-watching or other countryside studies.

- *Personal development* – the themes for these types of residentials are usually confidence or team building, communication or leadership orientated, for example.

- *Outdoor work* – this is more for those interested in preservation or conservation work.

Figure 7.6 *The leaflets illustrate just three providers of residentials in the Lake District*

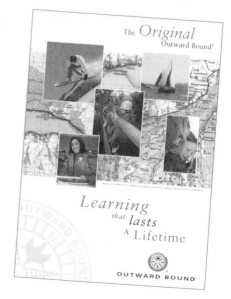

Let's do it!

Carry out some research of your own to identify some other types of courses not mentioned in the text, and classify them into the categories given, for example you might find one such as Camp Beaumont.

On all Multi-Activity holidays at our Isle of Wight Summer Camp!

CAMPS	2 FOR 1 DATES
Isle of Wight	9/8, 16/8 & 23/8

Bookings must be made and confirmed before 18th July 2003. Special offer places are limited, so acceptance is entirely on a first-come, first-served basis. In the case of two different holidays being booked, the free Multi-Activity holiday will be the cheapest of the two.

Book by 18th July 2003

CAMP BEAUMONT Tel: 01603 284280 WWW.CAMPBEAUMONT.COM

For bookings and more information please call

Residential providers

As was mentioned previously, all three sectors of the outdoor activity industry have organisations offering and running residentials. Closest to the public services sector might be army, RAF or Royal Navy centres, which are scattered around the UK and have connections to youth groups. They would tend to specialise in personal development or maybe adventure training.

Let's do it!

Do some research to find out which of these residential providers is closest to where you live.

Outward Bound is perhaps the most famous voluntary sector provider, with not only a set of UK centres such as Aberdovey in Wales, Ullswater in the Lake District and Loch Eil in Scotland, but a network worldwide, for example in Germany, Africa, USA. Outward Bound has a range of courses for personal development, skills improvement and adventure.

Case study

Open and tailor-made programmes at Outward Bound

Outward Bound regularly provides programmes for individuals, perhaps as many as 250 per year, with as many as 10,000 participants all over the world. The course content is directed at building confidence and self-belief, as well as improving decision making and problem solving, most of which is set in the outdoors. Open programmes range from one-week up to three-week courses, which reflects the traditional period of time the organisation began running its courses for, when they were first set up. Tailor-made programmes are very flexible to meet a range of needs, as for

- primary pupils
- secondary students' needs, for example A levels, PE, field trips
- skills and improvers' courses in adventure sports.

Think about it

What do you think would attract young people to go on these types of courses?

The National Trust has locations and courses for young people so they can learn and contribute more to the countryside, particularly areas of outstanding natural beauty and heritage sites such as the Cleveland Way and Robin Hood's Bay on the Yorkshire coast.

In the sections on projects on pages 250 to 253 examples were given of other organisations – Raleigh International and Fairbridge.

Let's do it!

Carry out some research on the YHA site to assess what residentials it has to offer and compare it to other large providers.

Private businesses around the country offer residentials too, such as the large providers PGL and Acorn or smaller ones such as Sutherland and Carlton Lodges in North Yorkshire. If you contact the British Activity Holiday Association they will be able to give you a list of approved providers who can tailor their programmes to suit your group's makeup and needs.

Keeping a record of your experiences on a residential is an important part of this unit. Try the next task to help prepare for doing this.

Let's do it!

Design a log book you could use for your residential experience to record

- arrangements
- kit list
- your thoughts and feelings about each activity and day
- your contributions
- your team
- any highs and lows
- any new achievements.

Compare your ideas with these of others in your class to get the best design, then word process all the pages and put them into a folder ready for use.

Benefits

As was mentioned in the previous section, residentials can be tailored to suit group needs and aims. The three main areas of focus which can be used to set appropriate objectives are:

1. Benefits from different activities, for example skills improvement, confidence building. This might be achieved by setting the skills level just above what everyone can manage and coaching people to attain the new standard, thereby giving them more confidence too.

2. Benefits for organisations, for example for those working to conserve the countryside. This might be achieved by groups undertaking the rebuilding of a broken down boundary wall or pathway. You could also expect some team-building benefits here too as group members cooperate to complete the task.

3. Benefits for individuals, for example development of teamwork and confidence. This could be achieved with a programme that incorporated adventure activities where participants had to perhaps find their own way or make their own camp and cook their own supper. Perhaps as part of an expedition.

A lot will, however, depend on the skills and abilities of the leaders or instructors to create the right contexts and facilitate the right kind of learning. You should always check that the centre you are going to use has staff experienced not only in the activities, but also in personal and team development.

Organisers' responsibilities

On page 264, in the section on community projects, it was made clear that the responsibilities of organisers were very important to the success of a

271

project or group activity. These need to often be carried out well in advance of the day and were not always apparent to participants. In this section we shall investigate a few of the most necessary for a residential or outdoor experience.

Health and safety

This is probably that factor uppermost in most parents' minds when their children go off on a residential which involves adventurous activities. Group leaders have to act in the role of 'loco parentis' as if they were parents, to ensure that no harm comes to children in their care. Health and safety covers a range of issues or 'hazards' which we don't have space to explore here, but we will highlight those most relevant to a residential as this section progresses.

Risk assessment is the process that all leaders should carry out with regard to aspects of the residential, such as transport, accommodation, activities. It involves five stages:

Assess what 'hazards' could occur, e.g. fire in the building, trips and falls on activities

Assess who might be harmed by these hazards, e.g. individuals, the whole group

Assess how likely these hazards are to occur and how severe they might be, e.g. a rope breaking or canoe capsizing — unlikely/likely — only affecting one person — serious though

Assess whether the measures in place are adequate, e.g. equipment is checked, fire appliances are present and in good working order, staff are qualified

Where you are not satisfied that all has been done, make some proposals to improve the health and safety measures, e.g. call in an expert, ask for more resources or staff

Figure 7.7 *The leaders of groups of young people about to engage in activities must make a risk assessment of the activities at the time they will be doing them, an example being water-based ones*

Risk assessments for outdoor activities are lengthy processes, but under the law they must be carried out. Most centres will have an adventure activities licence and will have had an inspection to assess a great deal of their provision, and you can check when this was last done by the AALA.

Staff or leaders should check the following (as an absolute minimum) when they arrive at the centre or ideally during the planning stage before you all leave. They should check that

- adequate fire appliances are present and have had a recent maintenance check
- staff are trained in first-aid practice and that sufficient boxes are positioned around the centre or are taken on an activity with groups
- all equipment to be used is in good working order and has been inspected recently, for example ropes for damage, lifejackets for buoyancy
- the programme and activities are right for the group and the conditions.

Where any gaps in provision are identified staff at the centre or from the group should ensure that measures are taken to bring things up to an acceptable safety level, for example correct equipment is bought or brought in (hired), hardware is given a proper service.

Failing that, a substitute activity replaces the one which staff are not happy to include for whatever reason. You may even go as far as cancelling the booking or finding a new provider or changing the course content. Be flexible and be safe.

A centre and the group need to have the right kind of insurance (see previous section) to cover travel accidents and personal possessions, for example. Some providers will include this in the cost.

Let's do it!

Carry out some research to find how much it would cost for

- accident insurance for a five-day hill-walking trip living under canva on Dartmoor
- a conservation project staying in a hostel in Wales
- travel insurance for a group of 10 to go from your home town to Scotland for three days in a minibus to work with disadvantaged children at a camp in the Borders.

Staff training and qualifications are key areas for organisers to check, particularly if you are using a private or voluntary provider. Organisers need to check that

- sufficient, qualified staff will accompany the group as per the governing body recommendations, for example for canoeing or hill-walking, that is they have BCU and MLTB awards
- staff have been trained to know the local area, for example routes, conditions, weather and tides; have adequate skills and know-how to use equipment to effect a rescue or evacuation; are trained to deal with participants who have an anxiety attack, for example in a cave.

Participants with special medical, dietary or even phobia needs have to have special consideration before the trip begins. This sort of information is usually gathered on a form at the planning stage, along with other information such as emergency contact numbers and home address.

Personal details	
Name: Age:	Address: Tel:
Person to contact in an emergency:	Address: Tel:
Special dietary needs:	Medical conditions:
Parental consent:	Signature:

Think about it

What else do you think could be added to the form for a week's outdoor activity residential?

Parents need to give permission for young people under 18 to go on a residential, so organisers need to issue a detailed breakdown of

- the content of the residential
- timings for departure and return
- contact details
- things to bring.

If there is a need to make parents aware of responsibilities organisers cannot take, then as well as giving a signature of approval parents may need to sign to say they will permit first aid to be given and not hold the organisers liable for certain aspects. This is called a disclaimer. It would not be reasonable to expect organisers to look after every possession each person has to take, for example, or to take responsibility for breakages.

Finally, organisers need to plan for contingencies such as bad weather or transport being delayed. In these cases you could plan an indoor activity to replace an outdoor one or some games to play while the transport arrived.

Let's do it!

Try to suggest some 'wet weather alternatives' for the following scenarios, for which you are the group leader:

1   Twenty boys from a scout troop have to spend an extra night in a log cabin in the forest due to torrential rain and flooded paths. What could you do to feed them, entertain them and reassure parents?

2   Nineteen girl guides are expecting their coach to arrive to take them home after a residential, but they receive a call to say it will be over three hours late. The weather is not good, but you cannot use the centre as it is being cleaned for the next group. How could you keep them dry and occupied?

Think about it

We live in a world where suing people for negligence is common. What impact do you think this might have on the attitudes of organisers towards residentials?

In summary

- Residentials are enjoyable ways to explore the countryside, learn new activities, improve your personal skills, and make a contribution to preservation.
- Centres exist all around the country that are willing to host residentials and can tailor their programmes to suit the nature of the party and its aims.
- Organisers have quite a few important responsibilities to carry out before, during and after a project or residential has been run.

Figure 7.8 *There are many benefits to be gained from doing land-based activities*

Assessment activity

For whatever grade you are working towards you need to describe the different benefits to individuals of participating in outdoor activity residentials.

CHECK WHAT YOU KNOW

1 List *three* outdoor activities which can be used for personal development.
2 How can going on an activity day help build teamwork?
3 Name *three* organisations which do voluntary work in the community.
4 Apart from team-building opportunities, what other abilities can be improved by doing an outdoor activity successfully?
5 Describe *three* main themes which youth projects offer the participants.
6 Identify three groups who can benefit from community projects.
7 Identify *three* benefits for the community in projects being successful.
8 Organisers have a great deal of responsibilities to carry out. Name two of these for (**a**) projects (**b**) residentials.
9 Describe a range of benefits which can accrue by taking part in a residential.
10 What is risk assessment?

Resources

Articles and books

Balazak, D (1995) *Outdoor and Adventure Activities for Juniors*, London, A & C Blackie

Beard, C M and Wilson G (2002) *The Power of Experiential Learning*, London, Kogan Page

Cloutier, K R (1998) *The Business of Adventure*, Kamlops BC Budhak Consultancy (USA)

Consalvo, C (1995) *Outdoor Games for Trainers*, London, Gower

Deknop, P and Standeven, J (1999) *Sport Tourism*, Leeds, Human Kinetics

Gartner, W *et al* (2000) *Trends in Outdoor Recreation and Tourism*, New York, CABI

Hall, C (1992) *Special Interest Tourism*, London, Belhaven Press

Lockren, I (1988) *Outdoor Pursuits*, London, A & C Blackie

Miles, J C and Preist, S (1999) *Adventure Programming*, Venture

Pigram, J and Jenkins, J (1999) *Outdoor Recreation Management*, London, Routledge

Roberts, L and Hall C (2001) *Rural Tourism and Recreation*, London, CABI

Ryan, C (1991) *Recreational Tourism*, London, Routledge

Tuson, M (1994) *Outdoor Training for Employee Effectiveness*, CIPD

Watt, D (1998) *Events Management in Leisure and Tourism*, Harlow, Longman

Journals

Climbing
Hiking
Journal of Adventure and Outdoor Learning
Leisure Studies/Sciences
Sailing
Skiing
Sports Management
Tourism Studies

Websites

Acorn Adventure – www.acornactivities.co.uk

Adventure Activities Licensing Authority – www.hmso.gov.uk

British Activity Holiday Association – www.baha.org.uk

British Canoe Union – www.bcu.org.uk

British Mountaineering Council – http://thebmc.co.uk

British Orienteering Federation – www.britishorienteering.org.uk

Central Council for Physical Recreation – www.ccpr.orpr.uk

PGL – www.pgl.co.uk

Royal Yachting Association – www.rya.org.uk

UK Sport – www.Uksport.gov.uk

Sport and recreation

Introduction

Sports and recreational activities have important roles to play with respect to peoples' lives and working in public services. They can benefit health, fitness and motivation, for example, both at work and away from it.

This unit takes you through a range of roles and uses to which sport and recreation are put, along with a focus on organising activities safely in different places. Towards the end a section is included on the planning and organising skills needed to stage effective activities.

The unit concludes with an investigation of benefits which accrue from regular participation, and a few summary questions to test your knowledge.

As you work through the unit it would be useful for you to refer to information in the following units:

- Unit 2 Public service skills
- Unit 3 Public sector fitness
- Unit 7 Outdoor activities and public services

As the unit is internally assessed, exercises will be integrated in the text at various points, so that you can build up your evidence and confidence.

How you will be assessed

To complete the assessment for this unit you need to have done some reading and research on the following before you present your evidence:

- The diverse roles of sport and recreation in today's society, that is some comparisons, motivations and uses.
- The importance of safety in a range of sports contexts, that is for individuals, groups and organisations or indoors and outdoors facilities.
- The benefits which can be gained from regular participation, that is personal benefits.
- The importance of planning and preparing well, that is for participation and hosting events.

- The value of keeping records of performance, that is attendance, PBs, improvements.

To access the higher grades your work will have to show that you have a really good understanding of the benefits of participating regularly and how to effectively plan and prepare for diverse sporting contexts found in the public services. Your work will need to be clearly and logically presented, with good use of terminology and evaluations, and analysis of the evidence. There are many opportunities to bring knowledge gained in other units into the assessment evidence such as Unit 2 Public service skills, Unit 3 Public service fitness and Unit 7 Outdoor activities and public services.

After completing this unit, you should be able to achieve the following outcomes:

1 Describe the role of sports and physical recreation activities and their uses within public services.
2 Investigate safety practices in sport and physical recreation activities for organisations and individuals.
3 Explain the importance of effective planning and preparation before participating in sport and physical recreation activities.
4 Participate regularly in a sporting or physical recreation activity and identify the benefits of participation for the individual.

The role and uses of sport and physical recreation within public services

Many different types of people work in the public services, and each one who participates in sport and physical recreation is likely not only to have a different reason (motivation) for taking part or using sports and recreation, but is also likely to choose a different activity too.

Let's do it!

Carry out a small survey with your class mates, family and relatives to assess the kind of people they are, what activities they prefer to do and why they choose to do these. Then enter your findings in the table below. One example is given to get you started. When complete, compare your survey with others in your group to assess the range of motivations and activities.

Category of person	Preferred activity	Reason for participating (motivation)
Teenager (brother)	Roller-blading	It appears cool and is done in fresh air
Adult		
Child		

Table 8.1

Hopefully your survey has given you an initial insight into users' preferences for certain activities. Let's look at some in more detail.

The role of sport and recreation activities

It will be helpful to clarify the differences between sport and physical recreation so that you are clear about the contexts for the purposes of this unit.

Sports are represented by games and competition such as football, cricket and tennis, involving the concept of winners and losers. Physical recreation describes equally skilful activities, but ones that are generally non-competitive and have different motivations, such as pleasure, challenge or exploration, with no real concepts of winners and losers, just enjoyment. Activities such as walking, skiing and diving could fit this category. With this in mind, let us explore the roles that sport and recreation plays in people's lives.

Fitness

Participants may choose to undertake a sport or recreational activity to get fit, stay fit, or improve their fitness levels. This may have been something you found out in your survey.

Case study

Improving fitness

Joe

Joe is a young adult who has found himself a new job, but finds some of the duties quite strenuous compared to being a student, such as lifting equipment or being on his feet all day. He feels that his stamina needs improving. To do this he decides to take up a sport 'to get fit' in terms of improving his strength and endurance. So he needs to choose an activity to achieve this.

Shirley

Shirley, a middle-aged woman working in the public sector, has always tried to 'stay fit' to help with her busy daily routine by doing a weekly aerobics session. She now wants to add a new sport to keep up her all-round fitness.

Harry

Harry is a 30-year-old fireman who is coming back to work after an injury and wants to 'improve his fitness' gradually.

1 What activities might suit what Joe wants to achieve?
2 What choices would you recommend for Shirley?
3 What range of activities could you recommend for Harry so that he improves gradually across a range of sports?

Stress reduction

Exercise has beneficial effects (psychological) through the endorphins which are released in our brains when we exercise. So we keep returning to our exercise routines to experience that feeling. In today's busy world many people, as they try to achieve a work–life balance, use their sport or physical activity to relieve stress created at work. Sometimes they see their activity as an escape route into a new less stressful world (for a while anyway). Why might this be so? Here are some examples.

Some people feel that working up a sweat, such as in an aerobics session or playing a game of squash, helps to clean the toxins out of their system and relieve stress. They can put the pressure of work to the back of their minds for a while and after having a hot shower their spirits are lifted and tensions eased.

Think about it

Have you ever experienced the sensations described above?

Other people may undertake a less strenuous route to tension relief such as a gentle swim followed by a dip in a Jacuzzi or a steam room session, or even a massage.

In both cases people try to create a different physical environment and activity as a contrast to their work environment. These are at opposite ends of simple activity spectrums, for example

Low impact activities ←——————————→ High impact activities

Non-competitive ←——————————→ Highly competitive

Case study

Assessing recruits for fitness

Potential recruits for the navy are being assessed by LA Fitness in a joint scheme with the Royal Navy. The scheme is aimed at preparing recruits for the Royal Navy's basic training so that they have an idea of how well they might do, or how much harder they need to train. Gyms around the country close to recruiting centres will be used for this service and should save many being disappointed at the first hurdle.

To access their sports and recreation activities people will use facilities run by organisations in one of three sectors:

- Public – local authority provision
- Private – limited companies such as Next Generation
- Voluntary (sometimes called the 'not for profit' sector) – local clubs and teams.

These are represented by facilities such as

- pools, pitches and play areas
- centres, clubs and country parks
- tracks, courts and bowling greens.

Figure 8.1 *Facilities need to be provided for people to participate in sport and recreation*

Skill levels and abilities vary enormously, but motivation and enjoyment are usually high.

In recent years certain social trends have developed to affect how we view and take our sports and recreation. Some of these include

- changes in working lifestyles and leisure time, giving some of us more time and different times
- higher levels of income, so more to spend on sport and recreational goods
- better transport systems, both public and personal, help access
- more awareness of the importance of health and exercise through education
- massive promotion of sports in the media.

 Think about it

Can you add other trends you have noticed?

In general there are more opportunities to play sport or take recreational activities for most people in the public services, through more courses, more centres, more coaches and instructors and development schemes. Although access and provision is far from equal for everyone, and fitness, ability and resources can restrict involvement for some people, sports organisations continue to add to the range most people can choose from, with new sports and locations being created year by year, much of it in recent years due to lottery funding.

 Think about it

Can you list three new sports or activities which have become 'fashionable' and name three new locations in your region which have recently opened?

Let's do it!

Using the results of your survey and the explanations given, identify a range of roles sports and physical recreation have in today's society.

Uses by different groups

You should now be able to identify that different groups of people use sport and physical recreation in different ways for different reasons. In this next section we shall look at six such groups in a little more detail. Our focus will be on

- children
- adults
- elderly
- youth
- disabled
- disadvantaged.

1 *Children* Children probably participate more in sport and recreation than any other group. It can form part of their play, their school curriculum and after-school clubs, even holidays. (Working with children is often the first voluntary task or job opportunity for young people working in the public services.) The motives can be diverse, such as play, competition, skills improvement, teamwork and social or developmental aims. We will look at these in more depth later.

Let's do it!

Create a list of sport and recreation activities for each of the previous roles, for example play, education, competition, skills.

2 *Adults* In adults, you might also identify the same motives of recreation, skills improvement, competition, but also the need to escape and relax.

Adults participate in the whole range of sports and recreation there is on offer in the UK, from low-key rambling to high-powered kick boxing. They use local authority sports centres, private gyms and compete at every level of sport from the village cricket team up to the Olympics.

Over a typical weekend there might be as many as 8 million adults engaged in some form of sport and recreation activity, some professionally, but more as enthusiastic amateurs.

3   *Elderly groups* For these participants some of the motives and the range of activities for doing sport and recreation are different. We might suggest they are less dynamic in nature, such as bowling or walking, but motivations could be the same, for example play, skill improvement, socialisation, which are common to many sports and recreational activities, but in the main we would expect health and fitness to be a prime role.

Let's do it!

Carry out some online research to identify what sport and recreation activities are on offer around the country in three public sector facilities (those run by local authorities) for the over-50s.

4   *Youth* Youth clubs and development projects use sport and recreation to engage young people in purposeful activities. This is often called social inclusion. The range is narrower as resources and space can be limited,

Figure 8.2 *Outdoor activities play an important role in the social development of young people*

for example in village or church halls. This category of user also tends to go into the countryside for outdoor activities such as camping and hiking, perhaps to do activities towards gaining an award, for example the Duke of Edinburgh Award.

Let's do it!

Can you identify other awards which youth groups might gain indoors and outdoors which are sport and recreation related?

5 *Disabled and disadvantaged* (e.g. low income or unemployed people)
These groups tend to have fewer opportunities and so for them access to sport and recreation can be an issue. However, sections of the public services will specifically target these groups to help bring them into sport in some way, for example sports development officers. Their feelings of success may be even higher than able-bodied or better-off participants, as in many cases they have to overcome bigger challenges to participate.

Case study

Health and fitness for the disabled

The government is really pushing for targets set in its strategy document *Game Plan*, and making sure that disabled people can also participate in attaining health and fitness targets.

A lottery-funded scheme was launched in the Autumn of 2003 to promote opportunities for disabled people to access health and fitness locations and programmes. It is run by a section of the English Federation of Disability Sport at 150 centres around the country. The aim of the scheme is to provide staff with training in sports development, use of equipment and how to market activities for the disabled. The scheme has been allocated £5 million.

Think about it

How would you judge the success of the above type of initiative to ensure the £5 million was well spent?

Let's do it!

Can you identify four types of disability and suggest sports which might suit the needs of the disabled?

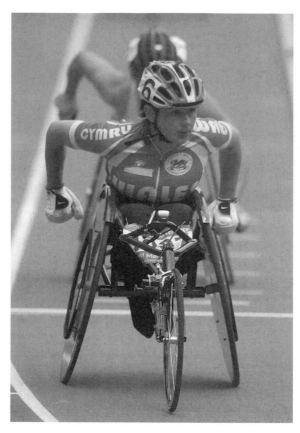

Figure 8.3 *Given the facilities, disabled people can achieve amazing feats, even winning gold medals at the Paraolympics, as in the case of Tanni Grey Thompson*

Non-sporting roles

Sport and recreation activities can contribute to other aspects of people's lives, particularly social and physical development and the opportunity they afford for travel and meeting new people and creating friendships. These are important factors worth considering a little more.

- *Social development* This means an individual's ability to develop personal skills on the field of play, but also outside the activity. This can actually mean
  - being able to act fairly and equitably with everyone in the team or opposition
  - being assertive, but not aggressive or manipulative
  - communicating clearly and fluently, without shouting
  - caring for others
  - being a good listener
  - developing leadership skills.

Let's do it!

Create some short examples in a sporting context to represent each of the above.

Physical development Sport and recreation covers aspects of physical development such as body shape, fitness, muscle tone and stamina and general health. Feeling good about yourself and your abilities gives confidence, and having good eating habits, training and practising regularly may well help you to develop to your full potential.

Opportunities for travel Those who play sport in a team are likely to travel to away matches during their season. This gives them a chance to see new areas of the UK or even Europe. Those who play in big competitions may even be given the chance to play further away than Europe. Recreationalists, as well as players, have an equal opportunity to travel as they follow their sporting interests, for example skiing, sailing and hill-walking.

Meeting new people This aspect goes with the previous one. Players and participants obviously meet other players and participants. If you are playing abroad you can also broaden your horizons by observing other cultures, perhaps becoming a tourist for a few days after your event or sports trip has ended. Many host clubs will provide hospitality after the game, giving another opportunity to socialise.

Case study

One way of meeting new people

LA Fitness is launching a speed dating service at some of its gyms around the UK. This is based on a survey that found that 63% of users felt they had a good chance of meeting a new partner at the gym. The marketing department of LA Fitness certainly believes this is true too, as it has been tried out at several clubs in Birmingham and London. Maybe they are hoping to host the wedding reception too?

What benefits do you think can be gained from meeting new people in this way?

Making new friends This is probably the most beneficial part of playing sport. Some athletes who compete against each other regularly build up friendships which last for life. In mixed gender groups friendships can blossom and may lead to marriage.

Let's do it!

Can you list two couples who have met and married through sport? This can be friends or famous people.

In summary

Sport and physical recreation have very diverse roles to play in our lives. They
- contribute to our well-being
- provide skills and confidence for other aspects of life
- motivate and provide fun and achievements
- facilitate travel and friendships
- are accessible to all ages and types.

Uses of sport and recreation in public services

People working in the public services may have some of the best access to sport and recreation because of the value that such organisations place on them and the resources they make available. There are benefits to an organisation providing sport and recreation facilities for its staff. We now explore some of these.

Maintaining staff fitness

A fit and healthy staff usually means fewer injuries and illnesses, the staff working more effectively and, probably, creating a good image to the public. For the more strenuous roles in the uniformed services, such as working in the fire, police or armed forces, maintaining fitness is crucial.

Case study

Working out

In Scarborough the local fire service teams work out regularly at the local authority sports centre in the town, in its fitness suite. The crews, in better weather, also enjoy a game of volleyball outdoors on the university playing fields or five-a-side football on its multi-play area. The crews take their fire engines with them and are in constant contact with their base should a call come in.

Reducing sickness

A fit workforce is far less likely to have days off for sickness. Keeping fit also involves looking after your diet, sleeping habits and exercise routine. When these are 'in balance' you are probably at your best for work as your immune system is raised by healthy eating and exercise and you are less likely to catch a 'bug' (see Unit 3).

Flu and other contagious illnesses easily spread amongst staff working closely together, so producing a chain-reaction as the bug 'does the rounds' in affecting other staff. The result could be disruption to work and shift patterns and stretching the other staff who have to cover for those off sick. Those who work even when they are sick are likely to have lower concentration levels and stamina, so could be a liability to themselves and others.

Anyone stressed by work might be able to relieve that stress by engaging in sport and physical recreation, as an escape from the pressures of work. The following phrases tend to capture the purpose of sport and recreation as a way of

- 'letting off steam', by having a competitive squash match
- 'getting away from it all', by going for walk in the country
- 'recharging batteries', by taking a short activity break.

Let's do it!

In small goups, think of two other problems created by staff being off sick and two other problems caused by being at work and not fully fit?

Teamworking

Sport and recreation are recognised as good team-building activities for public service staff. This is because

- sport allows some people to develop their leadership skills
- recreational activities done together help build relationships as people get to know each other better
- playing games according to rules helps with issues of fair play and equity
- post-match social activities help cement friendships away from work
- key aspects of sport such as tactics, cooperation and communication are just as relevant at work
- abilities learned through physical activities may transfer into the work context, for example giving, taking and following instructions, patience, and perseverance.

Figure 8.4 *You can learn a lot by being a member of a team. What might this photo show?*

Let's do it!

On you own, rank each of the aspects mentioned in order of importance for teamworking. Compare your list with those of others and discuss reasons for any differences.

Morale building

Many aspects mentioned in the teamworking section will contribute to the morale of staff working in public services, however some further dimensions are worth considering.

A successful sports team such as a cup-winning police football team, will create in that particular police station or in the local town a 'feel good factor' which improves morale. An individual officer's success may also build morale amongst his or her colleagues. Examples might be an outstanding marathon run or a win in a badminton tournament. The general feeling of well-being after a successful activity may carry over into work on a Monday morning, keeping morale high. On the downside, morale may be affected by poor performances, bad sportsmanship, defeats and disappointments.

For those in the public services the opportunities 'to compete' are high, both within their services and more widely, as in the police, RAF, fire, army and navy. Those services understand the benefits to morale building which can result.

Building confidence and life skills

A national scheme called 'Goalseekers' has been running successfully in Scotland since the summer of 2003. It is aimed at boosting motivation and self-esteem amongst disadvantaged teenagers and hopes to give them a boost towards employment too. The scheme is a partnership run jointly by Tulip Hotels, Careers Scotland, Glasgow City Council and Allsports, who are a group of coaches and teachers. The scheme uses team sports, such a football, and other physical activities (water-based) to build confidence and help develop life skills amongst the young people. It is hoped that behaviour and attitudes can be changed for the better.

Do you think this type of scheme could work elsewhere in the UK?

Community involvement

Many public service organisations play teams in local leagues or get involved in local tournaments. They may even host these events as they often have good sports facilities on site and good resources to support events.

The benefits of this type of community involvement are multifold:

- It gives something back to the community that supports them or, for example, for those who live close to a large military base.
- The image of the organisation is enhanced amongst local people.
- It helps to break down barriers, stereotypes and to build bridges between the service and the local community.

Let's do it!

Carry out some research (perhaps in the local press) to identify some public services teams that play in local leagues. What range of sports do they cover?

Staff development sport and recreation

Sport and recreation offers many opportunities to set challenges for staff, both personal ones and group-based ones.

Personal challenges include setting new targets in terms of 'best times', 'maximum repetitions', new levels or skills, overcoming fears and achievement of awards. Group-based challenges might include setting higher success targets, making fewer errors, using resources more effectively, meeting deadlines. Many of these can be achieved directly through sport, others through recreational activities, with the hope that good practice in this context might benefit or transfer to work modes too.

Let's do it!

Read more on the particular motivational theory conceived by Maslow, as this fits into this discussion.

Figure 8.5 *Maslow's model of motivation levels and factors*

Testing skills and abilities

Testing skills and abilities is likely to set challenging targets for staff. Good levels of fitness and adeptness at carrying out a specific task might mean, for example, that firefighters can put out a fire more quickly, or climb ladders fast, but safely. Good use of communications skills can defuse confrontations. These skills might be picked up on the football pitch, and used just as well in a prison conflict situation. Strength and endurance abilities might mean the difference between life and death if people need to be evacuated from a burning building. Calmness and control on the sports field might help you to cope better when under pressure at work. Cool-headed individuals are highly valued and much respected both at work and when the pressure is on during a sports event.

Let's do it!

Captaining a team takes ability and needs skills of decision-making, negotiation and tactical awareness, fairness, conflict resolution, setting targets, motivating others and good communication. Which of these skills would be useful in a work context and why? Put them in a priority list.

Encouraging people to join the public services

The public services need to find fresh new recruits every year, so if a public service has the image of a fit and healthy staff this can greatly encourage others to join that service. Opportunities to participate in sports and other physical activities can often be an important factor in helping new recruits to make up their minds whether to join a service or not. Because of this, it is a factor often used in adverts about joining the services.

Let's do it!

Using recruitment magazines or by carrying out an online search, identify how many services use the above approach in advertising to recruit new staff?

Similarities and differences in sports provision and physical recreation between services

Some services have identified that maintaining exercise routines and fitness activities are essential to carrying out the job. In the army, fire service and navy it is compulsory, so considerable provision is made to maintain exercise and fitness.

Other services do give basic training, but place the onus of responsibility on individuals to keep up their fitness through sport and physical recreation and don't often provide comprehensive facilities or schemes, as in the case of the police, ambulance and prison services.

At the lower end of the exercise and fitness ladder are groups such as the St John's or Red Cross ambulance members. They do concentrate on first-aid techniques, but usually don't have the facilities or expertise to keep their members fit. The volunteers who make up these services have to take care of their own fitness, as they may have to carry casualties, move over rough terrain to reach them and are often on site for long periods of time, until an event is over. All of this makes stamina, strength and speed important personal fitness factors.

Facilities provided

Some organisations provide sports facilities or recreational areas, with pitches, courts, gyms and recreation rooms. This however is often historical, that is the playing areas have been inherited. Fire stations often have a small gym, hospitals often have grounds with pitches, but RAF, navy and army bases always have greater provision, as 'fitness to fight' is a key concept in such services, a value that goes back to the origins of sport and recreation, maybe to Greek and Roman times.

Case study

Military-style training

Military-type training helped to give us modern gymnastics and exercise/training regimes and patterns, in those days called 'drill'. These drill sessions might even be remembered by your grandparents as the early name for PE! Routines were developed to get troops and recruits fit. However, after the wars these were still used by ex-forces fitness instructors as they became sports coaches or PE teachers. You can also trace fitness and skills for fighting in many of the Chinese martial arts and other combat sports, which today represent some peoples' recreation.

Can you think of any other sports today that have a military or fighting origin?

Let's do it!

Working in small groups, identify public service organisations and each group carry out a survey of the sport and recreation provision to assess the level of provision. Rank the organisations in order, with the most comprehensive first.

Assessment activity

For whatever grade you are working towards you will need to prepare a short presentation designed to describe 'The role of sports and recreational activities in the public services today'. Use illustrations and explanations for a range of different examples to support your points.

For a *pass* (P1, P2) you will need to describe the role and identify how public services use sports and recreational activities; for a *merit* (M1) you need to compare how the different public services use the activities; and for a *distinction* (D1) you need to show whether the use of these activities is justified.

Safety practices for organisations

We live in an increasingly complex society in which there are many laws, regulations and codes of practice to cover health and safety at work. The failure of an organisation to provide adequate safe working conditions according to law can leave them open to legal action by anyone who is injured as a result of that failure.

The application of correct procedures and safety measures is just as important for the public services as any other organisation. It could be said that the public sector should lead by example, setting the highest standards and enforcing them rigorously.

Much of our current requirements for safe practices stems from EU regulations and standards, brought in through UK legislation and overseen by the Health and Safety Executive (HSE). Most of the rest stems from common sense and best practice evolved over many years, however some are the result of bad accidents.

Employers are responsible for making sure the workplace is safe, and so are the employees. Here we will investigate a few key areas in sport and recreation that are most relevant to the public services.

Organisations

An organisation needs to make a risk assessment of the hazards which could occur in the workplace, such as poor electrical connections or boxes piled up in corridors, noting these and checking what measures are in place to prevent or minimise them. If these are inadequate in any way, then better ones need to be instigated, such as having the electrics fully checked and removing the boxes altogether.

In sport and physical recreation contexts, hazards may be even more common as many sports include combat or physical contact and many recreational activities include dangers such as falling off cliffs or drowning.

Let's do it!

List five sports and three physical recreation activities and opposite each identify two hazards. Create a chart to present your findings.

Risk assessment also requires that you weigh up who might be hurt (Chart 1), how likely the hazard is to cause a problem and how severe this might be (Chart 2). This process allows you to develop a time scale and priority list for any safety changes which need to be made (Chart 3).

Chart 1 The five steps to risk assessment

1 Review the location to be used and list the hazards you can find.
2 Identify the types of people who might be harmed.
3 Assess the adequacy of measures in place to prevent harm.
4 Propose or find out what improvements need to be made to the measures.
5 Implement these and review them as necessary.

Chart 2 Plotting the 'risk level' of each hazard

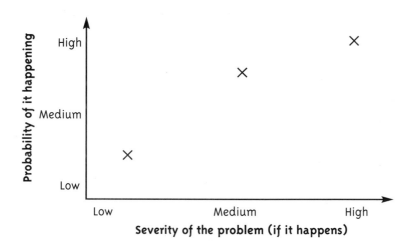

Chart 3 Evaluation of outcomes in Chart 2 (Scale of measures needed)

Type of hazard	Risk	Action
	High (probability)/ high (severity)	Urgent action needed immediately or stop!
	Medium (probability)/ medium (severity)	Action needed quite quickly
	Low (probability)/ low (severity)	Some action but a tolerable risk
	High (probability)/ low (severity)	?
	Low (probability)/ high (severity)	?

Table 8.2

Let's do it!

Try and insert an example of a hazard to fit all the blanks in Chart 3, then discuss what action would you prescribe for the two blank combinations in the chart.

We will now deal with some of the common hazards to help you understand the sort of public services measures and contexts in which they are dealt with.

1 *Provision of appropriate clothing* This is covered by the EU Personal Protective Clothing regulation. The clothing might be hard hats and boots in the workplace, safety helmets and harnesses in the outdoors, gum shields, padded helmets and shirts on the rugby pitch.

Let's do it!

In the following scenarios, what protective clothing would you recommend for
- fire personnel at the scene
- police in a busy town centre
- soldiers in training
- pit crew at a motor race track
- sailors who are ocean racing?

2 *Equipment needs to be used correctly and maintained to keep it safe for use* Whatever the situation at work or in a sporting or recreational context, there are always instructions on how best to use equipment. Sometimes this means following the instructions provided by the manufacturer, such as setting up a trampoline for a session or lighting a stove when camping. In other situations there may simply be a code or best practice to follow, such as when erecting a tent or preparing a dinghy for sailing.

Maintenance of equipment is a key safety factor in sports contexts, for poorly maintained equipment can jam up, break or fall apart, for example if it has not been oiled or stored correctly or had regular checks on its moving parts.

Organisations need to put in place procedures to make sure these requirements are followed by training staff in correct usage and maintenance.

Let's do it!

What safety requirements would you recommend for the following?
- A new piece of gym equipment which no one has seen or used before.
- New walkie-talkies issued to staff.
- Quad bikes to be used to cover difficult terrain.

3 *Insurance* Many types of insurance are available both for the individual and an organisation. They need to cover a range of situations in which people or an organisation might be found liable or might want to make a claim. Some versions which are likely to be found in sports contexts (both at work and play) include

- third party or public liability – to cover accidents to people while on the premises
- buildings and contents – to cover the fabric of the building and its fixtures and fittings
- accident – particularly sports injuries.

Failure to carry insurance can mean you are liable to fines, closure, imprisonment if you are found negligent; without insurance your possessions may be taken as payment if a court finds against you.

4 *Safe playing and working facilities (accommodation)* Nowadays the EU sets out standards for playing surfaces in terms of friction, rebound characteristics, texture and materials.

Governing bodies of sport will specify what the best surfaces are for their sport, so in this context things are well covered. If in using the wrong surface something was to go wrong, such as twisted knees or bruised heads after a fall, whoever was in charge might be found liable. A simple example might be an over-keen cleaner who polishes the sports hall floor to the slipperiness of a skating rink that has to be used the next day for playing badminton.

The correct parameters are also needed for sport and leisure, for example the run-off area, space around a court, roof height, lack of protrusions and obstacles. Too often equipment is stored around the perimeter of a sports hall creating hazards for players.

Think about it

Can you think of any examples of such hazards from your school days?

Organisers and owners of buildings are required to carry our risk assessments (as on page 298). In law they have 'a duty of care' for people on their premises.

Risk assessments

Examples of recommendations for measures to ensure safety in the public services are

- first-aid provision
- firefighting equipment
- trained staff
- briefings and practices
- regular checks.

First-aid provision usually requires qualified staff to be on duty and first-aid boxes to be in prominent places in the facility. The contents of a first-aid box usually includes

- sterile adhesive dressings
- sterile eye pads
- triangular bandages
- safety pins
- wound dressings
- cleaning wipes.

For general firefighting equipment you would expect to find

- water-based appliances
- appliances to fight chemical fires
- appliances to combat electrical fires
- fire blankets.

Staff training could cover a range of contingencies such as

- evacuation
- crowd control
- bomb scares
- injuries
- incidents
- theft
- violence and abuse
- attempted fraud.

Given all the above, there will still need to be dry runs and rehearsals, and retraining when changes are made to equipment or to legislation or to best practice. Organisers and organisations should have a planned programme and procedures for the year ahead, with updates and briefings either when necessary or perhaps on a monthly basis.

Case study

Safety, child protection and operational competences

One organisation you can contact for training in these types of needs is the new Sports Sector Skills Council. 'Skills Active', as they are called, will try to work with employees and employers who work in sport recreation, to improve the quality of training for staff in areas such as health and safety, child protection and customer service. This should also help develop motivation and stronger technical skills for staff as well.

What other skills do you think a member of staff running sports or recreational activities should have?

Let's do it!

In conjunction with your tutor, try to arrange a visit to a local police, fire or ambulance station or an armed forces base to assess how often they retrain staff, carry out maintenance and brief staff on equipment or safety processes. Evaluate and compare each organisation. Ask where they go for their skills improvement.

Dealing with contingencies

Some risk assessments or safety reviews have to be done while activities are in progress because of the possibility of changes in circumstances, such as a change in the weather, so that you can adjust the plans that have been made to take in the changes. These types of changes to plans are called contingencies and they can test your powers of decision-making, quick thinking and judgement. For example, if a storm was forecast to arrive in two hours and you were about to begin a sports day for 100 children, what decisions do you have to make? Who would you need to inform? What actions do you need to take immediately or in an hour?

The consequences of changing plans and making new arrangements can have quite an impact. Good leaders anticipate some of the possibilities and have contingency plans in mind, but there are always happenings that no one can predict. A range of impacts or consequences are considered below.

- *Changing the venue* The impact here will depend on how much notice you have about the change. A few days will give you time to organise to let participants know, even time to let spectators know, however any less time than this and you are faced with cancelling because there is just not enough time to re-arrange things.

- *Cancellation* This can have serious implications, such as your reputation being damaged, loss of revenue (unless insured), disappointments all round and maybe no chance to re-arrange the fixture.

- *Changing the route or course* This can occur in the case of a race, an expedition, a regatta, a climb because of bad weather or for other safety reasons such as congestion or bottlenecks. The crucial thing is to make the decision as early as possible, not to keep people waiting till the last minute, causing uncertainty and annoyance.

Information about participants

A key part of the planning stage is to gather participants' personal details to

- give you advance warning of any medical, physical, dietary or special needs
- leave behind as a data base
- provide communication details for emergencies.

A form like the one that follows could be filled in to provide required information about a participant.

Personal details form (all information will be kept in confidence)

Name _____ Age _____ Sex _____

Address _____

Tel (h) _____ (mob) _____

Emergency contact name _____ Address _____

Relationship _____ Tel _____

Dietary needs:

Medical conditions:

Medication or allergies:

Parental consent signature _____

Signature _____ Date _____

Think about it

Are there any other categories you could add to the form above?

If you are working with children under 18, then as a leader you are operating 'in loco parentis' (in place of parents) and must ensure a number of aspects of safety are covered. Parental consent must be sought for any activities or travel. Details of the leader's plans need to be left with a responsible person, for example route cards, check-in points, return times, names of those in charge. The department for education and skills and a number of other organisations, such as NSPCC, offer guidance on taking youngsters on trips of all sorts. When working in sport and other aspects of the public services your leadership skills and actions will be under the spotlight. Many organisations forget this and are pilloried in the press for their amateur approaches. Remember, always follow the published codes of practice.

Case study

Encouraging children to play more

The government has issued a paper called *Every Child Matters* which indicates that it thinks that children should be encouraged to play more, including more sport.

The government is proposing that a children's commissioner should be appointed to ensure that structured and unstructured play is encouraged more, both at and after school.

The Institute for Leisure and Amenity Management (ILAM) comment that more local authority leisure services should get involved to provide more opportunities for out of school play. (The ILAM website is also a useful place to visit for your studies in this unit.) Ministers in the government often speak out about the importance of physical activity as part of the health agenda, so it is welcome to read that a proposal is coming forward.

What might be the problems with the type of scheme mentioned in the case study?

Let's do it!

Carry out research online to find a code of practice for taking children on trips, sporting or otherwise. Compare your findings with those of others for similarities and differences.

Safety practices for individuals

Individuals are just as much at risk from negligent and poor practices as organisations, so many of the same principles apply. They are liable to be fined, disciplined, sacked, or even imprisoned, for unsafe practices – severe consequences. Under the law we have an obligation to follow safe working and sporting codes or procedures. There are a number of checks which can be made or practices that keep you on the right track, and we will consider a few in the next section.

Having a set of checklists for a range of occasions is a good method of ensuring you don't miss anything at the preparation stage.

One check you can carry out if using an outside provider is on the actual organisation itself. In the case of a sports provider you could check the

- qualifications of the instructors or coaches, to make sure they are on the Register of Exercise Professionals, for example
- suitability of the facilities
- safety record.

For an outdoor activity provider you should check

- whether they are licensed by the Adventure Activities Licensing Authority (AALA)
- the quality/suitability of equipment to be used
- the staffing ratios to be used.

Let's do it!

In small groups, suggest what checks can be made by an organisation that runs holiday football camps for children.

If you are a group leader you might devise a code of conduct for participants such as

- always follow the coach's instructions
- be polite and fair at all times to other players
- be on time for deadlines
- listen to the instructor's directions and descriptions.

Prior to any activity, it is the instructor's job to check that the equipment is safe and in good working order. If faults are found the instructor must report or record these and leave the piece of kit behind for repair or scrapping.

The use of equipment in sports contexts is very diverse. This means you can't always be an expert on its suitability, and may need to consult a more experienced or expert person. Don't take the risk of doing it yourself if you are not sure!

Figure 8.6 *Before setting out on any activity you need to have an expert check out the equipment to make sure it is safe to use, especially where lives could be at risk*

Here are some examples to give you a guide on checking equipment before going on an activity.

In preparing for a canoe trip you should

- check all the boats for damage or defects
- ensure the buoyancy is intact
- check all paddles for weaknesses
- check all buoyancy aids/lifejackets and helmets
- carry out a detailed check of the safety equipment staff can use, for example that the first-aid kit is in a waterproof container, throw lines are sound, flares are in date, radios, if carried, are charged up and all other emergency gear is stowed safely.

Think about it

Can you add anything more to this list? Try using the British Canoe Union website – www.bcu.org.uk

Let's do it!

Working with a partner and using the same principles above, create a checklist for a public services team travelling away for a hockey or football match and a group going for a day's hike on the moors.

One other good principle to follow before undertaking a new sport, event or activity is to take some preliminary instruction. Never assume everyone will be OK. There are certain benefits to be gained from a practice beforehand.

1. It helps everyone's confidence and shows the leader or coach who is not confident and might need extra practice or support.
2. It helps you learn the language of the sport or skills, so that if you are given a verbal command or instruction you know what it means and can do it.
3. Participants become familiar with the equipment and team mates.
4. Skill levels are usually increased giving more competence and allowing more enjoyment on the day.

Other basic rules can be followed which are fairly universal. These are

- leave details of your plans with a responsible contactable person, for example route, ETAs, emergency numbers
- collate everyone's personal details onto a form and leave these too
- check the weather forecast if the weather could affect your event or trip

- charge your mobile phone and key in some emergency numbers before you go
- pack a small personal safety kit (plasters, knife, wipes, string etc.).

Think about it

Discuss with a partner what one other 'golden rule' you would add to our list above.

Figure 8.7 *Before setting out on a trip you should make sure that you follow some basic rules on safety*

Assessment activity

For whatever grade you are working towards you will have to do the following activity. Working with a partner, prepare a report with three sections. Section 1 is to cover a description of the need for safety factors in sport and recreation. Section 2 is to cover the types of safety procedures organisations in the public services have to adhere to when doing sport or recreational activities. Section 3 is to cover what factors an individual needs to be aware of or follow when participating in or leading a sports event. Your report should clearly show which sections you each covered so that a balanced input is achieved.

To gain a *pass* (P4) you need to recognise there are differences in safety practices for individuals and organisations for sport and recreation activities; for a *merit* (M3) you need to specify what these differences are; and for a *distinction* (D2) you need evaluate these differences.

Effective planning and preparation

Here we will expand on the safety preparations and checklists that were covered in the previous section, which are just as important in the public services as elsewhere.

Keep the following motto in mind:

> PLANNING AND PREPARATION PRODUCE PERFECT PERFORMANCES

Planning

If you are working in a group or team (once you know your objectives) one of the best starting points is to create a team structure to cover everyone's roles and all the tasks which might need doing, such as finance, travel, kit, legal aspects. Figure 8.8 shows a typical structure, which could be adapted for a range of sports or services contexts.

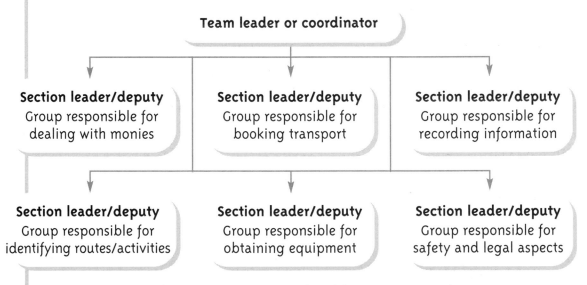

Team leader or coordinator

| **Section leader/deputy** Group responsible for dealing with monies | **Section leader/deputy** Group responsible for booking transport | **Section leader/deputy** Group responsible for recording information |

| **Section leader/deputy** Group responsible for identifying routes/activities | **Section leader/deputy** Group responsible for obtaining equipment | **Section leader/deputy** Group responsible for safety and legal aspects |

Figure 8.8 *This team structure can be adapted for use in a variety of contexts*

The second main challenge for a team in preparation for a sporting event or physical activity is to identify all the tasks it will need to perform (as part of its plan) to make it a success. This can be done by sitting down and making a list, for example by brainstorming all the activities and tasks in each area of the structure. The team can then decide on priorities and the order in which things need to get done. Out of this it is possible to create a 'flow chart of activities' such as the one on page 309.

Set objectives for the sporting
event or physical activity

↓

List all tasks/roles and
responsibilities needed

↓

Allocate roles and responsibilities

↓

Draw up a plan of action and
resources and a timetable

↓

After the event or activity evaluate
the initial objectives: what went well
and where the group/team could have
done better

Using our team structure we will investigate roles and responsibilities in a
little more depth and relate this to the flow chart plan wherever possible.

Team leader/coordinator

This person needs to have a clear idea of what the event/project/sports
activity is all about so that they can keep the individuals and teams on
track. Doing this requires a range of personal skills and clear objectives.
The personal skills are likely to be

- clear logical thinker
- good communicator
- commands everyone's respect
- can motivate and control people and activities.

The coordination will require

- a clear set of plans
- achievable objectives
- realistic deadlines.

 Think about it

What do you think are the attributes a good leader requires? Give a real example of
someone you feel is a good leader and say why.

Dealing with monies

In a sport and recreation context money will be needed for a range of purposes, for example to pay for fees, for transport, food, accommodation and kit washing. A budget should be set based on costs gathered from the team's areas of responsibility. It is important to stick to the budget agreed.

Money will flow into the club or team from subscriptions and perhaps sponsorship or donations. So the group dealing with monies needs to keep track of the flow of money and the amounts. This is probably best done with a simple income and expenditure account or cash-flow book, where all amounts and movements are recorded. This can be checked at any time to help other team members know whether they are within their budget limits for spending in the area of responsibility, for example transport. At the end of the activity or sporting event the group responsible for dealing with monies can report on the state of the account.

Income				Expenditure		
Item	Date	Cost		Item	Date	Cost
1				1		
2				2		
3				3		
		Total				Total
Balance				Balance		

Figure 8.9 *Example of a cash-flow book*

Booking transport

Most groups and teams are transported by mini-bus or coach and therefore sensible checks need to be made before making a booking, such as

- whether there are seat belts for everyone
- are the drivers properly qualified
- what amenities are onboard (e.g. video, music, toilets)
- how much storage space there is for luggage and kit
- is the vehicle/company insured
- what happens if there is a breakdown.

The company or drivers will need to know

- destination
- time of departure, arrival and return
- how many passengers
- how much kit there is to be carried
- any disabilities.

The group managing transport clearly needs to liaise with the monies group to report on costs.

Recording information

This role may well be important before, during and after the event.

Before the event

For example

- they may well need to create a list of personal gear players need to bring
- a list of names and personal details is needed
- travel details may need publishing
- contact numbers are required
- details of the opposition or venue/location for the event should be circulated
- preparing a copy of the 'plan' for everyone
- writing for permissions
- creating a risk assessment chart.

During the event

For example

- scores and scorers, performances and achievements need recording
- any post-match arrangements need circulating or posting up
- copying down any useful information
- keeping statistics.

After the event

For example

- sending letters of thanks
- reporting the event or match (press release)
- writing up official reports
- doing some satisfaction surveys
- submitting results.

 Think about it

What else can you add to the examples above from your own personal experiences of travelling to sports events, maybe with a public service youth group?

Identifying routes

It is particularly important when taking groups away to choose a suitable route. This might be discussed by the leaders, but it is likely to be dependent on a range of factors which the people organising the route need to take into consideration, such as:

- The nature of the trip, for example a hillwalk. In this case the route has to be interesting and achievable in the time. In the case of playing an away fixture of a football match, the route probably has to be the shortest and easiest way by road (coach/car) or by train. In the case of visiting a sports event, the route has to offer such things as stop-offs and good parking at the other end.

- The makeup of the group, for example youths or adults, mixed or single sex, how many there are, as each will have different requirements, such as the types of stop-offs.

- Duration of the visit/excursion, for example a short fixture close by will not have the same needs as a three-day tournament in another city.

The role of those preparing the route will be to make sure everyone, and especially drivers, have a note of the directions and venues or meeting/departure points; the time schedule; the contingency plans, for example phone numbers to make contact if held up.

In special cases, such as a hillwalk, the route needs to take account of the party's capabilities, weather prospects, escape routes, camping areas if this is a feature of the trip, drop-off and pick-up points and any natural hazards. A route card should be left with a responsible person giving details of paths to be followed, expected timings and escape routes, with a list of walkers and maybe a mobile phone number.

Let's do it!

Devise a contingency plan that you could use if a carload of team members had not arrived at the fixture half an hour before the start.

Obtaining equipment and clothing

The group or person organising this aspect is really in charge of important resources and needs to have an eye for details, as each person in the party might have specific needs apart from the team needs. In sport and physical recreation contexts the remit here could be very broad, so whoever is selected for this role needs to have a good knowledge of the sport or activity which is going to be pursued so that they can plan appropriately well in advance.

Figure 8.10 *The appropriate clothing is vital for whatever activity you choose to do*

A checklist is given below to provide some guidance on good basic principles of managing resources such as equipment and clothing.

You need to check

1 *Who* will be travelling/playing.
2 *What* kit will be required and where it is kept.
3 *Where* the kit is at the moment.
4 *How* you will get access to it and transport it.
5 *When* you need to have it ready by and returned by.
6 *If* you need to give individual/personal lists to participants.
7 *Which* participants have special needs.

Think about it

Can you add any other suggestions to the above list?

Joining a club and membership fees

Most clubs will have a constitution and a committee which runs its affairs. They are also likely to have a membership scheme which will involve you, if you join the club, in following certain rules or codes and paying an annual membership fee. The membership fee can cover things like

- insurance
- contributions to the club's funds/fixtures
- affiliation to a sports governing body (player registration)
- costs of a coach
- running costs of the club
- cleaning of kit
- travel expenses.

Joining a club means you have certain responsibilities towards that club and the other members. You would be expected to behave correctly, play fairly, not bring the club or your sport into disrepute and perhaps wear their uniform/strip/tie with pride. Should you transgress the club rules you might be disciplined, fined, dropped from a team, banned or even thrown out of the club altogether.

Think about it

Joining a club involves certain responsibilities and expectations which cannot be ignored. Which ones are these?

If we put this into the context of our planning and preparation section, the group taking fees and handling memberships needs to make it clear to applicants what is expected of them once they join, for example what standards of behaviour and contributions are required. They might devise a small club or group handbook to show these requirements, along with fixtures or outings and costs in a calendar format, which could be given out when fees are paid.

Seeking permissions from landowners

Getting permission to play on or use a piece of land is not just a politeness, but a requirement in some cases under the law, otherwise you may be accused of trespassing and causing damage – serious offences. The group or person organising this aspect will probably have to do so well in advance in order to ensure that permission is given in time.

For sports fixtures there are usually simple processes to go through to make bookings, as in the case of arranging to use local authority courts and pitches. This can be done with a simple phone call or by filling in an application form. Where spectators might attend, check that the venue is suitable for them too.

For physical recreation in the countryside, the permission process can be lengthier. Hiking across someone's land needs permission, camping in a farmer's field needs permission and paddling down someone's stretch of river also needs permission. Access agreements are usually in place for more popular routes, but no permission is needed if you are using public land or a recognised pathway. Where permission has to be sought a polite letter well in advance should secure a positive response, but always have a backup route in mind in case of a refusal. Farmers sometimes refuse permission in the lambing season and landowners who shoot for sport may do this in the shooting season. Fishing clubs may refuse the right to paddle down a piece of river if it is a popular fishing spot.

Think about it

For what other reasons might an organisation refuse access?

The best advice for organisers in charge of permissions is to make contact early and do their homework about what is possible.

Assessing safety factors

In the section on health and safety, pages 297 to 301, we covered risk assessment, which is the basis of how you assess risk these days. You can refer back to these pages to follow the model given.

Organisers in charge of safety need to apply the models on page 298 to every situation in turn, such as transport, the actual event, children's needs, equipment, the venue being used or the trail being followed, participants and spectators or parents. The measures in place can then be assessed as adequate or inadequate and adjustments or recommendations and changes made. When the organisers are not sure an expert opinion can be sought.

Let's do it!

Using the situations quoted above, make a list of factors you would wish to check for safety purposes.

Preparation

Planning gives you the 'blueprint' to follow for your sport or physical recreation experience. Preparation is actually doing something in real terms before you go which will help you be ready or see the project through. Some general factors which would nearly always count for public service related organisations would be fitness and resources.

Fitness

As any athlete or coach will tell you, getting fit and staying at the peak of your fitness is the key to giving great performances, however it's not just about fitness. Nutrition, sleeping habits, lifestyle and exercise patterns all count as well.

Having an appropriate and progressive exercise routine will enable you, or a team, to keep your potential high. This is usually combined with skills practice to keep sessions enjoyable and up to competition standards. Every sport or physical activity has its own prerequisites, just as every coach has his or her preferences for the content of a session. Important factors in a training session which covers skills and exercise and aims to improve fitness are likely to be

- an appropriate aerobic warm up
- balance and coordination skills
- speed training
- some endurance activities
- flexibility
- personal skills
- team tactics
- specific leg or arm work
- specific 'game' skills
- an appropriate cool down session.

Figure 8.11 *It is important to warm up before exercises and to cool down after doing them*

Case study

Commit to get fit

One of the best examples of a commitment to get fit has been a campaign by that very name launched by the Fitness Industry Association in 2003. Launched at the beginning of the summer the scheme encourages people to sign up for a taster period, but with charity fund-raising motives as well. The programme was run in fitness centres around the UK and the funds raised went to the Marie Curie Foundation in the first year (2004). Awards were given for the highest number of converts, the most innovative scheme for fund raising and the largest amount of money raised.

After training sessions, players and athletes should also allow some time for resting, taking care of their dietary and injury needs and of course enjoying themselves before the next session.

 Key point

Balance is the key word in preparation, which means a balanced diet, sleep and exercise/fitness programme, blended with a training regime that allows you to peak at the right times.

Let's do it!

Working with a colleague, devise a training regime for one of the following athletes or players for a pre-season period of eight weeks.

- A swimmer competing at club level.
- An 800-metre county standard runner.
- A football player playing in a local league.
- An international netball player.

Equipment checks

Another key element in preparation for public service groups is 'attention to detail'. The more you get ready before an activity the less you will be running round trying to do things on the day! We have discussed equipment checks previously, on pages 305 to 306, but here are some generic reminders. You should check whether

- things work
- you have enough (and maybe some spares)
- you can get replacements in time
- proper maintenance has been undertaken
- all the parts are there.

If the resources include kit (clothing mainly) of any sort here are some other reminders. Kit should be

- clean and complete
- the right colours (home or away)
- fit for purpose
- in good repair.

 Think about it

Can you add any relevant reminders to the two checklists?

The benefits of regular participation

As we mentioned previously, taking part in sport or physical recreation has more than just fitness and skills benefits, it enables you to meet or play against other people. Some people, particularly older ones, enjoy the social aspects perhaps more than the activity side. You may have different motives from others in your class for participating in sport or recreational activities and you may find you have an identity as someone who represents a particular sport or club with pride. These concepts are worth exploring further.

Regular participation

Regular participation will always be valued by public service organisations. You can participate regularly in a range of ways by

- attending courses – these could be player improvement, exercise and fitness, performance enhancement types of courses
- joining an activity club, such as those which exist for outdoor activities – canoeing, climbing, sailing, windsurfing, diving, skiing.

Figure 8.12 *There are plenty of facilities offering the opportunity to participate in sport and leisure activities*

Let's do it!

Identify an example of each of the above types of club in your area.

- joining a sports club, such as a rugby, football, cricket, hockey or netball club – these tend to be what we call 'the grass roots clubs', representing the main way in which people in this country partake in sport
- taking out a gym (fitness centre) membership – in recent years thousands of people have taken up exercise with a public or private gym as the interest in health and fitness has spread throughout the country

Let's do it!

Identify how many private and public gyms there are in your town or local area and find out what the average membership costs are in each type.

Regular attendance of course means going more than once a week. To get real benefit out of exercise you need to take part at least three times a week for at least half an hour each time. With more of us leading sedentary lives this sort of regularity helps to keep health and lifestyle in balance.

Benefits for individuals of regular participation

The benefits of exercise for individuals are physical, social and mental. No two people are likely to have identical benefits because of their individuality, nonetheless we can summarise the general benefits for those who participate regularly. The following shows some of the benefits. You can use this table to build up more examples for analysis.

Benefit	Types of sport or physical activity offering this
Increased fitness	Aerobics, running
Stamina	Marathon running, long-distance canoeing
Strength	Weightlifting, Sumo wrestling
Understanding others	Team games, representative matches
Relaxation	Yoga, walking
Friendship	Team games, pairs events
Additional skills	Better balance, improved coordination
Confidence	Judo, team captaincy

Table 8.3

Let's do it!

Add two more examples of benefits in the contexts boxes of the table.

We can look in more detail at the benefit of 'understanding others' in the following case study, which sheds some light on this aspect.

Case study

Benefits for disaffected young people

A scheme to help disaffected young people get back in touch with themselves and society has received the support of the Sports minister. PE teachers are being encouraged to try and re-engage disaffected youngsters using sport as a medium. They are being helped by other organisations such as the Youth Sport Trust and BSkyB. The government has a behaviour improvement scheme which is run through local authorities and the success of PE teachers in recapturing these disaffected youngsters is being monitored. The focus is on understanding others through sports activities, to help share values and give better standards of behaviour.

1 What are the weaknesses of this type of programme?
2 How do you think it will affect the target group?
3 How could the public services help in a scheme like this?

Key point

A great deal of research has shown that we are getting more obese as a nation, taking our leisure in less active ways (e.g. solo electronic modes), living 24/7 lives and eating poorer diets. The benefits of regular exercise, good diets and a regular sleep pattern are highly valued for long active lifestyles and the demands made of people working in the public services.

Assessment activity

For whatever grade you are working towards you will have to do the following activity. For a *pass* (P5) choose an activity and prepare a report on how you would plan and prepare for taking part in this activitiy. For a *pass* (P6, p7) complete a diary of your personal experiences in participating in sport regularly and show the benefits you feel you gained. In a short essay explain for a *merit* (M4) and evaluate for a *distinction* (D3) the benefits individuals and organisations can gain from regular sporting or recreational participation.

CHECK WHAT YOU KNOW

1 Explain the basic differences between sport and physical recreation activities.
2 Describe a range of roles sport and physical recreation can play in people's lives.
3 Identify some traditional sports facilities and some new ones, then describe what lifestyle trends these might reflect.
4 List some personal and work-related benefits that can accrue from regular participation.
5 What are the *five* stages of risk assessment?
6 Write down a list of the information you would collate prior to a group going on a trip.

7   Explain the phrase 'loco parentis'.
8   What can you use checklists and flow charts for?
9   Make up 'five golden rules' for planning a sports event.
10 Describe *four* benefits from participation: two mental and two physical.

Resources

Books

BAALPE (1990) *Safe Practices in PE*, City of Chester

Barker R *et al* (2204) *BTEC National Sport*, Oxford, Heinemann

Scott, T (2001) *GCSE PE for Edexcel*, Oxford, Heinemann

Beashel P and Taylor J (2000) *Understanding Sport*, Cheltenham, Nelson Thornes

CCPR (1994) *Expedition Handbook*, London, CCPR

English Sports Council (1997) *How to Find Out about Sport and Recreation*, London

Houliham B (2003) *Sport and Society*, London, Sage

Outhart A, Taylor L, Watt D and Barker R (1999) *Intermediate GNVQ Leisure and Tourism*, London, Harper Collins

Journals

Leisure Management

Leisure Manager

Navy News

Police News

Royal Air Force

Soldier

Sports Management

Websites

Sport England – www.sportengland.org.uk

Sportscoach UK – www.sportscoachuk.org.uk

Central Council for Physical Recreation (CCPR) – www.ccpr.org.uk

Adventure Activities Licensing Authority (AALA) – www.aala.org.uk

British Activities Holidays Association (BAHA) – www.baha.org.uk

Health and Safety Executive (HSE) – www.hse.gov.uk

Institute for Leisure and Amenity Management (ILAM) – www.ilam.org.uk

Institute for Sport and Recreation Management (ISRM) – www.isrm.co.uk

Crime and its effects

Introduction

This unit is designed to help you understand the impact crime can have on the lives of individuals, communities and society at large. This includes looking at services provided for victims by the government and charities and the cost of these to the taxpayer. The unit also looks at the various methods of reporting and recording crime and the statistics compiled from recorded crime. It also examines how crime statistics can be used to understand crime trends which can help in the detection and investigation of crime. You will also examine how offenders are managed once they have passed through the criminal justice system. This includes a look at the prison and the probation services and the various methods of sentencing that are available to the courts when dealing with offenders. Finally, you will consider the implications of the Crime and Disorder Act 1998 and look at how this piece of legislation aims to reduce crime and improve local communities. You will look at these different topics in order to be able to tackle your assignment which is based around the learning outcomes.

After completing this unit, you should be able to achieve the following outcomes:

1 Identify the effects of crime on the community and the individual.
2 Explain the crime recording and reporting system.
3 Examine the methods of offender management.
4 Explore the crime and disorder legislation and the strategies to improve the community.

Crime and its effects

Understanding the impact of crime is very important in most public service jobs. The emergency services, such as the police service, fire service and paramedics, deal either with the victims of crime or with the consequences of crime every day. In addition, the armed services are used increasingly as international peacekeepers and often have contact with civilians in other countries who have suffered appalling human rights abuses during times of war or internal conflict. So whatever service you intend to join, you will learn to understand crime and its effects and be able to deal with victims of crime in a sensitive and responsible manner.

 Think about it

Do you think an understanding of crime is important in the service you wish to join? Explain your reasons.

In addition to being able to deal with the emotional reactions to crime, such as anger, fear and resentment, you must appreciate that studying crime can tell you a great deal about how and why it happened and how the public services can prevent further instances of the same crime. It is said that once a person has become a victim of crime they are much more likely to be victims of crime on subsequent occasions. This can be a problem particularly in the case of people who are seen as more vulnerable to crime than others, such as the elderly, children, women and ethnic minorities. However, this vulnerability doesn't mean that 'at risk' groups will actually become victims of crime, actually they may be less prone to crime because they are more aware of their vulnerability and therefore take less risks than others. We will now explore people's fears and concerns about crime and the services which are there to support them.

Perceptions

Fear of crime

People are naturally concerned about crime. It would be unusual if they were not, considering the way crime is represented in the media, particularly in police and crime shows on television. The fear of crime is a response to real or imagined threats, such as mugging or burglary. Remember, the threat doesn't have to be real: even imagined threats can make people very frightened. The fear may not be because there is an immediate danger, it could develop from being aware of environmental

Figure 11.1 *The sort of environment people live in can contribute to their fear of crime*

threats, such as street graffiti or poor street lighting. This can create considerable concern, especially among those living in high crime areas. So, fear of crime is not straightforward. People will be more or less afraid depending on whose company they are in, their location, the time of day and their own personal experiences of crime.

The degree of fear varies. Some offences cause more fear than others, for example the fear of sexual assault is much more frightening than fraud or vandalism. Some people feel more fear than others, for example pensioners feel more fear of crime than younger people, and parents feel more fear for their children than they do for themselves, especially when they hear about child abuse and the crimes of paedophiles.

According to a Home Office study conducted by Hough (1995), people in general worry most about burglary, rape and vehicle crime. This is because the majority of crimes committed in our society are property crimes. You may be surprised by this, given that most of the publicity has to do with violent crime; in fact your property is much more at risk of crime than you are.

Other key points that were made in this study are:

- Residents of towns and cities have more fear of crime than people in rural areas. This would seem to make sense since statistics show that the majority of crime is conducted in urban areas such as towns and cities.
- People aged 60 and over tend to worry more about personal safety than younger people. In addition to the study described above, a study

conducted by the charity Age Concern found that almost 50% of people aged 75 or older were too afraid to leave their homes after dark because they thought they would be subject to assault or abuse. Over 20% said that this fear of crime had contributed to a sense of loneliness and isolation from the wider community.

- Individuals with an Asian cultural heritage tend to worry more than the white population.

Why are people so frightened?

There are many reasons why people tend to be frightened of crime. The Home Office has produced a Crime Reduction Toolkit that contains the following reasons why individuals and communities tend to have strong concerns about crime.

1 *They live in a high crime area* The area they live in is subject to a great deal of interpersonal and property crime which causes people to have genuine concerns about their risk of becoming a victim.

2 *They have already been a victim of crime* Once a person has been a victim of crime they are more likely to be targeted again. Having a crime committed against you makes you much more frightened and concerned and this fear can affect every aspect of a person's life.

3 *They feel vulnerable* If a person feels that they are particularly vulnerable to crime they will be much more frightened than usual.

4 *They are poorly informed* Most people do not know their real risk of being a victim. The majority of the population has a very low risk of being a victim of crime, but they think they are at high risk because of the things they hear in the media and the stories they hear in the community.

5 *They feel powerless and isolated* If people feel that they are alone and can do nothing to defend themselves or their property they will feel more afraid of crime.

6 *They have been subject to anti-social behaviour* Anti-social behaviour, such as verbal abuse, nuisance neighbours or young people, can frighten many people and make them feel more vulnerable to crime. This is especially the case when trying to do something to stop the anti-social behaviour of others.

7 *State of the local environment* If a local environment looks run down, has lots of graffiti, poor street lighting, drug paraphernalia or boarded up windows, it gives an impression of a crime-ridden area and so increases people's fear of crime.

8 *Poor public transport* If public transport runs infrequently, then this can leave people feeling isolated and unable to escape from their local community unless they have their own transport. In addition, a lack of public transport might leave people with a very long walk home leaving them feeling very vulnerable during the journey, especially at night.

Think about it

Look at the list above. Can you think of any other reasons people might be frightened of crime?

What types of crime have people experienced?

You will understand the fear of crime better if you know what crimes are more common than others and which crimes people have experienced in their own life. There are several ways of finding out what kinds of crime individuals and communities are subject to. These are:

1 *Police statistics* These are the official figures of crime collected by the police and published by the Home Office.

2 *Victimisation surveys* These can be large-scale or small-scale surveys and involve asking people what crimes they have been a victim of in the last year. The best known large-scale survey in the UK is the British Crime Survey, which is conducted every year and asks about 40,000 individuals over the age of 16 about their experience of crime in order to build a picture of crime overall in the country.

Police figures and British Crime Survey statistics often differ in terms of how much crime they show and what kinds of crime appear to be the most frequent. There is now a report which combines the two sets of figures: Crime in England and Wales 2002/3 (Simmons *et al*) highlights the following information about fear of crime:

- 73% of people surveyed believed that crime had risen in the previous two years. This is despite the fact that the crime figures have shown an overall decrease in crime rates every year since 1995.

- Many people greatly overestimate the risks of being a victim of crime. The table below shows how likely people thought they were to be a victim of crime compared with the actual risk.

Crime	Perceived risk	Actual risk
Theft from a car	25%	6.8%
Burglary	19%	3.4%
Violent attack	13%	4.1%

Table 11.1

As you can see, the worry that people have over being a victim of crime is not the same as the actual level of risk. This means that the vast majority of people are a lot safer than they think they are. Nevertheless this fear of crime can have enormous consequences on the everyday lives of individuals and can prevent them from doing all kinds of things.

Let's do it!

Pick 10 common crimes and ask 20 people if they have been a victim of them in the last year. Which crimes are most common in your survey and which are least common? Why do you think this is? (Remember not to ask about extremely personal crimes such as domestic violence or sexual assault, or you may offend people.)

Fear of crime and its effects on lifestyle

Fear of crime can have a huge impact on lifestyle. The study by Hough described above found out that between 1 and 2% of the population *never* go out at night because they are frightened of crime. Imagine the impact of this on the social life of individuals and communities; it would prevent most of the socialising we take for granted such as trips to the cinema or pubs. The Crime in England and Wales 2002/3 study by Simmons found that 29% of people never walk alone in their area after dark in the autumn and winter and 7% of the population say that their lives are greatly restricted by fear of crime. These restrictions on people's lives include the following:

- 5% of people carried personal attack alarms
- 5% of people chose to carry weapons
- 30% of people usually travel with groups of friends for safety reasons
- 35% of people organise special transport arrangements, such as a taxi or a lift from a family member, rather than walk home or use public transport
- 40% of people avoided walking near people who they thought might be a threat

Figure 11.2 *The presence of street gangs and the fear of them can restrict the way people live*

In addition, people's lifestyles might also be affected because of stress-related health problems, anger and resentment towards the criminals and a withdrawal from social contact with others.

Think about it

What crime prevention precautions do you take in your day-to-day activities?

Let's do it!

Look at the list above that describes how people take precautions to protect their personal safety. Do you think they are sensible precautions or an overreaction? Explain your reasons.

Vulnerable members of the community

Victims of crime

The study of victims of crime is a relatively new area of research. Up until about thirty years ago the majority of research focused almost entirely on the offender, ignoring the victim. However, recently pressure groups which support victims have highlighted how important it is to understand why some people become victims and not others, and how important good quality support services are to help victims after they have experienced crime.

All kinds of people can be vulnerable to crime and some people are more vulnerable than others for certain crimes, for instance a car owner is vulnerable to car crime whereas someone who doesn't own a car is not. The idea of being a victim is connected with ideas of being passive and helpless, and typical victims are assumed to be especially in need of protection. These are:

- *Children* They are seen to be vulnerable to abuse, abduction and bullying.
- *The elderly* They are seen as vulnerable to distraction crimes (e.g. being distracted by a caller while an accomplice steals from them), street robbery and physical assault.
- *Individuals with disabilities* They are seen as more vulnerable to physical attack and robbery.
- *Ethnic minorities* They are considered vulnerable to racist attacks, graffiti, verbal abuse, property crime.
- *Lesbian/gay/bisexual/transgendered individuals* They are considered vulnerable to homophobic attacks and verbal abuse.
- *Women* They are seen as more vulnerable to physical and sexual attack.

Assessment activity

To gain a *pass* (P2) you need to be able to identify the vulnerable members of society and describe the types of crime they might become a victim of.

Key point

The term 'victim' is now considered inappropriate by many because of its negative associations; the phrase 'survivor of crime' is now often used instead.

The perceived vulnerability of the groups above is said to make them easier targets for crime. In fact the statistics seem to show that regardless of whether you belong to a vulnerable group or not, the main reason you will encounter crime is based on your lifestyle. This is because people who never go out are unlikely to have to deal with crime, whereas those who live, work or spend leisure time in public places are at increased risk. Ironically, the people who we see as being more at risk in the list above may actually be much safer than the people we view as being able to protect themselves! The 1982 British Crime Survey showed that the people with the highest risk of being a victim were

Figure 11.3 *Some people are more likely to be victims of crime than others*

Think about it

Beryl is a 63-year-old woman living in a wealthy rural area of Dorset. Beryl doesn't drink and only goes out to socialise with her children and grandchildren. What is her risk of being a victim of a crime?

Reducing fear of crime

There are many things that can be done to improve an individual's and a community's fear of crime. If you consider the eight main reasons why people are frightened of crime listed earlier in this unit on page 325, then you can come up with strategies designed to tackle them. These strategies are particularly appropriate for the police and local authorities to use in reducing fear of crime and they are adapted from the Home Office Crime Reduction Toolkit, which you can find at www.crimereduction.co.uk. The strategies are listed below.

Reasons for fear of crime	Ways to reduce fear
They live in a high crime area	• Introduce a programme of effective crime reduction measures • Communicate to ensure that the community is aware of the action you have taken
They have already been a victim of crime	• Intervene quickly after the first reported incident to try to prevent a second or third occurrence • Encourage the person to get in touch with Victim Support
They feel vulnerable	• Offer reassurance to individuals or groups who are considered to be vulnerable • Develop positive policies to tackle hate crime which often targets ethnic minorities and LGBT groups • Try to meet with vulnerable groups on a regular basis to let them know what is being done to help them feel safer • Talk to vulnerable groups to gather their ideas on what could be done to help them feel safer • Make sure police officers are visible in communities – it makes people feel safer • Show vulnerable groups how to keep themselves safer by taking sensible precautions to protect themselves • Make vulnerable groups feel comfortable reporting crime to the police

They are poorly informed	• Try to get crime success stories in the local newspapers and radio stations • Send out leaflets and flyers to residents letting them know what is being done to reduce crime • Make every effort to contact traditionally hard to reach groups such as minority ethnic elders and older women living on their own
They feel powerless and isolated	• Consider neighbourhood schemes, such as a New Neighbours Scheme, where newcomers are greeted by a resident and told about the new area, or neighbourhood watch schemes which empower residents to take responsibility for community safety • Gather the views of the local community to make them feel valued and involved in the efforts to make their community safer • Develop youth schemes which will have an impact on reducing youth nuisance and make young people less isolated
They have been subject to anti-social behaviour	• Anti-social behaviour can reduce the quality of life and in a local area it can be combated by measures such as increased police presence or the use of community wardens • Police can make visits to primary and secondary schools to warn children about the impact of anti-social behaviour on others
State of the local environment	• Ensure there is adequate street lighting • Encourage lots of open well kept highly visible spaces • Remove graffiti as soon as possible • Keep roads and pavements in good repair • Regular street cleaning patrols • Take away abandoned cars as soon as possible • Repair boarded-up windows • Hold discussions with local community groups • Use CCTV to monitor the environment where necessary
Poor transport facilities	• It is important to keep buses and trains safe for travelling and bus stops and train stations should be well kept, well lit and safe • Use CCTV and well trained transport staff to encourage users to feel safe. • Provide transport users with up-to-date information and timetables to enable them to plan their journey correctly and safely • Ensure telephones, staff locations and helplines are available to make transport users feel less isolated • Ensure all groups in a community have access to travel information, perhaps publishing it in some community languages or Braille • Ensure car parks are safe and secure, staffed and well lit

Table 11.2

Assessment activity

To gain a *pass* (P1) explain why people are afraid of crime and describe the measures which can be taken to reduce those fears.

Personal safety

Being sensible about your personal safety is a key method of avoiding becoming a victim of crime. There are many things that you can do on a day-to-day basis to enhance your personal safety without compromising your lifestyle too much. The list below describes some of the possible ways of keeping yourself and others safe:

Keep yourself safe

- You should think about how you would act in different situations before you are in them. This will help you plan for and deal with any potential crime situations you might encounter. For example, imagine how you would defend yourself if you were attacked or how you would get home if your car was stolen.
- Stick to bright and well-lit areas, avoid dark alleys or isolated areas where help might not be readily available if you need it.
- Do not look vulnerable to others who might want to commit a crime against you. If you are walking confidently and look capable they might be deterred from selecting you as a victim.
- Do not keep all your personal valuables in one place. This means that if you have your bag stolen the thief won't get everything.
- It is always better to run away if you can rather than stand and fight.
- If you are being mugged, let them have what they want, your property can be replaced – you cannot!
- Scream loudly and make lots of noise if you are being attacked.
- Don't wear headphones when you are out alone because you will not hear an attacker approach.
- Be sensible in your choice of clothing. High heels may look good but they won't help you run away from an attacker or defend yourself.
- Carry a personal attack alarm and don't be afraid to use it.
- Ensure someone always knows where you are and when you will be back.

- Never travel in an unlicensed taxi and always check the ID of any taxi driver you hire. Always sit behind the driver so that you can get out without incident if you feel threatened.
- Make sure you know when your last buses and trains are.
- Do not display your valuables – flashing expensive jewellery and mobile phones is an invitation to a thief.
- Don't drink and drive and do not get into a car with someone you suspect may be over the legal drink drive limit, or who has used drugs.
- If you drive make sure your vehicle is in a good state of repair and has plenty of petrol – you don't want to be stranded as it can increase your risk of becoming a victim of crime.
- Lock away your valuables in the boot of the car if you drive.
- Do not accept lifts from anyone you do not know.
- Do not allow strangers into your home.
- Be assertive with anyone who is making you feel uncomfortable or is invading your personal space.
- Many sexual assaults are committed by someone you know – be wise in your choice of aquaintance. If in any doubt leave the situation and don't worry about appearing impolite.
- If you feel you are being followed go straight to the nearest public place.
- Do not be afraid to report crime to the police.
- Never leave your drink unattended in a pub or a club as it can easily be spiked with drugs which will leave you helpless against an attack.
- Do not allow anyone to buy you a drink unless you trust them implicitly or you can see that it hasn't been tampered with.
- On nights out stay with your friends – you are less vulnerable in a group than you are on your own.
- Go to self-defence or martial arts classes.

As you can see there are lots of steps that you can take to make yourself safe. Paying attention to your personal safety and the safety of others is a crucial factor in preventing crime.

 Think about it

Should you have to take precautions to protect your safety or should the government and the police make society safe for you?

Victim support

The needs of victims

Survivors of crime can face a range of problems which can affect their lives in the aftermath of the crime. The difficulties individuals face will depend largely on the crime that has been committed against them. A victim of rape will face different issues than a victim of car crime, and so on. Generally, some of the issues faced by victims of crime and their families are as follows:

Figure 11.4 *The victims of crime may have to continue living with the consequences of what happened to them*

Victims of crime need a great deal of support to help them deal with some of the problems listed above. There are many agencies which exist to help them in their time of need.

If you are working towards a *merit* (M1) you will need to explain the impact crime has on the lives of its victims and identify appropriate preventative measures.

Services for victims

Services for victims largely fall into two categories: statutory and voluntary. A statutory service is provided by the government and delivered through the courts and police. A voluntary service is not usually government funded and often relies on charities and volunteers.

Statutory services

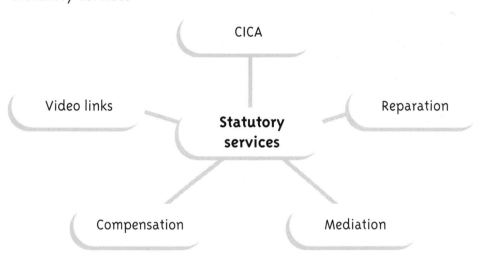

Figure 11.5 *There are official ways that victims of crime can be helped*

The role of the emergency services in supporting victims is shown in the table below.

Police	Fire	Ambulance
• Rescue • Crime prevention • Crime investigation • Crime detection • Referrals to Victim Support • Witness in court • Advice/Guidance • Reassurance	• Rescue • Putting out fires • Preserving evidence • Witness in court • First aid	• Medical treatment • Transport to hospital • Witness in court • First-aid training

Table 11.3

The Criminal Injuries Compensation Authority (CICA) This is a statutory government body that administers a compensation scheme for victims of crime. The role of the CICA is to decide how much compensation an injury resulting from crime is worth and provide an appropriate amount of money to compensate for it. Each individual injury is worth a set amount of money only. The list below details some of the amounts available on the current system.

- Fatal injury – £11,000
- Paraplegia (paralysis of lower limbs) – £175,000
- Permanent deafness in both ears – £44,000
- Loss of sight in both eyes – £110,000
- Sprained wrist (causes disability 6–13 wks) – £1000
- Severe permanent damage to genitalia – £11,000
- Sprained ankle lasting more than 13 weeks – £2500
- Quadraplegia (paralysis of all four limbs) – £250,000
- In addition other payments may be made in respect of long-term medical care for individuals who may need long-term private medical support.

Think about it

Do you think these amounts are suitable? What amounts would you give?

This scheme is of great benefit to victims of crime. Although no amount of money can replace a lost limb or repair damaged nerves, the money can at least provide for families in the event that a person cannot work for some time, and while it cannot bring back a loved one, it can at least cover funeral expenses. The CICA pays out around £200 million every year to injured victims of crime.

Reparation Reparation is the idea that the offender will repay the victim in the form of working for them. A limited system of reparation exists in the UK under community service orders. This is indirect reparation because the offender is helping the community at large, not just his or her actual victim. Systems of direct reparation do not exist to any large extent in the UK.

Mediation This aims to remove the hostility that exists between victims and their offenders by bringing them together using a mediator such as a social worker or community worker in order to discuss the situation face to face. A mediator is someone who helps people understand each other's point of view and resolve the problems between them. It can be enforced through a court order or remain a less formal arrangement. This method would not suit all victims, some of whom would be very frightened at the thought of meeting an offender and, like reparation, it is not widely used in the UK.

Think about it

How would you feel about meeting someone who had committed a crime against you?

Compensation The idea of the offender compensating their victim directly for injury caused has become very popular over the last twenty years or so and is supported by the government. Compensation orders can be given instead of and as well as any other sentence the court might want to give, but victims often do not know how to apply for a compensation order which would give them money directly from the pocket of the offender.

Think about it

Getting offenders to part with the money for compensation can be a problem. What would you do to make sure that they paid the money they owe?

Video links This is a particularly useful statutory service for child victims in violence and sexual abuse cases. As you can imagine a courtroom can be a very frightening place for children, so allowing them to give video-linked evidence rather than face their attacker, who may even be a family member, can remove some of the trauma involved in giving evidence.

Voluntary services

There are lots of voluntary agencies that provide support and information to victims of crime. Some of the main ones are described below:

Figure 11.6 *Voluntary services are available to help victims of crime*

Victim Support Victim Support is a registered charity which focuses on helping victims of crime in terms of emotional support and practical tasks, such as helping with insurance or compensation claims. It receives support from the police who refer victims to it and it receives funding from central government. Victim Support relies on the police to notify it of people who need its aid, however the police do not refer every victim to them, which means many victims receive no help at all.

Witness Service The Witness Service ensures that the process of giving evidence in court is as comfortable an experience as possible. It was established in 1989 and is managed and organised by its parent charity Victim Support. There is a Witness Service in every crown court in England and Wales and it performs several functions, which are

- to provide information on courtroom procedure to witnesses
- to accompany witnesses into the courtroom
- to help and reassure victims and witnesses.

Many witnesses may be very frightened at the thought of giving evidence, but without their evidence many prosecutions would fail and offenders would be able to walk free. It is in everyone's interest to support the Witness Service as good witnesses mean less criminals on the street. The Witness Service is not permitted to discuss the case itself or discuss the evidence the witness will give (this can only be discussed with the police or legal representatives), it can only offer moral support to the witness concerned. Cases of witness intimidation happen regularly, where the defendant tries to frighten the witness or their families to stop them giving evidence. In such cases there are some things the Witness Service can arrange to make the witness feel safer. They are

- screens between witness and accused so they cannot see each other
- live TV link to give evidence
- giving evidence privately.

The Witness Service can arrange for a victim or witness to visit the court in advance and to be told what to expect so that they feel more comfortable about the process.

Women's Aid Federation This organisation supports the survivors and families of domestic violence by providing them with a place to live in a refuge and offering practical and emotional support through volunteers and trained support workers. As with all charities it has limited funds and often struggles to cope with the demand for its services. The role of the organisation is to

- provide refuges and support for women and dependent children who have experienced domestic violence or who are in fear of domestic violence
- raise awareness of the issues surrounding domestic violence

- lobby government for changes in law and policy to protect victims of domestic violence
- train outreach workers to support victims
- share knowledge with other public services such as the police.

Each year over 50,000 women and children seek safety in Women's Aid refuges and many more seek help through telephone support lines such as the National Domestic Violence Helpline, which is also part of the Women's Aid Federation. As a charity Women's Aid must rely on the goodwill of volunteers if it is to survive. For its funding, it relies on charitable donations, grants and fundraising for all its income. It is an invaluable service for women and children who are victims of domestic violence.

Citizens Advice Bureau (CAB) The CAB began as an emergency measure during World War II and has now evolved into a much relied upon national agency. The CAB deals with around six million queries a year on a wide range of issues such as

- benefits
- debt
- consumer issues
- legal issues
- homelessness
- immigration.

It can help victims of crime by referring them to legal agencies, such as the police or a civil or criminal solicitor to represent them. They can also refer people to the Witness Service and Victim Support and give expert advice to victims on their legal rights.

Rape Crisis The first Rape Crisis centre was established in London in 1976 as a response to female victims of rape and sexual assault often being treated unfairly by the police and often blamed for causing the attack upon themselves. There are now many Rape Crisis centres around the country operating 'drop-in' centres and telephone support, and providing legal and medical information in a safe and emotionally supportive environment.

The Samaritans Victims often experience significant emotional trauma in the aftermath of a crime committed against them. They may develop depression, feelings of anxiety, irrational fears or even more serious problems such as post-traumatic stress disorder. The Samaritans are a voluntary organisation which operates a 24-hour service designed to help and support individuals who feel desperate or suicidal. The help is given primarily through a telephone support line.

The Samaritans also offer a service to prisoners who often feel isolated from any other source of support. They have also pioneered prisoner listener schemes where inmates are trained to befriend and listen to fellow prisoners who may be experiencing emotional difficulties. In a society where 160,000 people attempt suicide each year the Samaritans provide a vital and necessary service to victims of crime and many others who are troubled and suicidal.

Voluntary victim support schemes such as those discussed above are very underfunded and can't possibly help all the victims of crime who would benefit from their services. Also, government schemes can only help victims if people are properly informed about them. The public services are often unable to do much to help victims directly due to the limits on time and resources, but they can and do refer victims to support agencies where the support might be available, such as Victim Support or Rape Crisis.

In summary

- Victims of crime can experience all kinds of after-effects such as depression and anxiety.
- The risk of becoming a victim of crime is linked to the amount of time a person spends in public places.
- There are many things that individuals can do to reduce the risk of victimisation.
- Once a person has become a victim of crime it increases their risk of becoming a victim again.
- There are many agencies that exist to help victims, some are provided by the government and some are charity based.

Assessment activity

For a *pass* (P3) you need to explain the role of two statutory and two voluntary organisations who offer support to victims.

Assessment activity

If you are working towards a *distinction* (D1) you will need to design a 10-question survey to find out what effect crime has on the local community and put the questions to 10 people in your local area. You will also have to write a 150-word report on your results.

Crime reporting and recording

Crime reporting

Crime reporting and recording are important sources of information for the government and the police to examine problems of crime prevention and crime control. Without the statistics which come from reported and recorded crime it would be difficult for the police to know if they are having any impact in reducing crime. Reported crime is the amount of crime that gets reported to the police, recorded crime is the amount of reported crime that the police choose to record in official statistics. According to the government, about 70% of crimes reported to the police make their way into recorded crime statistics, the other 30% are either too trivial or there isn't enough information to take them forward. There are several ways that crime can be reported to the police. These are:

- *In person* You can go to the local or central police station and report the crime directly to the police. In addition, you can report a crime to a police officer who is on a school visit or on the beat.

- *By telephone* Most of us take this to mean dialling 999, however this is only for emergencies, and should not be used for reporting a broken window or a stolen car stereo. An emergency is when a crime is currently happening or there is immediate danger of one occurring. For non-emergencies you can contact the local police station on a local number and report the crime.

Alternative methods of crime reporting

- *Online* For reporting non-emergency crimes you can use the internet. The police service has a website which enables the public to report crimes such as theft, vandalism, criminal damage and vehicle theft and damage. On the website you are asked to key in details required for reporting the crime, including your personal details, type of crime, location, date/time and property involved. Minor crimes can be reported in about 10 minutes, saving the time that would otherwise be spent going to the police station. You can find the site at www.online.police.uk .

- *Self-report schemes* An offender may choose to report their crime themselves – but this is not common! Some types of crime are often self-reported, such as a traffic accident where a crime number is needed to claim on a car insurance policy, but most offenders would never go to a police station and admit what they have done. The exceptions are self-report schemes, which offer anonymity to offenders in exchange for information about their criminal habits. These schemes can help the police understand what motivates offenders to commit crime and this helps them stop it in future.

Reporting homophobic and racist incidents A homophobic incident is one in which a crime is committed by abusing or injuring someone because they are homosexual. The police service takes such offences very seriously and there are a variety of ways to report them. In addition to the methods outlined above, a report can be made in writing or by another person on behalf of the victim. Many regional police services also have a homophobic incident helpline through which non-emergency incidents can be reported. It is often very difficult for members of the gay/lesbian/bisexual/transgendered community to report crimes committed against them because of distrust of the police, fear of reprisals and having their sexuality 'outed'.

A similar problem occurs among ethnic minority communities, many of whom do not have particularly good relations with local police and would be reluctant to report a racist incident they have been a victim of. The police are trying very hard to be more supportive in dealing with racist incidents, particularly since the MacPherson Report on the murder of the black teenager Stephen Lawrence. The Report was highly critical of the way the Metropolitan Police dealt with the investigation of the murder and accused them of institutional racism. In order to encourage the reporting of racist incidents many police services have teams of officers dedicated to dealing with them. There are even specific report forms which can be used to report incidents such as the one in Figure 11.7.

Racist incident reporting form

1. Type of incident
   - [ ] Threatening behaviour   [ ] Verbal abuse   [ ] Written abuse
   - [ ] Email abuse   [ ] Physical abuse   [ ] Threat of assault
   - [ ] Damage to property   [ ] Racist graffiti   [ ] Other (please describe)

2. Are you the victim in the incident you are reporting?   [ ] Yes   [ ] No

3. (i) If you have answered **No** to question 2, please describe the nature of your relationship to the victim. Example: relative; friend; neighbour; employer; witness.

   (ii) Has the victim given their consent for you to report this incident?   [ ] Yes   [ ] No

4. Describe the incident and when and where it happened.

5. Do you want help to take action on the incident?   [ ] Yes   [ ] No

6. If you have answered **Yes** to question 5 please fill in the details below so that we can help you.
   Name _____   Address _____
   Postcode _____
   E-mail Address _____
   Telephone Numbers: Home _____   Work _____   Mobile _____

Thank you for taking the time to fill in this form. Your information will help us improve services to deal with racist incidents, offer victims support and enable us, where possible, to take action against people who carry out incidents. Please send it to the address below. You do not need a stamp.

Race Equality, Westminster City Council, 18th floor, Freepost LON17996, LONDON SW1E 6YT.

Data Protection Act 1998:
This information will only be used to record racist incidents. Please address any data protection enquiries to the Data Protection Officer, Information Services, 16th Floor, Westminster City Hall, 64 Victoria Street, London SW1E 6QP.

Office Use Only:
RESPOND Unique Reference Number:
Service Area/ Department:

00003-C-D-0203

Figure 11.7 *An example of a form for reporting racist incidents*

Assessment activity

If you are working towards a *merit* (M2), analyse and evaluate online reporting and the methods for reporting racist incidents. Are such alternatives needed and how effective are they?

Think about it

Do you think that ethnic minorities and members of the gay and lesbian community need alternative methods to report crime? Explain your answer.

Problems with reporting crime

A lot of crime never gets reported to the police. There are various reasons why people don't report crime. These include

- it is too trivial to bother reporting
- they are frightened of the offender and don't want to aggravate them
- the offender is a loved one and they don't want to get them in trouble
- they are too ashamed or embarrassed to tell anyone
- they don't trust the police
- they want to deal with it themselves
- they don't know that a crime has been committed against them
- they cannot report a crime because they have died as a result of the crime.

Crime recording

Recorded crime is the amount of crime the police choose to record into official statistics. At one time less than half the crimes that were reported to the police made it into the official statistics, however in April 2002 new National Crime Recording Standards (NCRS) were introduced by the government which meant that the police had to record much more crime. For instance, in the past when a pub fight took place and the parties involved did not want to press charges against one another, the incident would not have been recorded by the police and therefore wouldn't have entered the statistics. However, such an incident now has to be recorded as a violent crime. The NCRS was introduced to make it easier to compare the figures that each police service produces and to be more supportive of victims of crime. It will also highlight the true volume of work police officers have to deal with. The pie charts in Figure 11.8 show some of the categories of crime used by the police and the British Crime Survey in producing statistics.

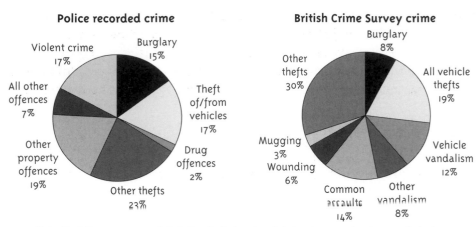

Police recorded crime

Violent crime 17%
Burglary 15%
All other offences 7%
Theft of/from vehicles 17%
Other property offences 19%
Drug offences 2%
Other thefts 23%

British Crime Survey crime

Burglary 8%
Other thefts 30%
All vehicle thefts 19%
Mugging 3%
Wounding 6%
Vehicle vandalism 12%
Common assaults 14%
Other vandalism 8%

Note: The BCS common assault definition includes minor injuries. From 2002/03 the recorded crime definition does not include minor injuries.

Figure 11.8 *Police recorded crime and BCS crime figures by types of crimes for 2002–2003*

As you can see, the statistics from the police and the British Crime Survey are different. This means that people will tell the BCS about crimes which they would not bother reporting to the police, such as vandalism. The BCS estimates that 57% of crime is never reported to the police.

 Key point

The new NCRS is a good idea as it gives a more realistic picture of the total amount of crime in society. However, using the new standards means there will appear to be more violent crime in England and Wales than before. This is because more violent crime is making it into the statistics, not because there is actually more violent crime.

The problem of course is that the public may not appreciate this and will believe there is more crime.

Statistics can be useful to the police and the government in that they

- reveal how much crime is in society
- tell the police where crime hotspots are
- show which crimes are a problem in which area
- show if the police are having any effect in reducing crime
- show the police where to target their officers and resources
- show how much crime there is in an area compared with other areas
- inform the public about their safety.

Statistics are also useful in helping the police know which crimes are reported and which are not, for example the majority of car crimes and burglaries are reported to the police because the victims will need a crime reference number in order to claim on their insurance – they can only get this number from the police, so they must report the crime. However, it is estimated that up to 90% of sexual assaults are not reported because the victims are too frightened and ashamed to come forward. Statistics help the police tackle problems such as this and encourage people to come forward.

Assessment activity

To achieve a *merit* (M3), describe how crime records are used to produce statistical data.

Systems of recording crime

Many police services use simple multi-page crime recording forms which are then faxed or scanned and sent to police headquarters, where a centralised data capture unit processes the forms using Intelligent Character Recognition (ICR) software, which creates statistics based on the forms that it processes. This data may be input into a database which can be accessed by police officers to help them detect and solve crimes. Examples of these databases are:

1   **Scottish Intelligence Database (SID)** This is a new database being developed in Scotland to help Scottish officers track and monitor offenders. It is likely to contain photographs of offenders, fingerprints, aliases and the MO (*modus operandi*) of offenders (how they commit particular crimes).

2   **Police National Computer (PNC)** This is one of the main sources of information for officers. It was created in 1974 and contains information on criminals, property and vehicles. The following are some of the ways it can be used:

- *Automatic Number Plate Recognition (ANPR)* This is used to scan the number plates of vehicles on the roads and motorways so that suspect ones can be identified.

Figure 11.9 *Police officers have access to centralised databases to help them in solving crimes*

- *Names Index* This has over six million records on criminals and missing persons.
- *Stolen Property Index* This has over 100,000 records of stolen property, so that if the police seize any stolen property in a raid on a suspect's property they can trace it back to its rightful owner.
- *Sex Offenders Register* This enables the police to track and monitor convicted sex offenders.

Think about it

Should the information the police have on known sex offenders be available to the public or should it remain confidential? Explain your answer.

In summary

- There are many ways of reporting a crime to the police, such as in person, by telephone or on the internet.
- Lots of crime doesn't get reported to the police.
- Recorded crime is that which has been reported to the police and then recorded by them into official statistics.
- New National Crime Recording Standards have changed the way the police record crime. They must now record more of the crimes that are reported to them.
- Police information on crime is used to create statistical data which can be used to improve the service they offer to the public.
- The police have many methods of storing crime information, such as the Police National Computer, which helps them in the fight against crime.

Assessment activity

To gain a *pass* (P4) you will need to give a detailed analysis of the systems used to report and record crime.

Offender management

It is important to understand what happens to offenders once they have been apprehended and found guilty. The first thing is that they are sentenced by the courts. The courts cannot just give any sentence they feel like, they must abide by a set of guidelines provided for them by the Sentencing Advisory Panel, which sets out suitable sentences for certain offences. It is important to have these guidelines so that each court in the country is sentencing in the same way. It would be very unfair if in Yorkshire an offender was given a fine, but in Surrey they were given a prison sentence for the same crime. There are a variety of possible sentences that the courts can use to punish offenders once they have been found guilty. These are listed below.

Sentence	Explanation
Absolute discharge	This is where an offender is found guilty or has admitted to being guilty but no further action is taken against them
Conditional discharge	The offender has no immediate action taken against them, but this is conditional upon them committing no further offences. If they commit further offences within a specific time period they can be brought back to court for sentencing
Fine	This is where the offender is required to pay a certain amount of money as punishment for the crime they committed
Compensation order	This is where an offender is required to pay a certain amount of money to their victim in compensation
Community rehabilitation order	The offender is required to attend regular meetings with a probation officer to ensure their behaviour is monitored
Community punishment order	The offender is required to do a certain number of hours service to the community, such as getting rid of graffiti or helping council workers landscape waste ground
Curfew order	This prevents individuals being out after a certain time, or stops them being in a certain area
Drug treatment and testing order	The probation service monitors drug rehabilitation and gives compulsory drug testing
Hospital order	A sentence available to be used for mentally disordered offenders, whereby they are placed in a specialist hospital unit so they can be assessed and treated
Prison sentence	A period of time spent in prison
Suspended prison sentence	A prison sentence that becomes active if the offender commits another offence

Table 11.4

The magistrates court guidelines provide advice on sentencing to magistrates on a wide variety of offences that they are likely to come across in court. The guidance they are given for each offence is in the form of a table like the example below.

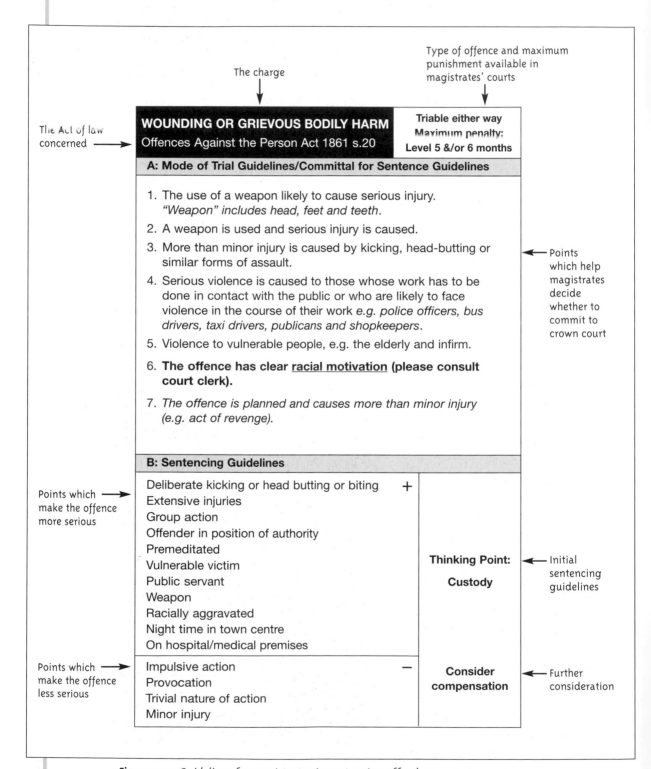

Figure 11.10 *Guidelines for magistrates in sentencing offenders*

Key point

The vast majority of magistrates are volunteers, about 30,000 of them. They are just like other people, albeit a little older (the minimum age for a magistrate is 27). They have no legal training and many hold full-time jobs in other fields such as teaching or business. It's no wonder they need the kind of guidance provided by the sort of sentencing guidelines as in the example above.

We will now look at the use of imprisonment as a form of punishment.

Prisons and the role of the prison service

There are 138 secure prisons in England and Wales, holding over 72,000 prisoners, and growing every year. The prison service has a very specific role, which is reflected in its mission statement:

HM Prison Service Statement of Purpose

Her Majesty's Prison Service serves the public by keeping in custody those committed by the courts. Our duty is to look after them with humanity and help them lead law-abiding and useful lives in custody and after release.

The prison service's purpose is not to treat prisoners badly or to punish them further. Prisoners should be treated with dignity and respect regardless of what they have done. However, many people believe prison should be made as hard as possible for offenders, but this is not the point of imprisonment. The point is to keep the public safe and punish the offender by taking away their freedom, and as long as this is what is done then the prisons are fulfilling their role.

One of the main aims of the prison service is to help rehabilitate prisoners so that when they leave prison they

Figure 11.11 *One of the purposes of prison is to keep the public safe from offenders*

do not have to resort to crime again. This can be achieved through the use of education and training to give them improved job skills.

Several categories of prison are used to house offenders depending on the level of risk they pose to the public and the likelihood of them trying to escape. These are:

Category A These are for prisoners who are very dangerous and would pose a real risk to the public and the police if they were to escape. These are maximum security prisons and house those who are guilty of the worst crimes, such as murder, rape or terrorism. They must not be able to escape under any circumstances.

Category B These are for prisoners who are dangerous, but less so than category A prisoners. Escape must be very difficult for these prisoners, so security is still very tight.

Category C These are for average prisoners who cannot be left in the community, but will probably not try a determined attempt to escape.

Category D These are for prisoners who can be reasonably trusted in open conditions. They may be allowed out during the week to work, but have to return to prison in the evenings and at weekends. They are a very low escape risk and they are not considered a danger to the public.

Let's do it!

Pick a category from the list above and design a suitable prison for the kind of inmate you would find in it.

The government has several aims and objectives which the prison service has to achieve. These are

- to carry out the sentence of the court in order to reduce offending and protect the public
- keep offenders in a safe, healthy and decent environment
- provide education and training to improve the chances of an offender going straight
- deal fairly with prisoners and respect their human rights
- support and promote equal opportunities and combat discrimination
- work in close cooperation with other agencies in the criminal justice system and other organisations that are interested in the welfare of offenders.

The prison environment

The prison environment varies depending on the category of prison. However, in general most prisons are overcrowded and do not have the facilities or staffing to allow prisoners very much time outside the cell environment. Most prisoners do not have a cell to themselves and may be bunked up with several other prisoners for most of the day. This means they have little privacy and any conflicts among cell mates can make it a difficult and sometimes threatening environment to be in. The prison environment runs on a strict timetable and by strict rules. Certain things are banned. For example, alcohol-based toiletries are banned because they might be drunk, wind-up radio's because they contain potential bomb-making equipment and banana skins because they can be smoked. Remand prisoners (those who are awaiting trial) can wear their own clothes, apart from football shirts which are confiscated because they might provoke fighting among rival supporters. A convicted prisoner must wear a prison uniform, which consists of a blue striped shirt, jeans and a maroon jumper.

Regardless of what the tabloid newspapers say, prisons are not like holiday camps; they are highly unpleasant places to have to spend any time. Prison officers and prison authorities work very hard to promote a positive environment. Despite this, problems do occur. Bullying is very common, particularly in young offender institutions (YOIs), and the use of drugs is an ongoing battle for prison authorities. Drug testing is carried out on prisoners in an attempt to stamp out the problem, however it is extremely difficult to stop.

 Think about it

Why would prison authorities be concerned about drug use in prison?

The probation service

The National Probation Service (NPS) was created in 2001 and supervises offenders who are completing their sentence in the community and those who are released early from their prison service on licence. The NPS has several roles to fulfil. These are:

- *Protecting the public* This involves assessing the risk an offender poses to the public and how likely they are to commit further offences. This assessment is presented to the courts so that they know whether to give a custodial sentence or a community one. The NPS produces about 90,000 offender reports for the courts each year. It also involves planning programmes of supervision for offenders who are being released early from prison, for example the NPS may decide that an offender needs to live in a hostel for a while and obey strict rules to prevent them re-offending.

- *Reducing re-offending* The NPS offers programmes of education to offenders so they will re-offend less. This includes drug treatment programmes in partnership with the National Health Service, since around 70% of crime is thought to be drug-related. Programmes such as these are very important in reducing crime.

- *The proper punishment of offenders in the community* Not all offenders have committed crimes that are serious enough for them to be sent to prison, but they still need to be punished for what they have done. The NPS runs programmes of punishment in the community such as helping the elderly, cleaning up the community and helping community projects. In this way offenders also give something back to the community – a win/win situation.

- *Ensuring offenders' awareness of the effects of crime on the victims of crime and the public* It is important that offenders understand the impact they have on the lives of their victims. The NPS helps with this by taking the views of victims seriously and operating programmes where the victim gets the chance to confront the offender.

- *Rehabilitation of offenders* The NPS helps offenders with employment opportunities, as they are less likely to offend again if they are in work. The NPS also helps prevent re-offending by offering counselling services, debt management, drug and alcohol abuse programmes and anger management courses. All of these things make it less likely that an offender will return to crime.

The probation service is an often forgotten part of the criminal justice system. Because it is not a uniformed service it is often not covered on your study course. However, the probation service supervises around 200,000 offenders every year, more than triple the number who are in prison at any one time. The types of offenders the probation service deals with are shown in Figure 11.13.

Figure 11.12 *The probation service plays a vital role in supervising offenders who have been released from prison back into society*

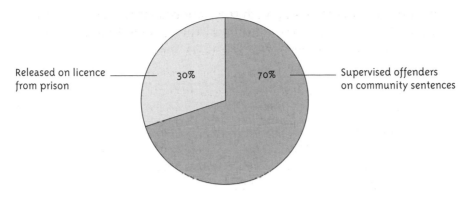

Figure 11.13 *These are the types of offenders the probation service deals with*

Think about it

Why is prison not the most suitable form of punishment for many offenders?

Community sentences

Most of the 70% of the NPS's workload in dealing with offenders who are completing community sentences will be on one of four main programmes:

Community rehabilitation order	This means an offender must serve a sentence in the community and must work under the supervision of probation officers to stop the causes of their criminal behaviour, such as drug or alcohol abuse
Community punishment order	This is when an offender must complete a certain number of hours doing work in the community, such as gardening, cleaning or removing graffiti. The maximum an offender can do is 240 hours
Community punishment and rehabilitation order	This order combines supervision by a probation officer to tackle the root causes of an offender's behaviour with some hours spent working in the community
Drug treatment and testing order	This is an order designed to help offenders who have problems with drug-related criminal activity. It tries to change the way offenders use drugs and reduce their offending. It involves medical assessment, twice-weekly drugs tests and advice on employment and health and fitness.

Home Office statistics show that community sentences are more effective than prison sentences in preventing re-offending. They show that probation-led community sentences reduced re-offending by 4.9%, whereas prison sentences only reduced re-offending by 3.3%. This is an interesting point because the public seems to want criminals sent to prison, but in the long term community sentences seem to reduce crime more.

If an offender fails to follow the programme provided by the probation service they risk being taken back to court and re-sentenced. This would probably mean a prison sentence in the case of many offenders.

The NPS operates in 42 areas across England and Wales and is a major player in multi-agency partnerships, as you will see in the next section.

Assessment activity

To gain a *pass* (P5) you need to analyse the methods of offender management and their effectiveness.

New prison and probation reforms

The prison and probation services were merged into a single service in June 2004. The new service is called the National Offender Management Service and will take responsibility for the rehabilitation and management of offenders both in and out of custody. The service will pioneer a new way of sentencing offenders, including weekend prison sentences and day fines. The aim of the new organisation is to reduce the prison population and to increase the use of community sentences instead.

Assessment activity

If you are working towards a *merit* (M4) you will have to explain the role of the probation service or prison service in offender rehabilitation.

Crime and disorder

Crime and Disorder Act 1998

Multi-agency partnerships

The Crime and Disorder Act 1998 placed a new duty on local authorities, police and other agencies to work together to reduce crime and disorder. This partnership involves statutory, voluntary, community and business groups working together to reduce crime, fear of crime and victimisation.

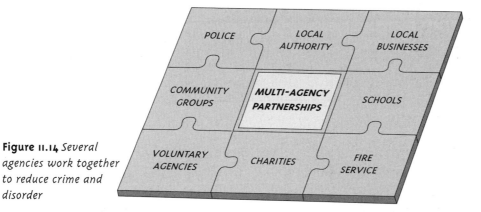

Figure 11.14 *Several agencies work together to reduce crime and disorder*

The Crime and Disorder Act 1998 created 376 local crime and disorder reduction partnerships in England and Wales. These partnerships have had to develop and implement ways to tackle crime in three-year cycles, the first cycle ran from 1999 to 2002 and the second cycle operates from 2002 to 2005. These strategies need to reflect local needs and priorities, which means that different crime and disorder partnerships around the country will be aiming to tackle different areas of crime depending on what is a problem locally.

Let's do it!

On your own, do research into what are the priorities of the strategies to fight crime in your local area.

The partnerships are made up of many different organisations, such as
- police
- community safety officers
- drug action teams
- youth offending teams
- local authorities
- health trusts

- probation service
- National Association for the Care and Resettlement of Offenders (NACRO)
- Victim Support
- educational establishments
- businesses
- housing associations.

The priorities addressed by a multi-agency partnership could be any of the following issues, depending on local needs:

Figure 11.15 *The priorities of a multi-agency partnership*

An example of a possible local crime and disorder reduction partnership according to the Home Office, would look something like this.

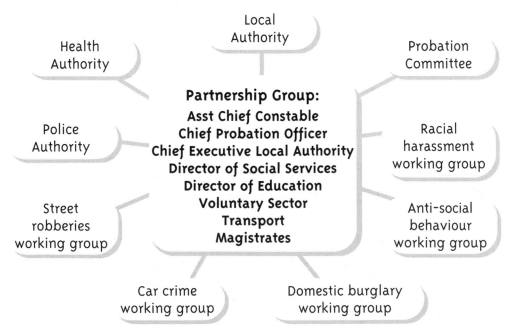

Figure 11.16 *A multi-agency partnership structure*

The first step a multi-agency partnership must take is a crime and disorder audit. The audit is a way of finding out what the local crime problems are. According to the Home Office, the audit serves several purposes:

- It ensures that all the groups in the multi-agency partnership are aware of the types of crimes and disorders that are being committed in their area.
- It identifies the needs of communities and addresses their concerns.
- It examines the wider impact of crime on communities.
- It helps to identify methods of reducing crime and disorder.

The crime audit is also another effective way for public service agencies to use crime statistics in order to target areas of high crime locally and predict future crime trends. Reducing crime and disorder in a local community can have a tremendous impact on the quality of life for residents. For example, reducing drug abuse in a local area can reduce the numbers of burglaries and street robberies committed by people who need to steal in order to feed their drugs habit. This in turn can improve the number of community activities in an area because people feel safe to leave their homes, and it may also encourage businesses into the area bringing employment and jobs.

Assessment activity

For a *pass* (P6) you will have to identify and describe in detail your local crime and disorder multi-agency partnership.

The priorities outlined earlier can be translated into specific schemes or initiatives to reduce crime. Such initiatives might be

- working with housing associations to improve estate management and remove persistent offenders from certain areas
- drug treatment programmes for offenders with a history of drug-related offending to feed their habit
- addressing problems caused by prostitution, including multi-agency tactics to keep prostitutes away from residential areas and deter kerb crawlers.

The setting of measurable targets like the ones above is a key issue for multi-agency partnerships. This ensures that projects to reduce crime and disorder have a clear aim and are value for money. Some examples of how crime and disorder legislation has been used to set targets are shown below in the case study.

Case study

Strategies for reducing crime and disorder

The following examples show how local crime and disorder partnerships set targets to reduce crime and disorder.

Manchester Crime and Disorder Reduction Strategy 2002–2005

- To reduce recorded crime in the city by 10% over three years.
- To increase by 6% the number of residents who feel safe alone after dark over three years.
- 15% reduction of violent offences in public places over three years.
- 15% reduction in youth nuisance over three years.

These are just some of the targets set by Manchester in their strategy for 2002–2005. They were identified by the use of a crime and disorder audit. All crime and disorder strategies operate along similar lines, for example

Charnwood Crime and Disorder Reduction Strategy 2003–2005

- To reduce burglaries of dwellings by 23% over three years.
- To reduce the incidence of theft from vehicles and damage to vehicles by 21% over three years.

Many crime and disorder partnerships make their strategy available on the internet. These are a valuable source of information in understanding the government's overall strategy on crime.

1 Do you think these targets will reduce fear of crime in Manchester and Charnwood?
2 Why do you think Manchester and Charnwood chose these targets?
3 Are these targets the same as the ones in your area? Why do you think this is?

Key point

The Crime and Disorder Act 1998 contains many sections that were specifically designed to help improve community safety, such as

- anti-social behaviour orders
- child curfew schemes
- child safety orders
- truancy
- parenting orders
- reparation orders
- tackling racism
- youth offending.

Anti-social behaviour order (ASBO)

The Crime and Disorder Act states that anti-social behaviour is that which causes or is likely to cause harassment, alarm or distress to one or more people who are not in the same household as the person causing the disturbance. Anti-social behaviour can be many things such as

- harassment of residents or passers-by
- begging
- verbal abuse
- criminal damage
- drug dealing
- vehicle crime
- vandalism
- noise nuisance
- graffiti
- dropping litter
- gang behaviour
- racial abuse
- kerb-crawling
- substance misuse
- drunken behaviour in public places
- joyriding
- throwing missiles
- assault
- prostitution.

Anti-social behaviour orders are intended to control the nuisance elements in a community to improve the quality of life for all the other residents. Sometimes one or two people on an estate can make things miserable for everyone else, and this is not fair. ASBOs are applied for by the police or local authority and if there is sufficient evidence a magistrate will grant the order. The order lasts for a minimum of two years and contains certain conditions which must be obeyed, such as staying out of a residential area, not associating with certain people, or not committing the same kind of behaviour again. Breaches of ASBOs can be punished with up to five years in prison, but it is unusual for this to happen, in fact one of the major problems with ASBOs is that they have no teeth and many people ignore them. In addition, the police and local authorities don't use them often; only 1337 ASBOs were reported to the Home Office for the period between 1 April 1999 and 30 June 2003.

 Think about it

Do you think ASBOs are a useful tool in preventing offending? Explain your reasons.

Curfews

A curfew is an order that children under a certain age must not be out on the streets after a certain time in the evening, this time is usually somewhere between 6–9 pm depending on the age group of the child. Like ASBOs, curfews were introduced by the Crime and Disorder Act 1998, although they had existed in Scotland since 1997. Curfews can be used against all young people under the age of sixteen and are applied for by local councils and enforced by the police, who have the power to take young people home who break their curfew and are caught on the street after a specific time. Curfew orders only last for 90 days, after this the council has to reapply for another order. The idea behind curfews is that with less young people on the streets there will be less juvenile crime committed and less young people will become victims of crime. However, curfews have not proved themselves particularly popular with local councils and they are not used with any great frequency.

Case study

Curfew in Corby, Northamptonshire

The town of Corby in Northamptonshire tried to impose a curfew on all young people aged 15 or under in 2002. The action was suggested in order to reduce the number of youth crimes in the area being committed at night. The curfew was scheduled to last from 9.00 pm to 6.00 am. However, the proposals were never carried out because of public complaints, which argued that you can't punish all young people for the actions of just a few.

1   When are curfews used?
2   What is your opinion on putting all young people under curfew in towns?
3   If you were the council leader in Corby what would you have done?
4   What are the human rights implications in putting curfews on all young people?
5   Do you think curfews work in reducing crime and disorder?

Youth offending teams

Youth offending teams (YOTs) are another aspect of the Crime and Disorder Act 1998 which has a big impact on youth crime. YOTs are made up of representatives from a variety of agencies, such as police, probation, health, education and local councils. The teams are designed to assess young offenders to find out why they commit crime and design programmes to help the young person stop their offending behaviour. This is yet another example of the multi-agency approach which is favoured by Tony Blair's Labour government. There is a youth offending team in every council area in England and Wales.

Parenting orders

Parenting orders were created by the Crime and Disorder Act in order to combat poor parenting being responsible for youth offending. They are applied for by the local council or local education authority and granted by the courts if a child has committed a criminal offence, played truant or behaved in an anti-social manner. The orders require the parents of the child to go to parenting classes and make sure their child goes to school and does not get into further trouble. The orders can last up to a year and can also be extended to cover children who behave badly at school. In addition to attending parenting classes, the parents can also be fined up to £1000, and in extreme circumstances they could be sent to prison. Like curfews, parenting orders are not popular with councils and it is a rare occasion when they are used.

Case study

Imprisoning parents

Patricia Amos was sentenced to 60 days in prison in 2002 for failing to ensure that her two daughters attended school regularly. One of her daughters had a 29% attendance rate and the other had attended school 34% of the time. Magistrates in Banbury decided that a prison sentence was the only option and it was the first sentence of its kind given in England. The sentence was later reduced to 28 days on appeal. The sentence had an large impact on the family as both the daughters pledged not to truant again and Ms Amos pledged that she would ensure her daughters attended school regularly.

1   Is it fair that parents are punished for their children's behaviour?
2   Why is truanting a serious problem?
3   How can children be encouraged to go to school?
4   How can parents be encouraged to take an interest in their children's education?
5   Is imprisonment taking punishment a step too far with regard to truanting?

Child safety order

This is a part of the Crime and Disorder Act which tries to prevent children under the age of ten becoming involved in anti-social and criminal behaviour. Children of this age cannot be prosecuted for the crimes they commit in this country as they are not considered responsible for their actions, so a child safety order is one of the few things that can be done to help resolve the problems the child is causing. The order can be used if a child under the age of ten has committed an offence, been anti-social or breached a curfew order. The order requires that a social worker or member of the youth offending team monitors the child and makes sure that they are being properly cared for and take action to stop the child re-offending. Child safety orders usually last for three months, but they can last longer in exceptional circumstances.

Think about it

Children under the age of 10 are not considered to be responsible for their criminal actions. What is your view on this?

Truancy

Another feature of the Act is to allow police officers to take children back to school if they believe that a child under the age of sixteen is absent without permission. Police can only use this power if the child is in a public place, they cannot enter a child's home and take them back to school.

Assessment activity

If you are working towards a *merit* (M5) and a *distinction* (D2) you will have to provide appropriate examples and assess the implications of how crime and disorder legislation impacts upon public services and local authorities.

Multi-agency partnership funding

Multi-agency partnerships are funded in a complicated way. The government makes some money available and distributes it to 10 Home Office crime reduction directors who give the money out to local areas. These officers are based in each of the nine government offices for England and one in the Welsh Assembly. Funding for each of the regions in 2002–2003 was as follows:

North East	£0.929 million
North West	£2.820 million
Yorkshire and Humberside	£1.869 million
East Midlands	£1.621 million
West Midlands	£2.194 million
Wales	£1.114 million
South West	£1.620 million
East	£1.583 million
South East	£2.550 million
London	£3.694 million

Some of the money is directly awarded to partnerships, but if they require extra funds they must develop schemes and initiatives like the ones already discussed and use them to bid for money to run them. If the bid isn't good enough, the Home Office will reject it and the money will go elsewhere. In addition, partnerships may bid for European funding or generate money from local businesses. Each council in the regions listed above gets a percentage of the available funds to use to combat crime and disorder in their area.

The initiatives and partnerships must be evaluated to assess how successful they have been and to see if they are providing the government with value for money. Evaluation is the process of checking that the strategies used are achieving their intended aims. Monitoring and evaluation identifies successful projects which can be shared with other partnerships and it also helps identify which strategies don't work so that they can be changed to perform better, or so that further time and money can be given to them.

CHECK WHAT YOU KNOW

1 What causes fear of crime?
2 What can be done to improve fear of crime?
3 List *six* groups in society who are vulnerable to victimisation?
4 In statistical terms what does a typical victim look like?
5 What are the methods a person can use to report crime?
6 Why do people choose not to report crime to the police?
7 What change will the new NCRS make to the levels of violent crime?
8 What are curfews?
9 What agencies take part in multi-agency crime and disorder partnerships?
10 What is the role of the prison service?

Resources

Books

Gray D *et al* (2004) *National Diploma in Public Services*, Oxford, Heinemann

Moore S (1988) *Investigating Deviance*, London, Harper Collins

Moore S (1996) *Investigating Crime and Deviance*, London, Harper Collins

Websites

www.crimereduction.gov.uk – a detailed government site on all aspects of crime reduction and fear of crime

www.edexcel.org.uk – this site allows you full access to the specifications for this unit

www.homeoffice.gov.uk/rds – the government's official site for the UK crime statistics

www.homeoffice.gov.uk/docs/sdaint1.html – an introductory guide to the Crime and Disorder Act 1998

www.hmprisonservice.gov.uk – the official site of the prison service

www.probation.home.office.gov.uk – the official site of the probation service

Expedition skills

Introduction

This unit identifies the skills and knowledge necessary to navigate safely and competently in open country. It will provide the background knowledge needed for selecting and maintaining the equipment appropriate to the activity being undertaken, especially overland expeditions which are an essential component of the training of members of the uniformed services. They will have the opportunity to experience a variety of different outdoor activities and evaluate the benefits of each. Students will also learn about environmental matters, including access rights and the work of the different countryside agencies and bodies.

In this unit students will learn the importance of teamwork, communication and leadership. They will also develop self-confidence, self-reliance and their own spirit of adventure.

How you will be assessed

An integral part of the unit is the completion of activities and tasks to help with understanding of the unit content. Case studies are also used for illustration and at the end of the unit there are assessment exercises to provide evidence for the learning objectives associated with the unit.

> ### Assessment activities
> Before you start this unit refer to the assessment activities on pages 398–399 to find out what you need to do to achieve the different grades for the unit.

After completing this unit, you should be able to achieve the following outcomes:
1 Identify and apply the skills required for carrying out expeditions in open country.
2 Identify and use effectively and safely the equipment appropriate to the type of expedition being undertaken.
3 Plan and carry out a multi-day expedition.
4 During the expedition evaluate individual and team performance.

Skills

Leadership skills

What is a leader and what makes a good leader? This is a vast subject, but every expedition and activity needs a recognised leader. This will be a person with the necessary qualifications and skills to inspire the members of the team to follow him/her in all situations. By following their instructions nothing much should go wrong.

The qualities of leadership are present in all of us, but may need to be brought out and encouraged. Taking a supervisory role in any group activity, such as organising a trip to a local sports centre or cinema for yourself and a few friends, will help you to start developing your own leadership skills. This can be followed up with helping to organise a more ambitious expedition, such as a weekend camping trip.

Leaders need to develop both hard and soft skills. Hard skills are the technical skills and knowledge needed to run an expedition, such as

- being able to pitch a tent in all weather conditions
- navigate in open country in all weather conditions
- knowing how to cope with emergencies
- being able to do safety procedures in a canoe
- being able to survive a night out in any weather conditions.

Soft skills are to do with teamwork, such as

- encouraging individuals to attempt new activities
- giving clear and unambiguous instructions
- keeping up team and individual morale when things go wrong or the weather is very bad
- encouraging and cheering up someone who is homesick
- knowing when to cut an activity short because people are bored, tired, wet, or cold.

Think about it

1 How many of these skills do you have?
2 How would you deal with the following situation?

You are out walking with a small group of friends on the North Yorkshire coast. When you set off it was a bright sunny morning but it has now started to rain and the wind has increased. One of your friends forgot his waterproof and is only wearing a T-shirt which is now soaking wet. He is also only wearing trainers and the path is becoming very muddy and slippery. You know that it will take at least an hour to reach the end of the walk and you are well past the point of no return. There is no alternative but to continue and finish the walk. Several members of the group are becoming fed up and the one who is wet is really grumbling and criticising you for choosing to attempt this walk.

3 How would you deal with the situation so that the walk is completed safely?

Interpersonal skills

These are the skills needed to work as a member of a team.

In the public services, teamwork is essential. It is very unusual for individuals to work alone; even in special forces operations, each individual is also a member of a team. In order to work as a member of a team, an individual needs to be able to get on with the other members of the team, through

- *cooperation* – the skills needed to work with other members of a team to achieve success
- *understanding* – the skills needed to know what other members of the team are feeling and thinking by looking at them and listening to them
- *patience* – this is the ability to wait for slower members of the team to complete a task without getting annoyed
- *motivation* – this is the ability to make all members of the team enthusiastic and keen even when they are tired; this is often achieved by praise
- *working as a member of a team* – this includes the ability to listen to others, to help other members of the team and to put forward ideas
- *assertiveness* – this means stating clearly and in a straightforward way what you want so that you get your own way, without hassle or aggression
- *dealing with conflict* – listening and talking often resolves conflict, but sometimes it is better to remove yourself from the situation for a 'cooling off' period; in extreme cases, the offending team member may have to leave the team
- *communication* – everyone needs to know what is happening, the individual, between individuals, between the team and a different level
- *commitment* – each individual must be fully committed to the best interests of the whole team
- *self-discipline* – an individual must be able to put the team's needs before their own. They must have the determination to make sure they do not forget their knowledge of basic skills.

Let's do it!

1 Your team has to work together as a group of sheep to be rounded up into a 2 × 2 metre pen in an open space about 10 × 10 metres.

You have to decide who is to be the 'shepherd', controlling the activity. Once the activity starts, all except the 'shepherd' are blindfolded and scattered around the open space, facing in different directions. The 'shepherd' cannot speak, but has to control the 'sheep' by means of any other sounds decided before the activity begins. You have 10 minutes to plan how you will carry out this exercise and a further 5 minutes to do it.

2 Describe how you carried out the exercise.

3 Comment on the success, or otherwise, of the exercise.

4 Analyse how you could improve your team's performance.

Case study

The need for leadership

You are a member of a group of army cadets on a Duke of Edinburgh silver expedition in the Peak District. There are five of you in the group and you have already spent one night camping. Unfortunately one of the group, John, was very reluctant to help with any of the camp chores and his reluctance was encouraging a rather unhappy atmosphere. This was not helped by there being only five of you, in three two-person tents, so John chose to sleep alone. Today it is really hot and sunny and the hills seem even higher and steeper than yesterday. You know you have to be at a certain checkpoint by midday to meet your assessor, but John is really lagging behind and everyone else is getting increasingly fed-up with him and muttering about letting him 'do his own thing'.

As the senior cadet in the group it is up to you to show your leadership qualities and make sure the group arrives at the checkpoint on time.

- How would you ensure that this happens?
- Which of the interpersonal skills will you need to use?

Organisational skills

The expedition team leader is responsible for planning the expedition, including

- researching or visiting the area where the expedition is to take place

- approval and booking of facilities
- ensuring that access is available
- logistics, transport, documentation
- planning activities which are safe but challenging within the capabilities of the group
- ensuring that the necessary equipment is available
- arranging insurance and medical cover
- planning for emergencies.

Let's do it!

You have been asked to organise an overnight cycling trip for half a dozen members of your cadet force detachment as a practice expedition before completing your Duke of Edinburgh silver award expedition by cycle in a couple of month's time. Produce a plan for this trip for approval by your detachment commander and Duke of Edinburgh officer.

Navigation skills

The skills associated with navigation in open country are essential when taking part in expeditions.

They are based on accurate map reading, but also include some extra navigation skills. (There is a section on navigation revision later in this unit). These skills are

- walking accurately on a bearing
- aiming-off or going slightly to the left or right of the objective
- handrailing or following a wall, stream, ridge or similar feature marked on the map and going in the required direction
- attack points or significant landmarks visited en route
- catching features or landmarks visible beyond the destination
- ticking-off features or landmarks passed to right or left of the route
- backbearings or bearings taken on landmarks behind the route and then converted into forward bearings
- the use of relocation techniques, which are used to find your position if you get lost; the easiest is to walk downhill, find a stream and follow it, or retrace your steps to your last known position.

An essential part of navigation is knowing how to send and recognise distress signals.

The international distress signal in mountains is

- *six* long flashes from a torch or *six* long whistle blasts or *six* shouts or waves, repeated at *one-minute* intervals
- answered by *three* long flashes/blasts/shouts/waves, repeated at *one-minute* intervals.

The international distress signal at sea is

- *seven* short blasts followed by *one* long blast on the ship's siren

or

- *Morse code SOS*, that is *three* short blasts/flashes, followed by *three* long blasts/flashes, followed by *three* short blasts/flashes, pause then repeat
- use of red flares or orange smoke
- raising and lowering of outstretched arms, slowly and repeatedly.

Case study

Signalling for help

You are walking in the Lake District when one of your group slips on the uneven ground and breaks a leg. She cannot walk on it and it would be impractical to try and carry her down the steep and rocky path. You decide that the best course of action is to make her as comfortable as possible and keep her warm until you can get help. You see a couple of adults climbing the crags across the valley so you blow your whistle using the recognised distress signal of six long whistle blasts, repeated at minute intervals until you have attracted their attention and they wave back to you three times to indicate that they know you want assistance. Through your binoculars you can see one of them using a mobile phone and then they begin to move in your direction. When they arrive they assess the situation and then use their mobile phone again to tell the mountain rescue team about the incident. Within a relatively short time, members of the mountain rescue team arrive and your injured friend is stretchered down the mountain and taken to hospital.

Revision of navigation

Before attempting an expedition you must be confident in the use of a map and compass. If you cannot navigate, you will not reach your destination!

Basic navigation skills are covered in Unit 9 of this course. Before moving on to higher level skills it is useful to revise the basics.

What is a map?

A map is a bird's-eye view of the ground drawn onto paper. A map is only accurate on the day it is drawn (a bit like an MOT certificate). Changes happen very quickly: new roads are built, houses are demolished, forests are planted. The only things that rarely change are hills, valleys and plains. It is important that you check the date that your map was drawn. The information is usually at the bottom right of an Ordnance Survey map. If your map is more than a few years old, be careful it may be completely out of date.

Scales and distances

The most useful maps of the United Kingdom are produced by the Ordnance Survey. OS maps cover the whole country and are widely available in good bookshops. The OS produces maps in a number of scales, the most common being 1:50,000 and 1:25,000. The *scale* of the map is the proportion which two points on the map bear to the same two points on the ground. On a map with a scale of 1:50,000, one centimetre represents 500 metres on the ground (therefore 2 centimetres on the map represent 1 kilometre on the ground). On a map with a scale of 1:25,000, one centimetre represents 250 metres (therefore 4 centimetres on the map represent 1 kilometre on the ground). No matter what the scale of a map, the distance between the grid lines is always 1 kilometre on the ground. The most useful maps for an expedition are the 1:25,000 maps. The scale is large enough to show a lot of detail yet the map itself represents a useful amount of land.

If you know the scale of a map you can work out the distance between points. At the bottom of the map, in the lower margin, there is a series of scales showing metres, kilometres, miles and nautical miles. If you need to calculate a distance, use a strip of paper and mark the distance between the points on your map, lay the paper against the scales at the bottom of the map and read off the distance. For a quick guide, remember grid lines are one kilometre apart.

The grid system

The entire country is divided into squares by the Ordnance Survey. This allows us to identify places with a grid reference. On an OS map, vertical lines numbered progressively from west to east are known as *Eastings*. Horizontal lines, numbered from south to north are known as *Northings*.

When you give a grid reference you must remember the following:

- A reference must always contain an even number of figures.
- A count must always be made first along the lines from east to west, and then from north to south.

Remember that the 3rd and 6th figures of a six-figure grid reference are estimations of distance between one grid line and the next. You need to estimate the number of 10ths between each grid line to establish a six-figure reference. If you cannot remember Unit 9, look at the right-hand margin of your map and all is explained. The *Romer* on your compass will help to make a more accurate estimate.

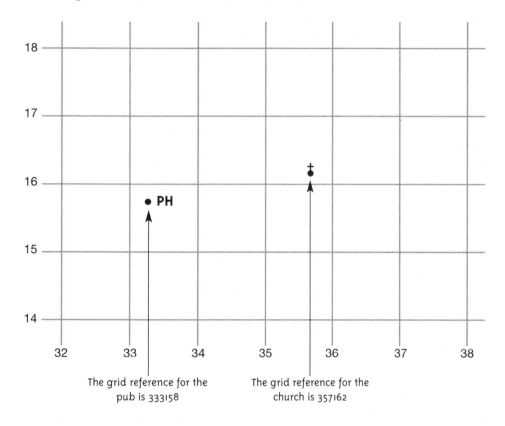

The grid reference for the pub is 333158

The grid reference for the church is 357162

Figure 14.1 *Grid references are used to identify where places are*

Conventional signs

It would be impractical to depict accurately objects on the ground. Map makers have devised a system of symbols to be used instead of accurate pictures. OS maps have a full list of these signs (called *conventional signs*) printed on the right-hand edge of the map. Revise these signs carefully, as you must know what to expect on an expedition.

Most signs are obvious and intuitive. For example, a thick black line is a railway, the sign for a windmill is almost a sketch.

The lightweight compass

There are two main types of lightweight compass, the *Suunto* compass and the *Silva* compass (the names just refer to the manufacturers). Either compass is suitable for navigation and in most respects they are very similar. Make sure that you acquire a compass calibrated in degrees; some military compasses are calibrated in mils and are not dealt with in this section.

The main purpose of a compass is that the red or black part of the needle will always point to the Magnetic North Pole. The Magnetic North Pole is a few degrees away from Grid North and True North. You will need to take account of the difference between Grid and Magnetic North later in this section. The transparent plastic plate of the compass also has a series of scales and measures, including Romers which are helpful when working out grid references.

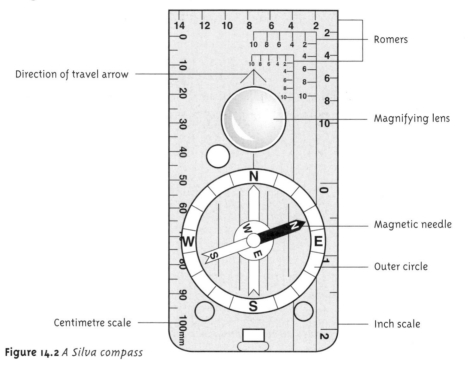

Figure 14.2 *A Silva compass*

Compasses are usually quite reliable although some common sense precautions are necessary when using them.

- When using a compass do not stand next to metal objects, like vehicles, or any electrical equipment that emits a magnetic field, they will attract the needle. Even a steel watch too close to the compass can deflect the needle.

- The magnetic needle housing is filled with liquid to prevent the needle from swinging wildly. If there is an air bubble in the housing the compass will be inaccurate.

- Compasses are generally very strong, but it is sensible to avoid giving them harsh treatment. Avoid dropping or heating your compass. In difficult circumstances your compass is the only way you have of finding direction, look after it.

North points

There are three north points:

- *True North* The actual direction to the geographical North Pole.
- *Grid North* The direction of the vertical grid lines on a map. For most purposes, True and Grid North are the same.
- *Magnetic North* The direction towards which a compass needle points. Magnetic North varies over time.

The difference between Magnetic and Grid North is significant for navigation. The difference is known as the grid magnetic angle (or magnetic variation) and it is given at the top of OS maps; its direction and rate of change is also given. The GMA for the United Kingdom in 2003 was 4° west.

Bearings

A bearing is a method of indicating direction. It is an angle measured in a clockwise direction from north. For example, due east is a bearing of 90° .

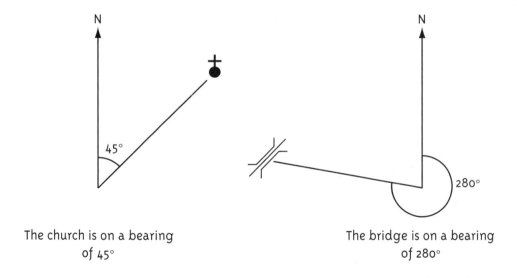

The church is on a bearing of 45°

The bridge is on a bearing of 280°

Figure 14.3 *A bearing is used to indicate the direction of travel*

An ability to use bearings gives an exact direction. You should be able to work out a bearing from one place to another on a map (a grid bearing) and on the ground (a magnetic bearing).

Taking a magnetic bearing

Hold your compass horizontally and point the direction of travel arrow at your objective. Keep the compass in this position and turn the outer circle housing so that the north arrow coincides with the north end of the magnetic needle. Read off the bearing at the direction of travel line.

Taking a grid bearing

When taking a grid bearing **ignore the magnetic needle**. Draw a line on your map between your position and your objective. Place the side edge of the compass base plate along this line with the direction of travel arrow pointing towards the objective. Keep the compass in this position. Turn the outer circle housing until the red parallel lines inside the housing are parallel with the north–south grid lines. Read off the bearing at the direction of travel line.

Converting a magnetic bearing to a grid bearing

If you take a bearing on the ground there are circumstances when you would need to draw that bearing on a map. You would then need to convert a magnetic bearing to a grid bearing. You need to know the grid magnetic angle – see the top of your map. Subtract the GMA from the magnetic bearing to get a grid bearing. For example,

Magnetic bearing	275°
GMA	4°
Grid bearing	271°

To convert a grid bearing to a magnetic bearing, all we now do is add the GMA. For example,

Grid bearing	60°
GMA	4°
Magnetic bearing	64°

Key point

For converting a magnetic bearing to a grid bearing:

- Mag to Grid = Rid (subtract the GMA)

For converting a grid bearing to a magnetic bearing:

- Grid to Mag = Add (add on the GMA)

Let's do it!

Convert:

- a magnetic bearing of 340° to a grid bearing
- a grid bearing of 73° to a magnetic bearing.

Back bearings

Back bearings are easy! They are also essential when you are calculating your position. The theory is straightforward. If you walked to a location and looked back to where you started from, what would be the bearing? It would be in exactly the opposite direction to the one you first took – there would be a difference of 180°.

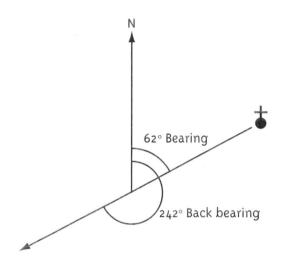

Figure 14.4 *Back bearings are used to calculate your position*

To calculate a back bearing, you must be able to add or subtract 180. If the original bearing is over 180°, you subtract 180. If the original bearing is under 180°, you add 180. For example,

- a bearing of 37° converts to a back bearing of 217° (add 180)
- a bearing of 225° converts to a back bearing of 45° (subtract 180).

Commonsense navigation

Most map reading is common sense mixed with a healthy dose of technical knowledge. In addition to the specific skills mentioned in this section there are a number of valuable tips which make navigation easier.

Aiming off

If you are aiming for a checkpoint on a linear feature like a gateway in a hedge, deliberately aim slightly off. If you know, for example, that you are to the left of your intended checkpoint when you hit the linear feature you turn right. Examples of linear features could include

- field boundaries
- roads

- rivers or streams
- well-defined edges of woodland
- coastlines.

Handrailing

Instead of slavishly following a bearing direct to your destination, it may make sense to follow a feature that leads in the right direction. For example,

- follow a winding stream instead of crossing and re-crossing if following a bearing
- follow a footpath if it leads in the right direction – you may need to use aiming off procedures at the end
- follow a ridge or well-defined physical feature.

Attack points

Attack points are significant and easily identifiable points you will visit on your route. Attack points are useful for

- providing definite objectives for the end of each leg
- giving a psychological boost as you pass them – people feel that they are making progress and such points confirm navigation accuracy.

Catching features

Catching features are landmarks that you can see beyond your destination. They are usually major landmarks like hills. They are useful for

- helping you to keep a check that you do not overshoot your objective
- giving you something to focus on beyond your next objective.

Tick-off features

Tick-off features are merely identifiable points that you pass on either side of your route. For example,

- easily identifiable buildings
- obvious physical features – like outcrops, confluence points.

They are similar to attack points in their effect.

Back bearings and bearings

Bearings taken on landmarks behind your route help to confirm direction when visibility ahead is limited. They should be part of your planning.

Relocation techniques

What to do when you get lost! Everyone who regularly goes into difficult country has at some time been lost. The real skill is being able to find yourself again! If you feel that you do not know where you are there are a number of things that you can do:

- Walk downhill. Roads and civilisation tend to be found in valleys. However, **do not use this technique if you are in an area of cliffs and scarps**. A bit of common sense is needed.
- Find a stream and follow it. This will have a similar effect to walking downhill. **Watch for waterfalls and deep water**.
- Go back to your last position. If you can, re-trace your steps to the last checkpoint where you were sure of your location.
- Apply position-finding techniques. For example, carry out a resection. This will locate your position without having to go further off route. However, you do need to be skilled and practised in the use of such techniques.

Distress signals

Re-read the opening sections of this unit and remind yourself of the most common international distress signals.

Preparation of a route card

It is essential that you prepare a route card before you start your expedition (see the planning sequence in this unit). A route card will give you the information you need to navigate accurately and it can be prepared in comfort in your own time. A route card is presented like a table of information, such as the following:

Leg	Start point	End point	Mag bearing	Distance	Time	Comments
1	Car park 893125	Ambly farm 899103	102	1.2 km	18 mins	Follow track Exit: Back to car park
2	Ambly farm 899103	Corner of wood 904076	162	3.8 km	1 hr	50 m climb, rough ground Exit: West to road
3	Corner of 904076	Trig point 873315	269	4.2 km	1 hr	Follow wood Exit: East to road then N to bridge

All the basic information is there: bearings, distances, brief descriptions of checkpoints and the route itself.

When preparing your route card, assume that a reasonably fit person carrying a rucksack or bergen can walk at an average of 4.5 kph. Add on an additional 1.5 minutes for every contour line crossed (up *or* down).

For each leg you should provide a safe exit route. This is the direction you will follow in case of emergency. It should be a simple instruction of direction and checkpoint. Often the safe exit route will be to retrace your steps.

> ## Checklist
>
> A route card should include:
>
> - A description of start and finish points for each leg. A statement of location will do.
> - The magnetic bearing to be used on each leg.
> - The distance to be travelled. This will allow you to calculate the approximate time for each leg. If you exceed your estimated time by 25%, you probably need to consider relocation techniques.
> - The time you expect to take. Don't forget to take account of going uphill or downhill.
> - Comments, which should include a brief description of the route and an indication of your emergency exit route.

Understanding vertical intervals

When out on an expedition it is important that you are able to 'read the ground' in order to work out your position. Also, when planning a route, it is important to be able to read a map and 'see' the ground through it. Contour lines and relief are ways you can use to help you do this.

- *Relief* – this shows the lie of the land, its rise and fall.
- *Contours* – these are the lines found on your map, usually coloured brown, to indicate the height of the ground in metres. The heights are written in figures in a way that they can be read facing up the slope. On 1:50,000 maps, the contour lines are shown at a vertical interval of 10 metres. Every 50 metres the contour line is shown by a bold line.
- *Features* – a feature is anything that stands out in the natural landscape, e.g. cliffs, scree slopes or outcrops, and are always shown in black.
- *Reading the contours* – not only do contours tell us the height of the land but they also tell us the shape. There are two simple rules:
  - The closer together the contours appear, the steeper the slope.
  - The further apart they are, the more gentle the slope.

You can also recognise particular features on the map from the shape of their contours:
- A ridge (see Figure 14.5)
- A spur (see Figure 14.6) (**Note:** the spur points *outwards* into the lower ground.)
- A re-entrant (see Figure 14.7) (**Note:** the re-entrant points *inwards,* into the higher ground.)
- A saddle (see Figure 14.8).

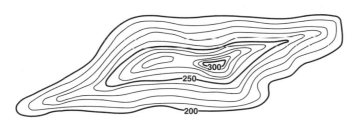

Figure 14.5 *A ridge*

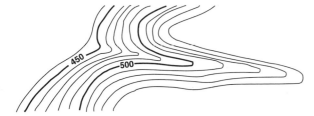

Figure 14.6 *A spur*

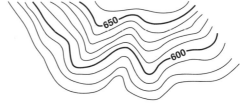

Figure 14.7 *A re-entrant*

Figure 14.8 *A saddle*

 Key point

It is also important that you know which is the top of the slope and which is the bottom, therefore you *must* check the contour figures. You can also use other features to help you, for example lakes, rivers, villages and railways are usually found at the bottom of a hill.

How to 'set' your map using a compass

Step 1 Look at the top of your map and locate the *Magnetic North arrow*.

Step 2 Place the compass on the map with the *direction of travel arrow* pointing in the same direction as the Magnetic North arrow line.

Step 3 Turn both the *map* and *compass* so that the *magnetic needle* in the compass is pointing the same way as the direction of travel arrow.

379

The map is now 'set'.

Another way of 'setting' your map is to lay the edge of the compass along an Easting (vertical) grid line. Now turn the map and compass until the magnetic needle in the compass is pointing the same way as the direction of travel arrow.

How to travel along a bearing

Step 1 Convert the *grid* bearing to a *magnetic* bearing. (**Remember:** Grid to Mag = Add the GMA.)

Step 2 Set the outer circle housing to read the *magnetic* bearing along the direction of travel arrow.

Step 3 Turn the compass until the *North* end of the needle is facing the same way as the *North arrow*.

Step 4 Hold the compass in front of you and walk in the direction of the direction of travel arrow. In order to keep on the bearing you must ensure the compass needle and the North arrow are pointing in the same direction.

How to move around obstacles

Obstacles, such as water features or buildings, often block your route and therefore you need to go round them without losing your bearing. To do this you should go round them at right angles (90°), as shown in the diagram below.

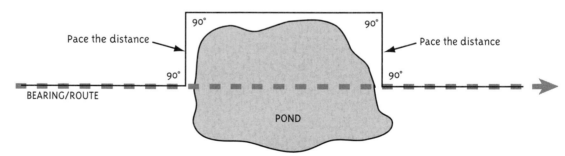

Figure 14.9 *Moving around an obstacle without losing your bearings*

How to find where you are using a resection

This is an accurate method of checking your position.

Step 1 Set the map.

Step 2 Check the ground and choose *two* clearly defined features, which can be easily located on the map. They should be a minimum of 1000 metres (one grid square), and at least 65 to 90° away from each other.

Step 3 Mark the features, e.g. 'Y' and 'Z'.

Step 4 Take a compass bearing on each object in turn.

The following is an example:

You are at position 'X'. The GMA is 4° and, because you are converting a *magnetic* bearing to a *grid* bearing, (Mag to Grid = Get Rid of the GMA), you will need to subtract 4° from each bearing.

- To point 'Y': 344° less 4° = 340°.
- To point 'X': 68° less 4° = 64°.

The bearings are now to be plotted on the map.

Step 5 Set the compass to the grid bearing for point 'Y'. Place a pencil vertically on the map at point 'Y' then place the compass edge against the pencil with the *direction of travel arrow* pointing in the direction of 'Y'. Make sure that the *North arrow* is pointing to the top of the map (Grid North).

Step 6 Pivot the compass around the pencil until the *North arrow* points towards *Grid North*. Now draw a line along the side of the compass.

Step 7 Repeat steps 5 and 6 to find the grid bearing for point 'Z'.

Step 8 Your position is at the point where the lines from points 'Y' and 'Z' cross. Make a note of the grid reference.

Equipment

The equipment used depends on the type of expedition being undertaken. It includes personal equipment and specialised equipment.

Figure 14.10 *Tents are an essential piece of equipment for many outdoor activities*

Hillwalking

The equipment for hillwalking is to be carried in a rucksack or bergen, with a waterproof liner, so weight is important but warmth and dryness are vital. A comfortable carrying weight would be no more than 15 kg. It is essential that you weigh your pack before setting off. If it is too heavy then you will get tired quickly.

Personal kit

The following is a list of personal equipment you need for hillwalking:

- walking boots (worn in, not new)
- two changes of underwear
- two changes of shirts
- three fleeces or pullovers
- waterproof jacket and trousers (in cold weather, extra thermal T-shirts)
- two pairs of thick socks
- thermal underwear
- two pairs of trousers
- woolly hat
- gloves

Do not miss out any of these items. Remember, you may get soaking wet and need a complete change of clothes. There may not be the opportunity to dry your wet clothes and you may need the second change as well! Cotton garments are not only heavier than polycottons, but take longer to dry. Nylon is both cold to wear and very uncomfortable when it gets wet. Wool keeps you warm, but is very heavy when it gets wet, whereas synthetic fleecy clothes are warm and dry quite quickly. Even in the middle of summer, the weather can change very quickly and a warm sunny day become wet and cold very quickly, especially in the hills or on the coast. The woolly hat, gloves and waterproofs are then essential.

In addition, you will need the following items of equipment:

- map
- tent
- carry-mat
- food (dried or dehydrated)
- water bottle/flask/hydration system
- knife, fork and spoon
- mess tins/plastic cup and plate
- personal first-aid kit
- plastic bin liners
- camera
- compass
- sleeping bag
- stove
- watch
- torch
- can opener
- small pocket knife
- money
- pen/pencil and notebook
- mobile phone

Remember, all these have to be carried by you, although some items, like the tent, stove and food, may be shared with other members of the group.

Safety equipment

Some of these may also be shared within the group:

- whistle
- survival/bivvy bag
- sunscreen
- emergency rations (chocolate bars, muesli bars, nuts and dried fruit)
- spare clothing
- group first-aid kit
- insect repellent
- sunglasses
- accident procedure/rescue call-out procedure

Canoeing and kayaking

The equipment is to be carried in the canoe so needs to be placed in a waterproof container. Weight, together with warmth and dryness, is important, otherwise your canoe will be unbalanced and difficult to paddle for any length of time.

Personal kit

The following is the personal kit you need:

- wetsuit
- thermal underwear
- change of underwear
- woolly hat
- helmet
- buoyancy aid
- dry bags

- wetsocks/boots
- fleeces
- thermal T-shirts
- waterproof gloves
- canoe bag
- spraydeck

The same comments as before apply to your clothing. It needs to be as lightweight and quick drying as possible. You will also need the following:

- waterproof containers (BDH)
- food
- maps/charts/guidebook
- headtorch
- sleeping bag
- mess tins/plastic mug and plate
- stove
- camera

- flask/water bottle
- compass
- watch
- tent
- carry-mat
- knife, fork and spoon
- can opener
- mobile phone

Again, some of the items, like tents, stove and food may be shared between group members.

Safety equipment

You will need the following safety equipment:

- canoe repair kit
- split paddles
- throw-line
- whistle
- survival/bivvy bag
- sunscreen
- accident/rescue call-out procedures
- emergency rations(chocolate or muesli bars, nuts and dried fruit)

- flares
- towing system
- sharp knife
- first-aid kit
- insect repellent
- sunglasses
- spare clothing

Camping

The equipment is to be carried in a rucksack or bergen, with a waterproof liner, so once again weight is important but warmth and dryness are vital. Again, a maximum comfortable carrying weight is about 15 kg. Packing and weighing your kit before an expedition is essential. Any tendency to put in additional items must be resisted!

Personal kit

You will need the following:

- tent (A-frame ridge, tunnel, dome, single pole)
- bivvy bag
- sleeping bag and liner
- karrimat/therma-rest
- stove and fuel (gas, methylated spirits, petrol, paraffin, hexi-burner)
- pans/mess tins (cooking/eating)
- water filter/sterilisation tablets
- other items as listed for other activities above
- clothing as for hillwalking

Safety equipment

The safety equipment is the same as for hillwalking, together with any specific guidelines provided by the organisation, national governing bodies, and the Health and Safety Executive.

General safety points

Before any expedition there are a number of things that need to be done to ensure that the expedition can be carried out safely. (Look at the expedition planning section at the end of this unit.)

- *Pre-expedition inspection and risk assessment of the area* If possible the area should be visited by a competent person, such as the DoE assessor or adult in charge of the activity, so that any possible dangers or hazards may be assessed and their risk removed or at least reduced. A full risk assessment should be completed and if the activity is found to exceed the acceptable limits, then the activity should be altered or abandoned.

- *Group and individual equipment checks* Before the activity takes place, the person with overall responsibility should check each individual's equipment to ensure that it contains the necessary equipment, is not too heavy and can be carried without difficulty. Any equipment deficiencies should be made good. Any group equipment should be shared out fairly at this stage.

- *Predicted weather forecasts for duration of expedition* The person with overall responsibility should ensure that the group is aware of the weather forecast for the duration of the expedition. This can be obtained by telephoning the local Meteorological Office, the number for which can be found in the Yellow Pages or at the front of the new local telephone directory under Weather Forecasting.

- *Respect for the environment/Country Code* During any expedition it is important to respect the environment. Such things as taking litter away with you, not leaving gates open, not walking through growing crops, not making fires and following other things in the Country Code are important. Remember, you are visiting the countryside and those who live there all the time do not want their area spoilt by your thoughtless behaviour.

- *Knowledge of first aid and effective treatment of possible injuries, both major and minor* You need to carry a first-aid kit on any expedition and you also need to know how to use it. You may very well get blisters from your boots. These should not be burst but instead you should use a plaster, preferably a pressure plaster, as soon as you are aware of the sore heel or toe. Cuts or scratches should be washed in clean running water (not a stream which may well be polluted) and then dried and covered with a plaster or lint dressing if they continue to bleed. Burns also need to be held under running water for at least ten minutes to cool them down. Major injuries like sprains or fractures should be immobilised and then treated professionally.

It is always a good idea to attend a recognised first-aid course such as a St John Lifesaver Plus or First Aid at Work course or an equivalent course from the Red Cross or St Andrew's in Scotland. This should provide the knowledge you need not only for expeditions but also for everyday situations.

Plan and carry out an expedition

In this part of the unit you will plan and carry out a multi-day expedition.

Planning

What is a multi-day expedition?

All this means is that your expedition will last for two (or more) days and will include at least one night out. It is assumed that most groups will opt for a night out under canvas (i.e. in a tent!) although it is acceptable to plan an expedition staying in hostels or camping barns.

Pre-planning

Before you start to consider organising an expedition there are important skills and knowledge that you must have. You must have basic navigation skills (see earlier in this course) and be aware of the Country Code. The Country Code is a commonsense list of things to do and things not to do when in the countryside. There are twelve things to remember.

1 Show respect for the countryside and those who live and work there. Agricultural and rural communities contribute to the nation as a whole and deserve respect and consideration.
2 Guard against fire. Do not discard matches and cigarettes carelessly. Make sure that fires and stoves are properly extinguished. Fire can destroy moors, woodland and farmland at great cost to individuals and the community.
3 Don't leave litter. Not only is litter unsightly, it can also harm wild and domestic animals.
4 Keep dogs under control. Dogs are hunting animals subject to their instincts. If a dog attacks farm animals it may be destroyed, wild animals can be left in pain to suffer a lingering death.
5 Protect water supplies. Do not pollute any water. After all you may end up drinking it if a supply feeds a reservoir.
6 Close all gates. Gates are there for a purpose, often to keep animals from straying. An open gate is useless.
7 Keep to paths. Do not walk through crops, paths often follow the edges of fields. If you are in difficult country, paths tend to follow the safe routes.
8 Do not damage fences, hedges or walls. If you need to cross a boundary, use a style or gate (remember point 6 above).

9 Leave livestock, crops and machinery alone. The countryside can be a dangerous place – many farm workers are injured or killed annually.

10 Protect wildlife, plants and trees. One of the reasons people go to the countryside is to enjoy the flora and fauna. If you abuse the natural world you deny people like yourself those pleasures and you may be committing a criminal act.

11 Keep noise to a minimum. Do not disturb those who live in the countryside, other recreational users or animals.

12 Take care on country roads. Roads are often narrow and winding. Drivers may have difficulty seeing over hedges. If you are a driver, slow down. If you are walking, face on-coming traffic.

- **Be safe – plan ahead and follow any signs**
  Even when going out locally, it's best to get the latest information about where and when you can go; for example, your rights to go onto some areas of open land may be restricted while work is carried out, for safety reasons or during breeding seasons. Follow advice and local signs, and be prepared for the unexpected.

- **Leave gates and property as you find them**
  Please respect the working life of the countryside, as our actions can affect people's livelihoods, our heritage, and the safety and welfare of animals and ourselves.

- **Protect plants and animals, and take your litter home**
  We have a responsibility to protect our countryside now and for future generations, so make sure you don't harm animals, birds, plants, or trees.

- **Keep dogs under close control**
  The countryside is a great place to exercise dogs, but it's every owner's duty to make sure their dog is not a danger or nuisance to farm animals, wildlife or other people.

- **Consider other people**
  Showing consideration and respect for other people makes the countryside a pleasant environment for everyone – at home, at work and at leisure.

Figure 14.11 *The National Trust Country Code*

Think about it

What type of expedition would you like to organise? What could you do? For example, you could travel by foot, by canoe, by mountain bike or on horse-back. It really depends on where you intend to go and the facilities and equipment available to your group.

Planning

Remember the six Ps: **Prior Planning Prevents Pathetically Poor Performance.** Without careful and considered planning you will make mistakes, mistakes that could put you or others in danger. Before starting the planning process, you need to define your aims and objectives. (**Remember**: Aims are more general, objectives are measurable.) Your overall aim will include completion of some of the assessment criteria for this unit. Your objectives may be, for example, to complete a planned route or practise and develop specific skills. Your objectives will be limited by a number of factors:

- The age, ability and physical fitness of your group
- The time you have available
- The equipment that you have available
- Your budget
- Safety.

It may be that you have a burning desire to organise a trekking and climbing expedition to the Himalayas. However, unless you have an experienced, fit and committed group with access to many thousands of pounds, such an expedition is unrealistic – dangerously so. If you are new to organising expeditions it is a good idea to 'think small and safe'.

A good starter objective would be to plan and complete a five-mile walk over public footpaths in an area you know well. As you become more confident and experienced you will be able to be more adventurous and consider more demanding activities leading up to a multi-day expedition. Objectives can include travelling specific distances, overnight camping in recognised sites or rough country or acquiring new skills (e.g. using a compass, climbing, sailing, canoeing or mountain biking).

Before considering any expedition you *must* know the capabilities of your group. Remember to take into account:

- *Age* – the very young or old may not be able to complete an arduous expedition
- *Experience* – beginners cannot do what more experienced people can

Specialists – do you have people who have the experience and qualifications to lead or support the group? – e.g. those who can prepare risk assessments, those qualified to lead expeditions in difficult country, on water etc. Do you have someone who is first aid qualified? Do you have a competent navigator?

Let's do it!

What expeditions could you organise in your area? Find out

- how many campsites there are within ten miles of your school or college
- if there are facilities for canoeing, horse riding, mountain biking, sailing or walking within ten miles of your school or college
- how much these facilities cost.

Key point

Before you go any further you should complete the navigation section of this unit.

Time to start for real!

When planning your first expedition don't forget to **KISS** (Keep It Simple, Stupid). If your first attempt is too complex or ambitious you could fail to reach your objectives through lack of experience. Failure disheartens everyone and your group members may be reluctant to attempt any more expeditions. Make sure that your first expedition is successful.

No matter how large or small, there are planning issues common to all expeditions. Planning must be written down and copies must be available to

- all members of the expedition
- a responsible person who is not part of the expedition and who will act as a point of contact for yourself and emergency services.

Planning sequence

1 Decide your objectives. Where are you going? When are you going? How will you travel? Who is going? Are your objectives realistic for the group and the resources you have?

2 Decide your command structure. Who will be in charge? Who will make decisions? Is your leader appropriately qualified and experienced?

3 Research the expedition area. Ideally you should make a visit. Identify potential dangers and prepare risk assessments. Identify campsites or hostels and find out how much they will cost.

Check availability for your preferred dates of accommodation and any other facilities you may need. Check mobile phone reception.

4   Ensure that you have adequate insurance. Your school or college may be able to help. Local education authorities can also assist and may have access to special policies.

5   Arrange transport and find out how much it will cost.

6   Get written consent for your expedition, especially from parents/guardians (participants under 18), participants themselves (if over 18), your school or college, landowners if you plan to go off public footpaths.

7   Gather information about any medical conditions suffered by your group. Do any participants have any extra needs (e.g. diet)? Ensure that someone in the group has at least a basic first-aid certificate and a first-aid kit.

8   Collate telephone numbers of all members of your group and publish a contact list. This list should be given to every member of the group and also left with a non-participating reliable person.

9   Prepare diet sheets. What are you going to eat? How much will you need to carry with you? Tinned food is heavy. Water is heavy and you could need up to 5 litres per person per day. How and where will you re-supply? If your expedition is particularly arduous you could need up to 3500 calories per person per day. Check Unit 3 for information on an appropriate diet.

10 Prepare route cards. Leave copies with your reliable contact (see navigation section of this unit).

11 Identify your support group and include them in all stages of planning. It is sensible to have a vehicle in support. You should plan to meet your support group regularly. Vehicles can carry heavy equipment, extra food and water and can also provide a safety back-up.

12 Prepare a detailed budget. Expeditions always cost more than you expect. When you have prepared a budget and found out how much everyone will have to pay you may need to modify your objectives if the cost is too high. Stick to these main headings:
    - *Transport* – vehicle hire, fuel etc.
    - *Accommodation costs* – campsites etc.
    - *Equipment costs* – you may need to buy additional kit, don't forget to include the costs of maps – they are not cheap.
    - *Food*
    - *Insurance*
    - *Pre-expedition recce* – it is helpful to check the area first.
    - *Administration* – stationery, photocopying, telephone calls, stamps.

13 Check the weather forecast for the expedition area. Your final weather check should be no more than 24 hours before you start the expedition.

14 Finalise your timings. Make sure that everyone knows where and when the expedition will start.

Case study

Budget for a two-day expedition

This is a budget prepared for a group of six students who spent two days walking in Yorkshire. Costs include two drivers/support staff.

Transport:
* College minibus — Free
* Diesel — £32.00

Campsite (8@£2.00) — £16.00

Equipment:
* Maps (3@£7.00) — £21.00
* Camping Gaz — £12.00
* First-aid kit — £7.00

Food (8@£2.50/day) — £40.00

Insurance (college policy) — £8.00

Recce (fuel for car) — £12.00

Administration:
* Photocopying — £2.40
* Telephone calls — £0.60
* Stamps — Nil
* Stationery — Free

Total — **£151.00**

Cost per person — **£18.88**

The cost of the above example was split between the expedition members and the two safety support staff. If the cost had fallen on the walkers alone the cost would have been £25.16 per person. You do need to consider if you are going to charge your support party, after all they are doing you a favour!

No matter how you split the costs, it can be quite expensive to organise an expedition. The example above did not include any specialist equipment or expert help. If you have to rent canoes, for example, and pay for a qualified instructor the price will rocket. Similarly, the example showed the students were able to borrow a minibus and had only to pay for fuel. If you have to hire transport you will find that it is very expensive. You can reduce individual costs by increasing the size of the party. However, the larger the party the more preparation is needed and the greater the problems. For example, communication between a group of six people is much easier than between a group of twenty-five. If you decide to plan for a large group, deciding the rules – especially who will make the decisions – is extremely important. In addition, if you start planning an expedition for a large group, do not be surprised if people drop out at the last minute.

Preparing equipment

Refer to the kit list at the beginning of this unit. Far too many people embark on expeditions with inadequate equipment. Your school or college may have a supply of tents and cookers that you can borrow, it is unlikely that you will be able to borrow personal clothing.

It is essential that your clothing and equipment are up to the task. It is also essential that you have the kit to cope with unexpected problems. Many 'wild' areas of the UK experience sudden changes in weather. However, if you intend to carry all of your equipment, weight is an important factor. As a general rule, if you are walking do not carry more than 15 kg. Bear in mind that as well as personal kit you will need to distribute shared equipment around the group. Tents can be heavy.

Remember the basics. You will need
- appropriate clothing (with dry spares – remember the plastic bags)
- appropriate footwear
- some form of shelter
- a sleeping bag
- food
- water
- safety equipment.

 Key point

Do not assume that all members of the group will have everything that they need. At least a week before leaving on an expedition, equipment must be inspected. It is a good idea to use a 'buddy' system. Participants should be organised into pairs, buddies should physically check and inspect their partner's equipment. They should check that kit is available and suitable for its intended use. At this stage, you will probably find that not everyone is fully equipped, and you will have time to acquire missing items and distribute communal equipment.

Let's do it!

As a group setting out on an expedition make the following checks.
- How well equipped are you at the moment?
- List all the items that you will need.
- List all the items that you have.
- How close are the two lists? How will you make good any shortfall of equipment?

During the expedition

If your expedition is to be successful you do need to follow some basic guidelines and rules.

- Think about the needs of others.
- Cooperate with the members of your team. Avoid arguments, if necessary 'turn the other cheek'. Take a full part in all activities, accept the decisions of your leader or the group as a whole, do your share of the chores.
- Think 'Tidy'. Keep your personal and group equipment well organised. Do not take things out of your rucksack if you don't need them, when you don't need them any more put things away immediately. Keep the campsite tidy and leave it that way when you depart.
- Stick to your planned routes. If you must deviate ensure that your safety support group knows where you are going. Do not deviate without re-planning your route.
- Everyone must know your safety arrangements and stick to them.
- Under no circumstances must a member of the expedition be left alone.
- Avoid alcohol at all costs. It makes you dehydrate. It also impairs decision-making.
- Do not be afraid to abandon your expedition, or part of it, if circumstances change, e.g. weather, injury.
- Eat and drink! It is essential that you have the energy to complete the expedition. When taking part in physically demanding activities you need more calories and more water than you think you will. Don't rely on sugary snacks and drinks. A high carbohydrate diet and water are much better. Refer to Unit 3 when preparing your diet sheets.

What to do if...

An important part of your planning and preparation will be to consider the actions you will take if you get into difficulty. Your risk assessments will have helped to identify potential hazards and your route card should include emergency routes to safety. However, in the event of more common problems you must establish standard operating procedures that are known and understood by all members of your expedition.

Think about it

Consider the following scenarios and decide how you would deal with them.

1 The weather suddenly worsens. You are in thick fog and cannot see your route.
2 A member of your group breaks an ankle.
3 You lose contact with your support group.
4 A member of your expedition is struck by hypothermia. You are five miles from the nearest road and your next planned meeting with your support group.

Possible solutions to the activity

1 Stay where you are. Erect a shelter and brew up! If you have mobile phone communication inform your support group.
2 Immobilise the ankle. If you are close to civilisation, take turns to help the victim. If you have a long distance to go or the ground is particularly difficult, leave someone with the injured party and two others go for help. (There's a lesson here – groups should have at least four people.)
3 Go to your next checkpoint and wait. If your support group has any sense, they will find you.
4 Hypothermia can be deadly. Erect a shelter, place the victim in a sleeping bag. Find a volunteer to get into the bag with the victim to provide body warmth, prepare a warm drink (not hot). If you have communications, call for help. If you do not have communications and there is no improvement in an hour, send two people for help (as in point 2).

Do not assume that all will go well, you must have systems in place to deal with the unexpected.

Evaluation

Evaluating an expedition

Recording your expedition

For successful completion of this unit you should produce written evidence of what you have done.

The evidence will be:

1 All your planning. This will demonstrate awareness of appropriate expeditions, equipment and leadership.
2 An evaluation of your expedition. Was it appropriate for your group? Did you achieve your objectives?
3 How did you perform? How did other members of the expedition perform? Are there skills that need refining?
4 How could you improve future performance?

Case study

Evaluation of an expedition

The following is an evaluation (points 2, 3 and 4 above) completed by Julia, a 17-year-old student who participated in a hillwalking expedition over two days in July, covering 28 miles in rough country.

We started our expedition in high spirits, we were all looking forward to spending time on the moors. Our objective was to complete the eastern section of the Lyke Wake Walk over the North Yorkshire Moors. The entire walk is 42 miles and is usually completed in 24 hours but we decided that we weren't fit enough to tackle the whole thing without some practice. The walking was very tough, much of it was over open moorland. Most of the group had some experience of walking and camping although no one had attempted this sort of distance before. Everyone in the group completed the walk, although two people had to leave most of their personal kit in the minibus on the second day because they found it hard to carry. We reached our objective without too much trouble, people generally knew what to expect. The expedition was about right for our group.

I found the first day's walking enjoyable. On the second day I was a bit stiff and it took an hour or two to get my muscles working properly. When it was my turn to navigate I had to rely on others quite a bit. I need more practice in using a compass and following a bearing. My kit was good. I had been able to borrow some bits from my older sister, although I ended up taking things that I didn't need. Other members of the group had mixed experiences. Some people would not do their share of jobs. Two people refused to carry any safety kit which I thought was selfish and stupid. A lot of us do need to improve our fitness before we try anything more difficult and have more practical navigation lessons.

Evaluation of Julia's report

Julia's report does consider objectives and how appropriate the expedition was for her group although there is no evidence that alternatives were considered. She does consider her own performance, although her evaluation is a little brief and lacks detail. She barely touches on the performance of others, except to be critical. Her style is a little too chatty, it should be more factual. She does suggest things that need to be done to improve future performance but she does not include an action plan which will lead to improved performance. There is little evidence of involvement in the planning process. Overall, Julia should achieve a *pass* grade for this part of Unit 14. If she hopes to achieve a *merit*, she needs to analyse the planning procedures and explain the roles of individuals in the expedition.

Case study

Another evaluation

Ronnie is also 17 and took part in the same expedition as Julia.

Before deciding where we would go, we considered a number of different types of expeditions. Pony trekking in Derbyshire and canoeing in West Yorkshire were popular but when we worked out the budget we found that we couldn't afford to hire the specialist equipment and instructors.

Walking part of the Lyke Wake Walk became an obvious choice. Two members of the group had quite a bit of experience of walking in the moors and knew the area well. We also felt that we could borrow the equipment that we did not already have. We decided to limit ourselves to about 28 miles over two days because we were not sure that we were fit enough to complete the entire course. In the end, our decision was right. By the end of the second day's walking two people were exhausted and could not have gone any further.

I have done some walking before and I knew what to expect. My clothing and boots were fine for this expedition, but if we try something similar during cold weather I will need to buy some decent thermal gear and waterproofs. The tent I have is too heavy, almost 4 kg. I had to leave it in the minibus after our lunch break on the first day. I enjoy map reading and my navigation skills are good. I always knew where we were and I was able to use a compass accurately. One member of the group did not understand that we had to work together. She would not help at the campsite and expected other people to look after her. The rest of the group cooperated well, doing the best they could, although most people need to brush up on map work and improve their general fitness.

Before our next expedition we need to get some better equipment. Decent tents are the main priority. We also need to practise camp cooking! We had a reasonable diet planned but by the time we got to our campsite we couldn't be bothered to follow it and ended up with cold beans and bread. Perhaps we need a bit more self-discipline.

Evaluation of Ronnie's report

Ronnie gives some insight into the planning process with a brief analysis of the reasons for their choice of expedition. He does not really assess whether the objectives were met although it is implied. He is able to assess his own performance and seems clear about his strengths and weaknesses, identifying what he needs to do and what the group needs to do for further successful expeditions. He also offers an evaluation of some of the equipment used. His comments about the rest of the group are mainly positive but lack detailed development. Overall, Ronnie should achieve a *merit* grade for this part of Unit 14. If he hopes for a *distinction*, he should justify the preparation needed to achieve the objectives and justify his role and responsibilities as well as the roles and responsibilities of others.

Finally

- Remember the six Ps
- Don't forget to KISS
- Think SAFETY.

Assessment activity

What you need to achieve for your assessments

1 In order to achieve a *pass* grade, you must do the following:
- Show that you are aware of the leadership, interpersonal and organisational skills needed for participation in a multi-day expedition. You must be able to explain to an assessor the skills that a good leader should have, how members of the group should act towards each other and what is required to organise a successful expedition.

- Contribute to the planning and preparation of a multi-day expedition. You do not need to do it all yourself but you must take some responsibility for the organisation. For example, you could be the person who books facilities or who arranges your safety cover.

- Identify and list the equipment needed for a multi-day expedition. This is self-explanatory, so decide what you will need and list it! Be prepared to explain your choices.

- Participate in a multi-day expedition identifying your own roles and responsibilities. It is not enough just to take part. You must be aware of your own part in the expedition, especially what you do to contribute to the success of the whole group. For example, you could be the main navigator, the cook or even the leader taking responsibility for decision-making.

- Record your performance and that of the group, identifying strengths and weaknesses. You should produce an expedition report, concentrating on how well you and your group achieved your objectives.

2   In order to achieve a *merit*, you must do the following:

- Satisfy all the *pass* criteria.

- Analyse the planning and preparation required for a multi-day expedition. You should be able to demonstrate to an assessor that you understand the planning process and that you understand why the process and individual parts of the process are essential.

- Describe your own performance and the performance of others, identifying weaknesses and areas for improvement. You should describe what you did, what others did and how that contributed to the expedition. It is important to be self-critical, you must be able to see how you, and others, could improve your performance.

3   In order to achieve a *distinction*, you must do the following:

- Satisfy all the *pass* and *merit* criteria.

- Evaluate the planning and preparation. Justify the preparation needed to achieve your objectives. As well as understanding the planning process you must demonstrate to an assessor that your planning was considered and appropriate for your expedition. In addition you must show that you have carefully considered how successful your planning was and that you have considered alternative approaches for your next expedition.

- Critically evaluate your performance and the performance of others, identifying weaknesses and areas for improvement. You not only need to be aware of how you can improve, you also need to be aware of what you will do to improve. A critical evaluation does not mean that you concentrate on your failures! (although you must be able to identify weaknesses for the assessment criteria). A critical evaluation should also explain what you did well.

Linked site: www.theaward.org (The Duke of Edinburgh's Award Scheme)

Appendix: Integrated Vocational Assignment (IVA)

What is an IVA?

The IVA is an assignment set by your awarding body Edexcel. It is not an examination, it is a normal assignment and will probably look a lot like the ones you are used to doing throughout your BTEC First. It is set externally to ensure that your qualification has equivalency with other Level 2 qualifications, such as GCSEs, and which have external tests. The IVA is marked by your tutors and then checked by examiners at Edexcel to ensure that your tutors are marking in the way they ought to be. You should not have to worry about an IVA any more than you would worry about another assignment. It is not intended to frighten or intimidate you, it is just another piece of work that you need to do in order to get your BTEC First. You must remember that your IVA is a compulsory part of your course – if you do not complete it you may not be eligible to pass your qualification.

Which subject is covered by the IVA?

For the BTEC First Diploma in Public Services your IVA will be set on Unit 01 – The Public Services.

How will I get my IVA?

A new IVA is issued every year. This ensures that you cannot copy the work of the previous year's class. Your college or school will issue you with the IVA at a time they choose, usually sometime between September and January. However, the IVA is released to the public on the Edexcel website earlier than many centres may give it to you. This means that you can go to the Edexcel website www.edexcel.org.uk and print it off from there if you want to have extra time to consider it or work on it. Be careful to ensure you are downloading the latest version; it would be a pity to work on an assignment which is out of date.

How long will I get to complete my IVA?

This depends on how long your centre gives you. Centres can be flexible when they give their assignment out and when they expect it in. The final deadline for submission of your work is usually at the end of March, but Edexcel does not specify a time that it should be given to you. This means that your tutors may provide you with the IVA at any point from September onwards. If you want to get a head start then there is nothing to stop you accessing the assignment direct from the website. However you must remember that your IVA has to be marked by your tutors before it goes off to Edexcel, so it is likely they will want it in by mid-March at the very latest.

What help will my tutors give me?

Your tutor should help and guide you in the same way they would for other units on your course. This means they may point you in the direction of useful resources, such as books, journals or websites. They may give you guidance on structure and presentation of your work, and some tutors may be happy to check your notes or drafts for spelling and grammar errors. It is important to remember that all the work you submit should be your own; your tutors cannot and will not complete the work for you.

What does the IVA consist of?

Your IVA consists of:

- *A set of general instructions* This is a list of around ten bullet points which provide you with guidance on how to complete the IVA. It would make good sense to read them thoroughly as they will help you approach your assignment in the correct way.
- *Your assignment scenario and tasks* This should be similar to assignments you already complete. It will consist of a hypothetical but realistic situation involving the public services and a series of tasks or questions you must complete which are based on the scenario. The work you have done in class should help you address these tasks, as will this book and your own research.
- *A summary of your tasks and what you should hand in* This is a description of what should be in your final package of work. Make sure you check this thoroughly to be certain you don't miss out parts of your assignment or forget to hand it in.
- *The assessment criteria for the unit* Always reference your answers to this set of criteria; it will provide you with as much guidance on what the

assignment requires as does the assignment brief itself. Look at the criteria and make sure that your assignment answers the set criteria as well as the assessment tasks.

- *Your IVA coversheet* This is the front cover of your assignment, it must be placed at the start of your assignment.

What happens if my IVA is late?

It is your responsibility to plan your academic workload sufficiently well so that none of your assignments are late. This is especially true for the IVA. Each college makes a decision as to whether it will accept late work and sets the grounds on which it will permit extensions. Your centre can submit your late work for re-marking but it may delay your achievement. You cannot resit your IVA.

How can I do well on my IVA?

You can achieve a high grade on your IVA in much the same way that you would achieve a high grade on any other assignment. The following points will help you work towards a successful outcome for all of your work, including the IVA.

1 Make sure you start your assignment as soon as you get it. Don't underestimate the length of time you will need to understand, research and write your work. It is likely that you will need several months to be able to do a creditable job of it. Leaving it until the last minute and rushing through it is a recipe for disaster.

2 Read your assignment thoroughly and ensure you understand what is required of you. If you just skim the assignment it is highly likely you will miss many relevant points which could have improved your grade. If you don't understand a question you must ask your tutors for clarification. There isn't any point in not understanding what you need to do and not doing anything about it – the only person to suffer will be you!

3 Do not be tempted to take the easy way out and simply reproduce work you have found in textbooks or on the internet. All your work must be your own, you may not copy anything you find, and if you do use work from external sources you must reference it within the body of your work and again in the bibliography. It is wholly unacceptable for you to submit copied work.

4 If you complete any aspect of your assignment as part of a group you must record your achievement individually. This means all of your contributions to the group task must be identified and your individual contribution must show that you have met all the outcomes.

5 It is important that you use a wide variety of resources in order to complete your work. Using one or two sources of information will not provide you with the depth and detail required for a high grade. Remember that you may use textbooks, journals, magazines, newspapers, internet, first-hand accounts from public services officers or other professionals, your own primary research and public service promotional information, to name but a few. The more sources you use the fuller your answers are likely to be and this will be reflected in your grade.

6 Try to produce work as professionally as possible. It is extremely difficult to mark work where the writing is illegible. If you know your handwriting is poor then it is in your interests to word process it. If your spelling and grammar is poor then have a dictionary handy or use the spelling and grammar checker on your PC. Your work should be focused and well organised with each task clearly labelled.

7 Pay attention to the key words in your tasks, such as *analyse*, *explain* or *describe*. These key words mean different things and it is important to know what they mean and how to interpret them in your assignment.

8 Consider creating an action plan that details how you will approach your assignment, with timescales. This will help you monitor how well you are doing and whether you are falling behind schedule in producing your work.

9 If you are having any kind of difficulty with the assignment, such as problems managing part-time work and study, health problems or home life difficulties, you should tell your tutor immediately so that they can offer you the support you need. Don't struggle alone. Most colleges have extensive support systems for students – make use of them.

10 Before you hand your work in check that you have included everything and not left out any parts by accident. This last check and read through may pick up other mistakes on your assignment you didn't spot while you were writing it.

11 If you use a word processor you should ensure you back up your work onto a hard drive or the college network if you are allowed access to your own network area. Don't just rely on a floppy disk to save your work, they can be damaged very easily and your assignment may be lost.

There may be some occasions where a student would be eligible for an extension to allow more time for work to be completed, such as bereavement or a serious illness. If you feel you qualify and would like to be awarded an extension you should speak to your tutors as soon as you become aware of the situation. Equally, you may feel your work should receive special consideration because of your personal circumstances. Your school or college will have an Edexcel form which they can complete on your behalf, so speak to your tutors as soon as you can about this if you feel it applies to you.

Remember that producing good quality work is important in all your assignments for your BTEC First Diploma, not just the IVA. If you can work hard it will stand you in good stead for joining the National Diploma in Public Services and also be a bonus if you decide to join a service straight from college. Remember that whatever service you decide to join your tutor will be asked to write a reference for you – handing in poor quality work won't impress them!

Index